PACIFIC WELL-BEING

Intersectionality and Theology Series

This series is a home for theologies that weave in the strands of gender, race, and class. Because weaving involves stripping the strands, this series makes room for plaiting sub- and minor- strands. Each volume of the series, as such, will exhibit the interwoven and intersectional natures of theology—theology is a weaving or intersection where words, images, schemes, stories, bodies, struggles, cultures, and more, meet and exchange. At this weaving/intersection, traditions, standards and ideals inspire, transpire, and some even expire.

OTHER WORKS IN THE INTERSECTIONALITY AND THEOLOGY SERIES:

Jin Young Choi and Joerg Rieger, eds, *Faith, Class, and Labor: Intersectional Approaches in a Global Context*

Jione Havea and Monica Jyotsna Melanchthon, eds, *Bible Blindspots: Dispersion and Othering*

S. Lily Mendoza and George Zachariah, eds, *Decolonizing Ecotheology: Indigenous and Subaltern Challenges*

Jione Havea and Y. T. Vinayaraj, eds, *Transgressing Race: Readings, Theologies, Belongings*

Jione Havea, ed, *Bordered Bodies, Bothered Voices: Native and Migrant Theologies*

PACIFIC WELL-BEING

(Is)Lands, Theologies, Worldviews

EDITED BY
Jione Havea

◦PICKWICK *Publications* • Eugene, Oregon

PACIFIC WELL-BEING
(Is)Lands, Theologies, Worldviews

Intersectionality and Theology Series

Copyright © 2024 Wipf and Stock Publishers. All rights reserved. Except for brief quotations in critical publications or reviews, no part of this book may be reproduced in any manner without prior written permission from the publisher. Write: Permissions, Wipf and Stock Publishers, 199 W. 8th Ave., Suite 3, Eugene, OR 97401.

Pickwick Publications
An Imprint of Wipf and Stock Publishers
199 W. 8th Ave., Suite 3
Eugene, OR 97401

www.wipfandstock.com

PAPERBACK ISBN: 978-1-6667-6217-4
HARDCOVER ISBN: 978-1-6667-6218-1
EBOOK ISBN: 978-1-6667-6219-8

Cataloguing-in-Publication data:

Names: Havea, Jione, editor.

Title: Pacific well-being : (is)lands, theologies, worldviews / edited by Jione Havea.

Description: Eugene, OR: Pickwick Publications, 2024. | Intersectionality and Theology Series. | Includes bibliographical references and index.

Identifiers: ISBN 978-1-6667-6217-4 (paperback). | ISBN 978-1-6667-6218-1 (hardcover). | ISBN 978-1-6667-6219-8 (ebook).

Subjects: LCSH: Worldview—Oceania. | Theology—Oceania. | Pacific Islanders—Religion.

Classification: BR1490 P15 2024 (print). | BR1490 (epub).

03/27/24

Scripture quotations marked NIV are taken from the Holy Bible, New International Version®, NIV®. Copyright © 1973, 1978, 1984, 2011 by Biblica, Inc.® Used by permission. All rights reserved worldwide.
Scripture quotations marked NRSV are taken from the New Revised Standard Version Bible, copyright @ 1989, Division of Christian Education of the National Council of the Churches of Christ in the United States in the United States of America. Used by permission. All rights reserved.
Scripture quotations marked NRSVUE are taken from the New Revised Standard Version, Updated Edition. Copyright © 2021 National Council of Churches of Christ in the United States of America. Used by permission. All rights reserved worldwide.
Cover Image: Tui Emma Gillies and Sulieti Fieme'a Burrows, *The Last Kai* (2022). Courtesy of the artists.
Figure 1.1: Tui Emma Gillies and Sulieti Fieme'a Burrows, *The Last Kai* (2022). Courtesy of the artists.
Figure 12.1: 'Elenoa Telefoni, *Sāpate Faē* (2012). Courtesy of the artist.

Work on this book was supported by
Council for World Mission through its DARE program
(Discernment and Radical Engagement)

CONTENTS

Foreword: I Am Daughter, I Am Child of the Ancient One | *Adi Mariana Waqa* | ix

Preface | xi

List of Contributors | xiii

1. Hol(e)y Well-Being | *Jione Havea* | 1

PART ONE: Well-Being of Bodies and (Is)lands

2. Translating Theology into Practice at the Front Line: MES-19 | *Alesana and Lemau Palaʿamo* | 17

3. Stranger in a Blue Land: Reimagining Theology in Place | *Dianne Rayson* | 27

4. A Sin of Omission: The Sinking Islands | *Tioti Timon* | 41

5. Reimagining Climate Change Education in the Pacific | *ʿElisapesi Hepi Havea and Lynley Tulloch* | 53

PART TWO: Well-Being of Traditions and Theologies

6. *Lotu-Noa*: Impact of Delusional Religiosity on Well-Being | *Nāsili Vakaʿuta* | 73

7. *Agasala*: Reimagining the Theology of Sin | *Rene Sau Maiava* | 96

8. Judas Greets Jesus with a *Sogi*? A *Talanoa* of Judas's Kiss (Mark 14), the Lover's Kiss (Song 8:1), and the *Sogi* of Limaleleimaʿoloa | *Brian Fiu Kolia* | 108

9. *Talanoa Suli o le Moana*: Re-Stor[e]ying Ishmael's Inheritance | *Iatuivai Kioa Latu* | 119

10. A Moment of *Tasi ae foi*? The Canaanite Woman Meets Jesus within Samoan Rhetoric | *Fatilua Fatilua* | 133

PART THREE: Well-Being of Imaginations and Worldviews

11. Reimagining Images of God for Multiethnic Pacific Women | *Therese Lautua* | 147

12. *Sāpate Faʻē*: Art and the reStorying of Theology | *ʻElenoa Telefoni* | 159

13. The *Tapu* of *Fanua* (Womb): A Sermon on 1 Thessalonians 4:1–8 | *Nikotemo Sopepa* | 164

14. "I Am Fearfully and Wonderfully Made": *Takatāpui* (LGBTQ+), God's Call, and the Church's Dis-Ease with the Bedroom | *Paul Reynolds* | 170

Index | 191

FOREWORD

I Am Daughter, I Am Child of the Ancient One

Adi Mariana Waqa

My heritage speaks. Though I silence it with rhetoric of my Fijian genealogy, my heritage speaks through my face, my color, and even through my hair. It whispers a faint echo of *Mālō e lelei*, but I quickly respond, "Hush! Be quiet and let me be! I do not know you, and you are a stranger to me. Leave me to partiality and lay no claim on my heritage. For I am estranged from you, and you will never own me."

I cling tightly to the shoreline of Fiji, but look, they do not know me either, and they refuse to claim me as one of their own! I am pushed, pushed away from the shoreline of my ancestral home. For the Vanua has forgotten me; she has spat me out as my taste is now foreign to her tongue.

I am thrown into the depths of Moana, and as I am submerged into her waters, I defiantly whisper, "Moana, I will drown you with my tears! Your depths cannot contain the sorrows of my heart, the oceans within me are furious, and they will roar through my eyes! For I have been rejected and I am in exile from both my land and my people."

Moana sustains me with her waters, she has heard the wail of my heart. I float upon her surface with my face toward the deep blue sky. I breathe in her salty fragrance as my bitter tears slide into her seas. Moana comforts me through the gentle lapping of her waves, she rocks me in her watery embrace. She recognizes that I am a daughter, I am a child of the Ancient One.

"Wash me!" I cry, "Wash away my foreign flavor so that I may return!" But Moana drowns out my pleading with the sound of her waters. She has refused to interfere with my rejection and she is deaf to my pleas. So I call out to my Vanua, I plead for her to remember me. "How can I remember you?" She replies, "When you do not even remember yourself." These words cut me, and fatally wound me. My tears now burn in temperature, and the weight of my heart sinks beneath the weight of Moana's oceans. "But it's not fair!" I cry, "For I had no say in leaving you! And yes, yes, I did try to forget you, it was easier that way. Can't you see? I had to find a new place to belong, and though I missed you, time soon eradicated parts of my aching."

My wounds are deep, and they bleed openly into Moana. The smell of my own blood intoxicates me with sadness. Surely, if I do not drown first with the tears that I cry, then death will claim me through the streaming of my blood. I am dying, I know it, my spirit is fading. The sharks gather around me, but they will not drink my blood, nor will they devour my body, for an ancient covenant repels their natural instincts towards me. I am daughter, I am child of the Ancient One.

But wait, what's this? *Sa qoqolou na Vanua* . . . I hear the Vanua wailing, so I open my eyes and see that Moana has washed my blood upon the land; reddening its sand and drenching the coconut trees in the shade of my blood. I am faint, the breath of life is weak within me, but in one mighty surge Moana throws me back towards the crimson hued shoreline of my ancestral land. I lie face down upon the beach, for Moana has refused to be my watery grave.

The earth trembles beneath me, "Oh no! She's about to spit me out again!" But instead the Vanua responds, "You are foreign in flavor and sound, but through your blood upon my shores, I now remember that you are mine."

I smile faintly through my final breath; I am home now though I am near death. "Take me into your earthy crevice and cover my grave with the wildest of flowers. Put me to sleep in the tomb of your soil, and fragrance my body with sandalwood oil." The Vanua obeys my final request, and embraces me fully as I enter her rest.

PREFACE

THIS WORK PUTS INTO visible, written words the conviction that the well-being of Pasifika (alt. Pasifiki, Pasefika)[1] depends on the well-being of bodies and (is)lands, the well-being of theologies and traditions, and the well-being of imaginations and mindsets—hence the three clusters of essays in this book. Put differently: the well-being of the daughters and sons of the Ancient One (see the foreword) depends on the well-being of seas, (is)lands, customs and longings of all creatures—human- and other-kinds—in the Pasifika world/views.

The wind behind this book was the Talanoa Oceania biannual conference held at Trinity Methodist Theological College (St. John's, Auckland, Aotearoa New Zealand), September 10–11, 2022. Several of the authors (Fatilua, Havea and Tulloch, Kolia, Latu, Lautua, Maiava, Pala'amo and Pala'amo, Rayson, Reynolds, and Telefoni) presented at this conference and received feedback from one another and from other participants, and they then revised their papers and submitted for this *kaupapa* (cause, book project). Not all submissions completed the peer review processes, and four more authors (Sopepa, Timon, Vaka'uta, and Waqa) joined to spotlight further directions to and commitments for the well-being of Pasifika.

This work comes as an invitation for further conversations and collaborations toward *Pacific Well-Being*.

---

1. Pasifika refers to the region known as the Pacific or Oceania. It is a wide and broad region, dominated by wind and (salt)water, with diverse creatures, values, and ways.

CONTRIBUTORS

Fatilua Fatilua is lecturer in New Testament studies at Malua Theological College, in Samoa. An ordained minister of the Congregational Christian Church Samoa, his research interests include Samoan rhetoric, Pacific Island contextual biblical hermeneutics, politics, economics, and new institutionalism.

'Elisapesi Hepi Havea is senior lecturer at the Waikato Institute of Technology. Her PhD research focused on climate change education in Tonga. She presented *talanoa* as a culturally responsive pedagogy for teaching and learning about climate change in the Pacific. 'Elisapesi's research interest revolves around the role of education in climate change mitigation and adaptation.

Jione Havea is co-parent for Diya Lākai—a polycultural daughter; native pastor (Methodist Church, Tonga); and senior research fellow with Trinity Theological College (Aotearoa New Zealand) and with Centre for Religion, Ethics and Society (Charles Sturt University, Australia). An activist on the ground and in meeting- and class-rooms, Jione pushes back at bullies and suckers, and flips (at) shitstems, in and around scripturalized (con)texts.

Brian Fiu Kolia is a second-generation Australian-born Samoan. He hails from the Samoan villages of Sili, Satapuala, Faleaseela, and Tufutafoe. He is an ordained minister of the Congregational Christian Church Samoa and a lecturer in Hebrew Bible/Old Testament at Malua Theological College. He holds a PhD from the University of Divinity, in Naarm/Melbourne, Australia. His research interests are in Hebrew Bible and reading the text from diasporic, decolonizing, Pasifika/Moana cultural, and indigenous/native perspectives. More importantly, he is a husband to Tanaria and a father to Elichai.

Iatuivai Kioa Latu is a *suli* of Piula Theological College and *tautua* of the Methodist Church of Samoa and of Moana theologies and hermeneutics, and recently submitted his PhD dissertation at the University of Otago. Latu's research topic is "*Suli* Hermeneutics: reStor[e]ying Inheritance in Scriptures in/from the Moana."

Therese Lautua is a Tomokanga Postdoctoral Research Fellow at the University of Auckland/Waipapa Taumata Rau. Proudly from South Auckland, New Zealand, her cultural heritage spans across the villages of Lalomanu, Amaile, Samusu, and Poutasi in Samoa as well as Ireland and Switzerland. Therese loves the challenge of being a wife and mother and serving her local Catholic parish and community.

Rene Sau Maiava is Samoan, born and raised in Aotearoa/New Zealand, primary carer for her mum, and senior researcher with Moana Connect, and started her theological doctoral studies at the Waipapa Taumata Rau, University of Auckland, in 2023. Her research areas include Pasifika and Pacific views on racism, patriarchy, decolonization, relational hermeneutics, and the doctrine of sin. Rene's PhD research focuses on Pacific women's understandings of love in its virtues and distortions as influenced by their ethnic culture and churches.

Alesana and Lemau Pala'amo serve at the Malua Theological College in Samoa. Alesana is HOD for practical theology. An ordained minister of the Congregational Christian Church Samoa, his teaching and research areas include Christian ministry, youth and social ministries, practical theology, research methodologies, and pastoral counselling. In addition, Alesana and Lemau founded a nongovernmental organization called Soul Talk Samoa Trust, which runs rehabilitation programs and provides pastoral counselling and social services for church groups and individuals, couples, and families.

Dianne Rayson is an ecotheologian and senior lecturer at Pacific Theological College, Suva, Fiji. Her home is on Biripi country in NSW, Australia, where she raised her children and grows vegetables. Her research focusses on the theology of Dietrich Bonhoeffer. Di is a public theologian engaged in social issues and often appears in Australian media. She writes liturgy and preaches across several denominations. She is a singer and cellist.

Paul Reynolds is a *kaiako* (lecturer) and research fellow and director of Te Piri Poho, the 3-Tikanga Research Centre at St. John's Theological College, Auckland, Aotearoa. He is a Te Haahi Mihinare priest, *kaupapa* Māori health researcher, and a fledgling Indigenous theologian. He belongs to the *iwi* of Nga Puhi, Ngati Tuwharetoa, Whanganui, and is a son, *moko*, father, and uncle.

Nikotemo Sopepa is an ordained minister of the Ekalesia Kelisiano Tuvalu who was the former moderator of the Presbyterian Church of Fiji and the Pacific regional secretary for Council for World Mission. He is currently a PhD candidate at Pacific Theological College, Suva, Fiji. He hails from the island of Kioa, in the Fijian province of Cakaudrove. He is married with two children.

'Elenoa Telefoni is a mother of five and wife. She is art teacher at Tamaki College, Glen Innes, Auckland, as well as youth assistant, Sunday School teacher, and lay preacher at Me'a'ofafungani Methodist Church, Auckland, New Zealand. 'Elenoa is involved in the freedom of expression of creativity through visual arts to enhance understanding of discrimination within community and theological contexts.

Tioti Timon serves as both a pastor and the principal of the Kiribati Uniting Church's Theological College. With a profound sense of concern, he devotes himself to addressing the far-reaching impacts of climatic conditions on low-lying islands. Acknowledging the urgency of the matter, Timon actively integrates climate change and environmental resilience into the college's curriculum, ensuring that aspiring pastors and theologians are equipped with the necessary knowledge and skills to tackle these critical challenges within their communities.

Lynley Tulloch is an early childhood education lecturer at Auckland University of Technology. She has a PhD in the field of sustainability education and ideologies of nature. Lynley taught environmental and sustainability education at the University of Waikato between 2006 and 2017. Her research interests focus on early childhood education, climate change education, policy discourse analysis, critical animal studies, and sustainability education.

Nāsili Vaka'uta is principal and Ranston Lecturer in Biblical Studies, Trinity Methodist Theological College (Auckland, New Zealand). He earlier served as a faculty member of the School of Theology, University of Auckland, New Zealand. Vaka'uta is author of *Reading Ezra 9–10 Tu'a-wise: Rethinking Biblical Interpretation in Oceania* (2011), editor of *Talanoa Rhythms: Voices from Oceania* (2011), and coeditor of *Bible and Art, Perspectives from Oceania* (2017) and has contributed to numerous academic journals and book volumes.

Adi Mariana Waqa is a Fijian who grew up in Australia. She is a curious thinker, part-time rebel, introvert, lover of waterfalls, and proud daughter of the Pacific. She is also the founder of Vunilagi Book Club—a small NGO set up on the outskirts of Suva, Fiji's capital, to encourage reading and literacy in marginalized communities—and currently works to develop the child protection program of the Pacific Conference of Churches (Fiji).

1

HOL(E)Y WELL-BEING

Jione Havea

SIZE DOES NOT SIGNAL well-being. A big body may be a sign of prosperity and abundance, but it also signals overconsumption, possible genetic glitches, and unhealthy lifestyles. Big may be beautiful on many shores across Pasifika (Pacific, Oceania),[1] and valued by people who live in tight and small (is)land spaces across the globe, but it is not necessarily a proof of well-being. Along the same line, a smaller body could be strong and healthy. Size matters, but size does not necessarily indicate well-being.

Notwithstanding, native Pasifika islanders (are encouraged to) think big. For instance, Epeli Hauʻofa preached that we should think of ourselves as inhabitants of a *sea of islands*, and i[2] have answered his *alter call* with testimonies to our native *sea of readings* and *sea of theologies*.[3] We think big,

---

1. Pasifika (alt. Pasefika, Pasifiki, etc.) is one of the native renderings of the label *Pacific* that Europeans gave to our waters and islands. I use the term as a reminder of our colonial history, a history that has not ended.

2. I use the lowercase *i* (except at the beginning of a sentence) because i also use the lowercase with you, she, we, he, they, it, and other. This is a sign of my affirmation that i (as individual) do not exist without relating to others and to the surroundings, a sign of my resistance against the privileging of the so-called independent modern self, and a sign of my rebellion against the colonial English language.

3. See Hauʻofa, *We Are Ocean*; Havea, *Sea of Readings*; Havea, *Theologies from the Pacific*.

broadly, and intersectionally—owing to our fluid island world/views (for world and worldviews). The fluidity of the Pasifika world is the inspiration for the intersectionality of Pasifika worldviews.

PASIFIKA WORLD/VIEWS

Fluidity and intersectionality are undercurrents that generate this book: The well-being of human bodies is tied up with the well-being of the (is)land and sea (read: context), with the well-being of traditions and theologies (read: history and cultures), with the well-being of the imaginations and worldviews (read: dreams and visions), vice versa and across. The health (or disease, and even death) of the body, mind, and soul (of humans) interweaves with and interdepends upon the health (or disease, and even death) of the *environment*—understood broadly as physical, ecological, psychological, cultural, religious environments. This intersecting way of thinking is reflected in the flow of this collection of essays, which i explain below.

To set up for that task, i first *out* one of the hidden agendas of this collection—to (re)set the table so that there are places for Pasifika voices, interests, and wisdoms, and for Pasifika ways of doing things. Put another way, this monograph is about taking a place at the table and influencing the items on and conversations at the table. And second, i will explain that the table needs to be (re)set because well-being is both *holy*—it is important, necessary, valuable, and critical—and *holey*—it has holes.

(re)Setting the Table

This monograph is another attempt (1) to make space for Pasifika contributions to academic conversations on critical topics and (2) to influence the conversations to account for, and thus reflect, Pasifika ways and modes. The critical topic that runs through the following chapters is *well-being*, and all the contributors are located (at the time of writing) in Pasifika—Aotearoa, Fiji, Kioa, Kiribati, Samoa, Tonga, Tuvalu. But as a collective, we do not claim to represent all of Pasifika. Pasifika is more than us; there are many more Pasifika voices and concerns than are represented in this collection. Nonetheless, the ways in which this monograph seeks to influence the conversations on well-being, in my humble opinion, reflect the intersectional modes of thinking that native Pasifika islanders share.

This monograph comes in the footsteps of an earlier monograph, *Pacific Identities and Well-Being: Cross-Cultural Perspectives*.[4] That earlier work aimed to bridge mental health–related research—that is, Western theories—with what happens on the ground in Pasifika and Māori communities. The range of topics discussed in that collection includes traditional and emerging Pasifika identities; working with Pasifika youth, adolescents, and adults; and supervision practices developed by Māori and Pasifika practitioners. The discussions include practice scenarios, research reports, analyses of topical issues,[5] discussions about the appropriateness of Western theories for other cultural contexts, and the creative works by Māori and Pasifika poets that give voice to the changing identities and contemporary challenges within Pasifika communities—primarily in Aotearoa New Zealand.

The contributions to the present monograph are not as concerned with Western theories,[6] nor with the divide between theory and practice. On the other hand, as a collection, this monograph is more concerned with telling (*talanoa*) and talking around (*talanoa*: conversing, interrogating) the stories (*talanoa*) of well-being in various platforms and struggles in Pasifika.[7] In these regards, this monograph is another attempt to (re)set the table in the interest of Pasifika peoples and our world/views.

The Last Kai (see figure 1.1) is also an attempt to (re)set the table. That artwork is a collaboration by Tui Emma Gillies and her mother, Sulieti Fieme'a Burrows. *The Last Kai* is their subversion of Leonardo Da Vinci's famous work, *The Last Supper*. Sulieti and Tui grew up seeing prints of Da Vinci's work in the living rooms of their relatives. *The Last Supper* is a work with which many Pasifika people have a special affinity, and it provided the urge for this team of daughter and mother to do their own version on Tongan *tapa* cloth.[8]

---

4. Agee et al., *Pacific Identities and Well-being*.

5. Of the contributors to this collection, i am the only one who contributed to that earlier collection. My chapter in that collection reflected on the subject and power of death.

6. I quickly clarify that all the contributions reflect awareness of Western theories, but re/presenting those is not the main drive of their contribution to this book. Moreover, several of the contributors engage with Western theories in other works and studies.

7. The term *talanoa* has three references: first, it refers to "story," bearing in mind that a story is usually a combination of several stories; second, it refers to the "telling" of a story, so it is about an act, or process; third, it also refers to the "interactions" (conversations, interrogations) in relation to the "story" and the "telling"—at this level, *talanoa* is a collaborative event that involves listening, hearing, questioning, and reStorying.

8. The painting was a mammoth task, a painstaking and labor-intensive endurance event as well as a creative firestorm that taught the artists so much about their chosen art practice. Sulieti used old *kupesi* stencils handed down from elders in Falevai for the background. The *kupesi* stencils are placed under the cloth, which is rubbed with brown

4   PACIFIC WELLBEING

Figure 1.1: Tui Emma Gillies and Sulieti Fieme'a Burrows, *The Last Kai* (beaten *tapa* cloth, *'umea*/earth dye, mangrove root dye, black Indian ink, acrylic and watercolors, 500 x 250 cm), 2022. Courtesy of the artists.

Tui and Sulieti made space at the table for women to sit. They locate the Last Supper in the context of the COVID pandemic, when people had to wear masks. The work represents the artists' expectation that, if the Last Supper were happening in the current time, women would be sitting around the table. The artists included women to show that they are equal and that they need fair representation.[9]

Like the attempt by Tui and Sulieti to give women a place at the table of the Last Supper, this monograph also makes space for Pasifika contributors to be at the tables where *well-being* is discussed. But unlike *The Last Kai*, this monograph brings Pasifika people without masks so that they can talk on— and talk back at—both Western and local world/views. Moreover, unlike *The Last Kai*—where the women figures are adorned with colorful outfits, but they all look formal—this monograph makes room for contributions

---

'umea dye made from red earth clay also from Falevai, Vava'u. Sulieti used traditional Tongan patterns for the borders and the flooring, while Tui focused on painting the supper itself in the glorious colors that Pasifika people love to wear.

9. Another critical (re)setting of the table is Susan Dorothea White's *The First Supper* (which may be viewed at http://www.susandwhite.com.au/enlarge.php?current=23&workID=94). All the characters are women; the center figure (Jesus) is an Aboriginal woman wearing a T-shirt with the Aboriginal flag; the figure at the position of Judas (in Da Vinci's work) is a blonde wearing a pink shirt and overalls.

from people who prefer to look formal, to look casual, or to look informal.[10] Pasifika is not one-size- or one-look-fits-all.

Resetting the table on the subject of well-being is critical because, in Pasifika, well-being is hol(e)y.

Hol(e)y Pasifika

I am here mixing two English words and their connotations—holy, holey—and i use these terms with my native Tongan mind. Playing with and problematizing English terms are part of my attempt to reset the table.

Holy is an English term applied to acts or objects that are sanctified. Along that line, the terms that move Pasifika spirits are *mana* and *tapu*. Each Pasifika community has *talanoa* on what *mana* (having to do with energy and vitality) and *tapu* (having to do with status and character) mean for them, and my intention here is not to squeeze our worldviews into one systematic definition. But i wish to assert here that "holey well-being" is evidence to the lack or death of *mana* and *tapu*. In that line of thinking, rekindling *mana* and *tapu* is needed for "holy well-being" to take shape.

Holey is a term that suggests that there are problems, that something meant to be secure and solid (or holy) is broken (it has holes). The Tongan terms that translate "holey"—*ava* (hole) and *avaava* (many holes)—invite attention, commitment, and involvement. One cannot be idle upon learning that something is *ava/avaava*. The Tongan terms may also be translated as *open* and *opening*—so stating that well-being is *ava/avaava* is both an admission that well-being has *holes* and an invitation to take those as *openings*/opportunities and obligations to do something in order to regenerate *mana* and *tapu*. This collection of essays does both—it admits that there are holes in the well-being of Pasifika, and it invites mending the holey/broken well-being of Pasifika.

In the following chapters, the authors give expression—in different ways, and with different Pasifika terms—to the presence or absence of *mana* and *tapu* in Pasifika circles. And most importantly, the following chapters bring the fruits of *mana* and *tapu* to the table where conversations on well-being (of Pasifika and beyond) take place.

---

10. In look and outfits, the contrasts between *The Last Kai* with Greg Semu's 2010 collection of works titled *The Last Cannibal Supper* (which may be viewed at http://www.gregsemu.photography/the-last-cannibal-supper) are suggestive.

FLOW OF THE BOOK

The essays are placed into three intersecting clusters: well-being of bodies and (is)lands; well-being of traditions and theologies; well-being of imaginations and worldviews. The rationale behind this arrangement—rearrangement and resetting of the table—is that the well-being of Pasifika requires attention to the present (bodies and islands), to the past (traditions and theologies), and to the future (imaginations and worldviews). These three points of attention are identified in temporal terms, but they are seen and felt in Pasifika spaces. In other words, the divorce of time from space is not a native item on the Pasifika table.

While the chapters could fit into two or all three of the clusters, they have been placed in one cluster to spark a Pasifika kind of conversation at the *table of well-being*. The chapters address Pasifika questions and concerns, and they are placed so that the conversations they spark could take place—free of the traps of Western theories and disciplines—with Pasifika accents and rhythms. Put crudely: the chapters answer our questions, and they invite and encourage *talanoa* in our ways.

Well-Being of Bodies and (Is)lands

The four chapters in this cluster move the conversation from the *front line* (ch. 2) to the *classroom* (ch. 5), via the struggles to belong meaningfully in a *blue land* (ch. 3) and to survive on *sinking islands* (ch. 4). At another level, this first cluster moves the conversation from the well-being of the body to the well-being of the soul, the island, and the mind—with the weight of the *talanoa* falling upon the well-being of the next generation.

Alesana and Lemau Pala'amo (ch. 2) retell the story of the measles epidemic at Samoa in 2019 (MES-19), from the perspective of a frontline *faifeau* (minister) and *faletua* (minister's wife) team. Seeing MES-19 as a "thief in the night" that stole lives at a time when most societies do not expect death from measles,[11] this epidemic claimed eighty-three Samoan lives, most of whom were young children. The mobilizing of the MHPSS (Mental Health Psycho Social Services) unit of the Ministry of Health of Samoa invited the coauthors to provide emotional and spiritual support to those impacted by the epidemic—to patients, to families, and to the health workers. It soon became clear to Alesana and Lemau that the resilience of

---

11. Lack of resources and access to measles vaccination made MES-19 an epidemic for Samoa.

Samoans was due largely to their faith in God (compare with the burden of "delusional religiosity" that Nāsili Vakaʻuta discusses in ch. 6).

Upon witnessing death move swiftly amid the efforts of local and foreign medical teams trying to save lives, efforts to provide spiritual and emotional support required Alesana and Lemau to be the visible "presence of God." Consequently, Alesana and Lemau call for the grounding of theology in *being present* as God's servants, for a hurting community. When MES-19 plateaued and the measles outbreak was contained in Samoa, COVID-19 came. The response was the same—be the presence of God among infected Samoans, so that theology rises from and moves upon (rather than over) the ground (compare with Dianne Rayson's notion of "groundedness" in ch. 3).

Dianne Rayson (ch. 3) shifts attention to the land on which one does theology, especially for theologians who are not native to that land. She interrogates the practice of doing theology in a strange place, "strange" in the sense that the land upon which she does theology is unknown to her. As such, she is also strange to the land (see also Mariana's Foreward).

Building on her earlier work around the notion of "groundedness" and relationship to land, a core tenet of her ecotheology, and of what she has described as *Earthly Christianity*, Dianne's chapter considers belonging to place and whether a white settler in Australia or in Fiji can ever really belong to country or place. She asks questions of theology in Pasifika as part of a globalized world facing existential threats from climate change and biodiversity loss. In attempting to "do theology well," she explores what it means to be in a new place and learn ancient wisdom in relationship and with permission.

Tioti Timon (ch. 4) comes to the subject of the land from a different angle: (is)land is a *point of connection* between the sea and the sky, and a *relative* to Pasifika islanders (see also the discussions of *vā* in other chapters). Land represents a sense of interconnectedness that is evident in the way that the people in Kiribati regard land as *te aba*, people or nation, and Fijians relate to the land (*vanua*) as mother.

In Pasifika, climate change has made the land (qua point of connection, and a relative) unwell. And sadly, neighbors from near and far have looked away from the sinking low-lying islands of Kiribati and Pasifika. To counteract this "sin of omission," Tioti proposes the Kiribati notion of *maneaba*—which is the name for the meetinghouse where communities gather to make decisions and build relationships. The name *maneaba* comes from *mwaneaba*, which is made up of two Kiribati words—*mwanea* and *(te) abamanea*—which combine to make a call "to accommodate or take care." In the context of climate change, for the sake of caring for the land as a relative and point of interconnections, Tioti encourages the provision of *maneaba* for sinking islands.

'Elisapesi Hepi Havea and Lynley Tulloch (ch. 5) propose another countermeasure—climate change education. Climate change education aims to address the impact of climate change both now and in the future. It aims to build knowledge and awareness of climate change, as well as to support students in problem-solving and decision-making. The action component is perhaps the most crucial in empowering students to make a difference in addressing climate change.

Most of the current models of climate change education are situated within Western pedagogies and epistemologies. For climate change education to be meaningful for Pasifika peoples we need to reimagine what it can look like in Pasifika contexts, in other words, to reset the table. 'Elisapesi and Lynley address this challenge by deconstructing and reconceptualizing core sustainability concepts from the point of view of Pasifika values and knowledge systems. They argue for a climate change education based on the principles of *talanoa*.

Talanoa enables people to co-learn, to co-construct new knowledge and solutions, and to talk from and with their hearts and beings. *Talanoa* strengthens the *vā*/relationship, in terms of both the *vā* among people and *vā* between people and nature (see also Tioti's conceiving of land as relative and point of connection). In climate change education, this *vā* empowers knowledge and understanding of how students are related to one another, together with associated responsibilities and obligations to address climate change.

Together, the essays in this first cluster suggest that the well-being of Pasifika bodies and (is)lands depends on the channels of *talanoa* being open, and the *vā*—between the infected bodies with their families and healers; between strangers with their home/land; between sinking islands with their neighbors; and between students and their climate-affected life context—being warm and thriving. To consider well-being of bodies and (is)lands, mindful of these intersecting concerns, is to (re)set the table in a Pasifika way.

Well-Being of Traditions and Theologies

The second cluster opens with reflections on the clamps of delusion (ch. 6) and sin (ch. 7) over against Pasifika faith communities, then offers three hermeneutical positionings—drawn from the Samoan world/views—that could redress such contagious traditions and theologies. First, the patience to reassess uncritical traditions (e.g., the assumption that the kiss by Judas at the garden was evidence that he was a betrayer; ch. 8). Second, the courage to take a stand against unjust theologies (e.g., the election of Isaac and rejection of Ishmael; ch. 9). Third, the zeal to promote healthy *vā*/relationship (e.g., in the embarrassing encounter between Jesus and the Syrophoenician woman; ch. 10).

Nāsili Vakaʻuta (ch. 6) reflects on one of the signals to the lack of *mana* and *tapu*, namely "delusional religiosity" (DR, a condition for which he gives a Tongan name, *lotu-noa*). DR is the upshot of religions not providing adherents with a sense of belonging and hope, but instead fueling division (between themselves) and intolerance (with people outside of the fold). Religious people are delusional when they are driven by strict dogmatic truth claims, visions of supremacy, cultures of intolerance, and urges to control. DR was strong during the COVID pandemic, among Christians who expected their faith, and the power of their Savior, to be strong enough that they did not need to be vaccinated. The DR positioning is opposite to the faith that Alesana and Lemau saw in the Samoan community during MES-19 (see ch. 2).

There are certain perspectives, actions, and outlooks within religious circles that are detrimental to communal well-being if not given urgent attention. Nāsili thus invites conversations at the intersection of religion and health care, and whether *lotu* (religion, faith) could support health-care providers.

Rene Sau Maiava (ch. 7) presents *agasala* (a Samoan term used to translate "sin") as a platform for reStorying the traditional Western theology of sin. As a New Zealand–born Samoan woman shaped by Western Christianity for most of her life, Rene struggles with the way that the conversations on the theology of sin conjure up "original sin" (St. Augustine of Hippo) and "humanity's total depravity" (Martin Luther). The theology of sin inadvertently takes an individualistic focus, privatizing the notion of sin to the extent that sin is seen narrowly as a personal insult against God—a vertical view framed within an anthropocentric focus.

Agasala on the other hand is an interrogation, reimagining and (re)embracing of sin with a Samoan Christian theological reconstruction. The intimate relationship God has with creation places the emphasis on the systemically destructive nature of sin in relationships that humanity has with each other and with creation. Attitudes and actions that are destructive toward one's neighbor and creation negatively impact one's relationship towards and in God. For Rene, *agasala* allows a reimagining of sin that renders social and climate injustice as systemic sin.

What *agasala* offers from a Samoan cultural theological perspective is another way of viewing sin horizontally. This horizontal view does not neglect God's involvement in the private or personal, for God is affected by the systemic and structural nature of sin that we personally and privately commit. The horizontal view holds humans to be more responsible for their *agasala*.

Brian Fiu Kolia (ch. 8) reassesses the ways that the kiss by Judas in the Synoptic Gospels has long been interpreted as an act of betrayal. But was it? A closer reading of Judas's kiss in Mark 14 suggests other possibilities. There are elements in Judas's kiss that echo the kiss of the lovers in the book of Song of Songs.

As a Samoan, Brian is intrigued by the use of the word *sogi* in the Samoan translation of the Bible. *Sogi* points to different nuances of "kissing" that resonate with the Māori *hongi*. *Sogi* is also the word for "smelling" or "breathing in," so *sogi* for Samoans is not just a planting of lips on the other person, but a breathing in of that person's scent and a breathing in of their spirit (like the Māori *hongi*).

Through this perspective of *sogi/hongi*, did Judas breathe in/suck out the spirit/life of Jesus? Does this mark a turning point in the Gospel narrative? These questions warrant a cross-textual *talanoa* between the biblical and cultural texts, and accordingly Brian rereads Judas's kiss in the garden at Gethsemane in Mark 14 from a Samoan/Pasifika perspective.

Latuivai Kioa Latu (ch. 9), also with the courage to reread, rejects the biblical agenda to expel Ishmael in Gen. 21:10 and to disinherit him from his right as a firstborn to Abraham's *tofi* (inheritance). Kioa offered a reStorying reading that restored Ishmael's identity and right to inheritance through a *Tagata o le Moana* (native or indigenous person of Moana, or Oceania) lens called *Suli* (Samoan for "offshoot" and "descendant") hermeneutics. The *Suli* perspective is cultural, theological, and biblical.

Similar to the law codes of the Ancient Near East, Samoa's custom and practice regarding rightful inheritor and inheriting are calculated by way of *tala le gafa* (genealogical explanation) to justify membership in the *āiga* (family), the right to *matai* title/name, and the privilege to inherit land. Determining those rights are done under three *Suli* categories: *tau-manava* (right of inheritance by birth), *vae-tama* (right of inheritance by adoption), or *tautua* (right of inheritance by service). On account of these three categories, Ishmael's *tofi* could be restored.

To use Nāsili's language, the texts, traditions, and theologies that reject Ishmael are delusional. Kioa thus seeks to restore Ishmael's rights and privileges through his *Suli* hermeneutics.

Fatilua Fatilua (ch. 10) appeals to Samoan rhetoric for navigating the intricacies of the *vā*/relationship. A critical consideration for the rhetor is how to save face in embarrassing moments or in an onslaught of insults. The primary interest is to maintain respect for the *vā*, bearing in mind that failure to do so leads to disharmony and disruption of relationship. And to some extent, it can lead to war and death.

Tasi ae foi le saunoaga is one rhetorical tool in Samoan culture. It is often used to "re-situate" an otherwise unsettling moment in a *talanoa*. While it is often utilized for deferment, it also serves an important function to diffuse a rather embarrassing moment in a manner that is consistent with respect in Samoan rhetoric.

Mindful of Samoan rhetoric, Fatilua explores the encounter between Jesus and the Syrophoenician woman in Matt 15:21–28. He re-situates the text within the Samoan rhetoric of *tasi ae foi le saunoaga* and offers an opportunity to explore the challenges that often come with navigating the *vā*. This approach offers insights into some of the intricacies of the space in between. It is also an opportunity to re-situate an often "embarrassing" biblical text, and to make sense of it from the perspective of the "embarrassed" one.

Reading this cluster of five chapters together, in sequence, suggests that well-being is possible and achievable when folx name unhealthy traditions and theologies (as Nāsili and Rene did), and then reassess (so Brian), resist (so Kioa), and relate anew (so Fatilua). It is not enough to expose unhealthy traditions and theologies; it is necessary to also lay stepping stones toward well-being—all chapters do both, in varying degrees.

Well-Being of Imaginations and Worldviews

This final cluster invites engaging with four subjects that could promote well-being in Pasifika and beyond: multiple belonging as inevitable and normal (ch. 11), art as a medium for re-membering and theological reflection (ch. 12), sex as *tapu* (ch. 13), and *takatāpui*/LGBTQ+ as *tapu* also (ch. 14). The chapters in this cluster seek the well-being of Pasifika imaginations and worldviews.

Therese Lautua (ch. 11) finds new generations of Pasifika young people living in Aotearoa to be more likely to have multiple ethnicities woven together in their genealogy. This presents a complex of new challenges and opportunities for church communities and families to *talanoa* and reimagine what images of God are meaningful to multiethnic women in particular. The image/s of God are important as they can harm or aid a positive state of mental well-being.

Therese draws on her unpublished doctoral research (completed in 2020) and focus-group interviews with sixty-four multiethnic, seventeen- to twenty-four-year-old Catholic women in Auckland. While this chapter is specific to the Catholic community in Aotearoa, it is relevant to any Christian community who are grappling with how to best build the mental resilience of Pasifika young peoples from a faith perspective. Social Trinitarianism is used as a model of intersectionality and a means to renew our understanding of what it means to live in and with the image/s of God. Radically equal relationships in one's identity with culture, family, spirituality, physical environment, and body generally equate to being mentally well.

'Elenoa Telefoni (ch. 12) presents ways in which art can awaken Pasifika theologies to the power of memory, and to the gifts of women. 'Elenoa unfolds her *talanoa* around an image of her late great-grandmother titled *Sāpate Fa'ē* (Mother's Day). The artwork helps rekindle memory (*remembering*) as well as provides an incentive to interrogate (*re-member*) unhealthy theologies (e.g., patriarchy, sacrifice).

Through art, Moana theologians could *remember* and *re-member* theological and cultural practices and worldviews. Art would be easier to digest and interrogate in local parishes and schools. However, in Pasifika schools and communities, art is not considered serious business.

Nikotemo Sopepa (ch. 13) offers a sermon based on 1 Thess 4:1–8, in the context of increasing sexual violence—especially against women, young and old—in Pasifika. Sexual acts are performed as expressions of power and domination, and the bodies of women are treated as targets (like in a firing range) for the discharging of perverts. And there are many perverts, some of whom violate their own blood and relatives.

Nikotemo invites *talanoa* on matters related to sex, which Pasifika people hesitate to discuss for cultural reasons. As such, Nikotemo encourages the changing of worldviews so that the *tapu* (as sacredness) of the body and of the womb are respected. The Tuvaluan term for "womb" is *fanua*, which is also the term for "land." There is accordingly an ecological aspect to Nikotemo's view, that the well-being of *fanua* applies to (is)land and women both.

Paul Reynolds (ch. 14) winds up this cluster with a reflection on stories of some of the faithful *takatāpui* (LGBTQ+) servants of God, amid their church's infatuation with what happens in their bedroom. Several *takatāpui* folx have received the call from God to join the ordain ministry, but the church refuses to recognize them mainly because of their sexuality—even though some are legally married.

There is an obvious tension within faith institutions with people who identify as *takatāpui*. However, *takatāpui* folx are still loyal and faithful servants in churches that do not totally accept them. With an indigenous Māori *takatāpui* perspective, Paul challenges those churches to rethink their stance on sexuality.

Churches and communities that discriminate against *takatāpui* folx, and that are silent in the face of sexual abuse, are not well. Those churches and communities are nowhere near *mana* and *tapu*. The same resolution applies to the smaller scale of families, and more broadly to island nations.

SO WHAT?

This monograph is a *talanoa* that answers our questions, in our ways: well-being is not just a mental, health, and/or spiritual state, but a weaving (intersecting) of many strands. Those strands include human bodies and praxes, (is)lands and ecologies, theologies and traditions, imaginations and worldviews, through and with learning and faith communities.[12] In a utopian state, each strand would be well and trimmed and their interweaving would be neat and tidy.

Utopia may come for a few moments, and the authors of the following chapters do not expect it to linger. At those fleeting moments, to borrow the words of Mariana (in the foreword), we get to experience and witness that we are children of the Ancient One. At those fleeting moments, *mana* and *tapu* are experienced and understood, and deemed livable. Our *opening* (*ava, avaava*, read: challenge, responsibility), therefore, is to make those moments possible for future generations of human- and other-kinds.

BIBLIOGRAPHY

Agee, Margaret Nelson, et al., eds. *Pacific Identities and Well-Being: Cross-Cultural Perspectives*. Routledge Monographs in Mental Health. New York: Routledge, 2013.

Hauʻofa, Epeli. *We Are the Ocean: Selected Works*. Honolulu: University of Hawaii Press, 2008.

Havea, Jione, ed. *Sea of Readings: The Bible in the South Pacific*. Semeia Studies 90. Atlanta: SBL Press, 2018.

———, ed. *Theologies from the Pacific*. Postcolonialism and Religions. Cham, Switzerland: Palgrave, 2021.

---

12. There are other strands not woven into this *talanoa*/book, such as fellow animals and other-kinds that also inhabit (is)land, sea, sky, and underworld; the fire that rumbles in the underworld; the wind that roams the skies and turns (is)lands and seas; the machines and matrixes of artificial intelligence. Those items also need to be set on tables where well-being is discussed and fellowshipped.

Part One

WELL-BEING OF BODIES AND (IS)LANDS

2

TRANSLATING THEOLOGY INTO PRACTICE AT THE FRONT LINE
MES-19

Alesana and Lemau Pala'amo

IT IS RARELY THE case that children of any nation become fatalities from measles in this modern era, given the worldwide vaccination programs that safeguard against measles, mumps, and rubella (MMR). Yet for Samoa at the end of 2019, this was a reality; the outbreak of measles across the island group led to many deaths.

This *talanoa* collects the experiences and reflections of being a *faifeau* (minister) and *faletua* (minister's wife), rallied as frontline workers to the measles outbreak by the Ministry of Health (MOH) of the Government of Samoa. The opportunity to align with the MOH in such a role during the state of emergency for Samoa was a humbling experience and a way to ground the theology taught at Malua Theological College. In doing so, our team of medical doctors, psychiatrists, psychologists, registered nurses, social workers, counselors, and clergy addressed the holistic wellness of Samoans in body, mind, and soul at a time when the people of Samoa—especially the children—were vulnerable and at high risk of becoming fatalities from the outbreak of measles.

Reflecting theologically upon witnessing death move swiftly amid the efforts of local and foreign medical teams trying to save lives, all pastoral efforts to provide spiritual and emotional support relied upon becoming the visible "presence of God" to a hurting people faced with death. This *talanoa* shares the grounding of our theology in knowing God by being present as God's servants of *faifeau* and *faletua* when such workers were sought in the face of uncertainty and the real possibility of death, especially amongst children.

MES-19 UNFOLDED

The acronym MES-19 refers in this *talanoa* to the Measles Epidemic in Samoa, which began around November 2019. The exact date the epidemic began is uncertain.

It is believed that the first patient of MES-19, labeled here as *patient zero*, was a traveler to Samoa who may have been infected at the measles outbreak in South Auckland, Aotearoa New Zealand, around the second Sunday of October 2019. This coincides with the celebration of White Sunday[1] by most Samoan churches locally and in the diaspora (Samoans living abroad, with large Samoan communities in Aotearoa New Zealand, Australia, Hawaii, and USA). This significant Sunday in the church calendar year[2] is a happy and joyous event for many Samoans. Yet, the following weeks and months resulted in heartache and pain, with eighty-three deaths, primarily children.

At the time of patient zero, Samoa experienced vast skepticism about the MMR vaccination for measles, mumps, and rubella.[3] Two years prior, two infants died from malpractice while being immunized for MMR, resulting in hesitation and fear amongst Samoans to vaccinate their children. Due to the low vaccination rate for MMR in Samoa, measles rapidly spread within the communities and developed into the epidemic it became. By the time the outbreak was eventually contained, the measles epidemic had recorded around 5,700 infections.[4]

---

1. On this special Sunday for children, observed annually, most Samoan churches celebrate children as God's gifts to families and villages. The worship services on this Sunday are led by children and youth who share the gospel of Christ in retelling Bible stories through drama, creative dance, and song.

2. Any mention of church/Samoan church in this essay, unless specified otherwise, is in reference to the Congregational Christian Church Samoa/Ekalesia Faapotopotoga Kerisiano Samoa (CCCS/EFKS).

3. It is understood that the vaccination rate for MMR in Samoa at the time was around 20 percent.

4. MacIntyre et al., "Potential Impact," 2.

TRANSLATING THEORY AND THEOLOGY INTO PRACTICE

Traditionally, the roles of *faifeau* and *faletua* in the ministry involve caring for the holistic well-being of parishioners in body, mind, and soul. This includes the preaching ministry from the pulpit, visitations and pastoral care, youth ministries, Sunday school, and any group ministries such as *Mafutaga Tinā* (Women's Fellowship) and *Mafutaga Tamā* (Men's Fellowship) as practiced in most parishes. These servants of God are called to pastor their flock and care for the members of their parish in the best way they can. Occasionally *faifeau* and *faletua* are called upon by various groups and associations to advocate and participate in social and community events. Considered community leaders, in addition to their inherent roles as pastoral counselors and social workers,[5] *faifeau* and *faletua* provide emotional and spiritual support for people under their care.

The work of *faifeau* and *faletua* aligns with the discipline of practical theology, understood as the study and understanding of God—and applying such knowledge to all areas of one's ministry. A more detailed definition of practical theology is considered as the "critical, theological reflection on the practices of the Church as they interact with the practices of the world, with a view to ensuring and enabling faithful participation in God's redemptive practices in, to, and for the world."[6] Through this critical and theological reflection, valuable insights are formulated, with the primary goal of guiding and transforming future practices that inform and shape the life of faith.[7]

"Translating theory and theology into practice"[8] is an expression that adequately sums up the work undertaken by *faifeau* and *faletua*. The theory and theological training of *faifeau* and *faletua* for the church ministry involves a four-year mandatory residential study at Malua Theological College in Samoa. The different academic programs offered by the college include a diploma of theology (level 6), a bachelor of theology (level 7), a bachelor of divinity with honors (level 8), and a master of theology (level 9). The spouses of students (also called *faletua*) study as well through the certificate of theological studies (level 4) and diploma in theological studies (level 5) offered by Malua Bible School, a subsidiary institution of the college open to the public. These programs take a holistic approach to the theory and theology taught by covering the five disciplines of Old Testament, New Testament,

---

5. Pala'amo, "Three-Dimensional Triangular Roles."
6. Swinton and Mowat, *Practical Theology*, 6.
7. Swinton and Mowat, *Practical Theology*, 12.
8. Kola, "New Goreku Community Presentation."

theology, church history, and practical theology. It then becomes the task of *faifeau* and *faletua* to take the theory and theology learned through their training at the college and apply these in their real-life church ministries.

"Translating" fits adequately with how *faifeau* and *faletua* apply their studies at the college to their respective ministries. Once called to their church or parish ministries, *faifeau* and *faletua* need to apply lessons learnt throughout their course of study into their real-life contexts. This process goes beyond the doing of contextual theology, which identifies culture to help understand God[9] and readapt meaning-making into one's context and immediate surroundings and environment. For any translation to make sense and to be considered adequate and understandable versions of the original message, the translator must have a sound understanding of both contexts—the context and language that the original message is translated from and equally necessary, the context and language that the message is translated into. In other words, the translator must be proficient in conveying the message.

Faifeau and *faletua* become translators who must study to understand the context of the biblical narratives and the theological readings of the sacred text, first and foremost, then translate this knowledge into practice. By doing so, *faifeau* and *faletua* play an essential role in conveying the messages of the biblical narratives and sacred text to become relevant and meaningful in the lives of their parishioners.

LINKING THE MINISTRY OF HEALTH WITH THE CHURCH

Following the public announcement of the measles outbreak in Samoa, the Mental Health Psycho-Social Services (MHPSS) unit of the Ministry of Health of Samoa was set up. Various local nongovernment organizations (NGOs) were invited to join MHPSS to assist in responding to the epidemic. Soul Talk Samoa (STS) Trust was an agency summoned to join MHPSS to provide emotional and spiritual support. The coauthors of this essay cofounded this agency in 2017, and since then, STS has provided pastoral counseling and social services for clients locally and abroad. STS is staffed by *faifeau*, *faletua*, theological students and their spouses who have both completed their studies, and trained counselors. By joining the MHPSS unit, staff of STS became translators of theory and theology and conveyed biblical messages to provide spiritual and emotional support for carers, families, and individuals impacted by the MES-19 epidemic.

9. Havea et al., "Dialogues," 300.

As *faifeau* and *faletua* on the staff of Malua Theological College in Samoa and cofounders of Soul Talk Samoa, joining the MHPSS unit at the outbreak of MES-19 was an inspiring and humbling experience. It allowed us to offer ourselves as frontline workers, to contribute where we could to the tragedy unfolding in Samoa. The resilience of the Samoan people inspired us during tragic times. Although faced with possible death once infected with measles, many Samoans still believed in God for peace despite their uncertainty. We were further moved by the immediate and professional response of the global EMTs (emergency medical technicians), and volunteers mobilized from different countries worldwide to help a crippled nation impacted by the disease.

The primary task of the MHPSS unit was to provide holistic support in body, mind, and soul, to those impacted by MES-19, through counseling, hospital visitations, and home visits. The Mental Health unit staff provided clinical support through doctors, nurses, and social workers. Alongside those, the selected NGOs like Soul Talk Samoa provided spiritual and emotional support for counselors, social workers, and community leaders such as *faifeau* and *faletua*. Teams were assigned at daily briefings by the leader of the MHPSS unit Seiuli Dr. George Tuitama. MHPSS was strengthened during MES-19 by visiting professionals from Pacific Island Medical Assistance Teams (PACMAT) and EMTs from Aotearoa New Zealand made up of psychiatrists, psychologists, and mental health nurses.

For our part in the MHPSS unit as frontline *faifeau* and *faletua*, we provided spiritual and emotional support through counseling of the people that we visited. We also identified any social needs that were presented during our visits. We unintentionally undertook roles as liaisons mediating between foreign EMTs and carers and families of patients due to the limited Samoan-speaking medical staff available when we turned up for our visits. In addition, the MHPSS unit received many requests for basic needs such as diapers, wipes, towels, and sheets, which our unit provided through the generous donations received locally and from abroad.

One significant contribution to the MHPSS unit and the Health Emergency Operations Centre (HEOC) was to begin daily briefings along with worship to God through prayer and singing hymns. When called upon by the director general of the MOH, Leausa Dr. Take Naseri, who headed up HEOC to open daily briefings in worship, it became a time to reflect upon scripture and seek God's blessings through prayer and hymns for the challenging daily tasks of finding resolve and peace amid the havoc of the epidemic. Such traditional practices highlight that Samoa is a God-worshiping nation, and that drawing strength and guidance from God daily is part and parcel of our way of life. During a crisis such as MES-19, worshipping and honoring God remains at the forefront of our work as a nation.

A TEMPORARY INTERNATIONAL HOSPITAL

Upon reflection, it was indeed a blessing to observe and work alongside the hundreds of international aid workers who flooded Samoa during MES-19 (in due course, the experience with MES-19 prepared the Ministry of Health to face COVID-19).[10] To the public, these medical professionals and teams from various countries were considered as *foma'i palagi* (Western/Caucasian doctors) and treated with respect and held in high regard as they worked together with our local medical professionals. The hospital wards were filled with our global helpers. One could easily have been mistaken as walking into a hospital in Australia, New Zealand, or the UK, with the noticeable presence of foreign EMTs working the wards. Often the English language became the preferred communication medium in hospital wards and communities.

At the same time, some patients and their carers required translation from local doctors and nurses and by our MHPSS teams. Several EMTs continued caring for Samoans until the last shift of their rotations in Samoa, saving lives. Logistically it was a mammoth task to coordinate the efforts of the foreign aid workers who volunteered their time, resources, and expertise towards a collective response to MES-19. The skilled personnel and representatives from the WHO regional office undertook the coordination task. By the time MES-19 plateaued and global EMTs started to return to their sending countries, forty-one different rotating teams from twelve countries, and nations from Europe and the United Kingdom, made up the 557 foreign personnel dispersed to help Samoa during this tragedy.[11]

We grew accustomed to seeing our global EMTs identified by their respective medical scrubs working the hospitals and out in the field: the AUSMAT team (Australians) had their sky-blue scrubs; NZMAT (New Zealanders) also had their sky-blue scrubs with khaki trousers; PACMAT (Pacific Island EMTs from New Zealand) had their dark blue scrubs; EMTs from Israel had their green scrubs; and many others. It was amazing the passion

---

10. Foreign countries that responded and sent EMT teams to Samoa during MES-19 include the following: Australia, New Zealand, Israel, Fiji, Hawaii, Japan, Kiribati, Norway, Papua New Guinea, Solomon Islands, Tahiti, USA, and nations from Europe and the United Kingdom. Regional representatives from WHO and UNESCO and global bodies such as Save the Children UK and Samoa Doctors Worldwide were also key responders to MES-19.

11. Government of Samoa Ministry of Health, *Heoc Situation Report*.

and love these medical professionals and volunteers from around the world had for the thousands of sick Samoans they dedicated their time and knowledge to save and restore to life. It was inspiring to see the care given to the sick during MES-19, comparable to any hospital in places like Australia, New Zealand, and the UK, given the many foreign teams who worked around the clock during their rotations. These teams offered their time, wisdom, and skills to help save and preserve the lives of the Samoan people.

The global EMTs who worked the wards acknowledged the work undertaken by the MHPSS unit, as they often commented to us during our hospital visits. It was humbling to receive such reports, especially from medical professionals from different faith backgrounds to our own who hold to their belief systems. Yet, they allowed teams from our unit to share time with patients and carers. Some of these foreign workers expressed how they noticed a difference in the patients, carers, and families that we visited, who displayed renewed spiritual and emotional strength following our visits. It was a blessing to be used by God in this way, to align with the MHPSS unit and become part of a team that offered coping strategies for Samoans in need. It was all worth the sacrifice to become frontline *faifeau* and *faletua* in joining the MHPSS unit and hearing accounts of our visits' impact on the lives of the carers of the sick and bereaved families.

From the local and international efforts in response to MES-19, the situation in Samoa began to improve, and some global response teams completed their rotations and returned to their respective countries. The director general of the Ministry of Health acknowledged their professionalism and expertise in containing the measles outbreak at the HEOC daily briefings that coincided with their departure. At the last HEOC meeting that we attended in mid-February 2020, MES-19 plateaued and all present celebrated by ending the gathering with a traditional Samoan dance—*taualuga*. This dance is a joyous and happy occasion often observed after festive gatherings for different events. In this case, the cause for celebration was that the measles outbreak in Samoa had plateaued and appeared contained.

At the very same HEOC daily briefing, the director general of the Ministry of Health advised the gathering that there was a possible new threat to Samoa, the coronavirus outbreak beginning to take shape in Wuhan, China. MES-19 taught many valuable lessons for Samoans, which led to the government of Samoa closing its international borders at the first hearing of the threat of the COVID-19 pandemic.

REFLECTIONS

As this *talanoa* approaches its end, we present two reflections that have made a lasting impression about being frontline *faifeau* and *faletua* in response to a tragedy that struck Samoa. The first we call *Dr. Tourist*, and the second involves being gifted *a pen from Israel's head of the EMT team*. These reflections sum up the experiences and lessons learnt from being frontline *faifeau* and *faletua* during MES-19.

Dr. Tourist

Being frontline responders to MES-19, we the coauthors dedicated all our time to the MHPSS unit. It became clear that we were putting our young sons at risk each time we returned home, despite taking strict measures to avoid bringing the virus home. We sent our young sons unaccompanied to Sydney to be cared for by our family members and away from the epidemic. When it became safe to return to Samoa, we made the trip to Sydney to bring our sons home. On this flight, we witnessed the dedication of one of our international friends who assisted Samoa during the epidemic.

The flight we boarded from Apia to Sydney included AUSMAT doctors, nurses, and team members who had completed their rotations in Samoa. These returning EMTs had foregone the usual medical scrubs we were accustomed to; now, they were in plain clothes. One of the young doctors from AUSMAT (called here Dr. Tourist), whom we had worked alongside in the ICU ward at the hospital, was returning to Sydney on the same flight. Around two hours into the flight, Alesana noticed this young doctor pacing slowly up and down the plane, looking at everyone seated in their places.

Once he reached at our seat, he recognized us and greeted us with "Reverend." Alesana then responded, "Doctor," and commented that we too should stretch our legs just as he appeared to be doing. The young doctor leaned over to us and whispered that he was checking whether anyone leaving Samoa showed any signs of illness.

While most fellow passengers were sleeping or glued to their entertainment screens, Dr. Tourist was still trying to save lives even while off duty and no longer on call. Most of the eighty-three fatalities to MES-19 had come through the ICU ward where this young doctor was stationed. To most passengers and airline staff, he was just an ordinary visitor, a tourist in jeans and a T-shirt returning from a trip to Samoa, stretching his legs walking up and down the plane; yet for us who knew him, he was responsible for saving so many young Samoan lives from the epidemic that without the efforts of EMTs like Dr. Tourist, the death toll would have been so much more.

A Pen

As mentioned in this *talanoa*, HEOC always opened its daily briefings in worship. One morning's daily gathering coincided with the end of the rotation for one of the doctors who headed up Israel's EMT team. As done so on similar occasions, the director general of the Ministry of Health acknowledged this doctor's contribution to Samoa's combined international and local effort to respond to MES-19. Words of encouragement and gratitude were exchanged, and the departing doctor gave gifts on behalf of members of the Israel EMT team returning home. For our part in the MHPSS team and leading worship during the HEOC daily briefings, the doctor from Israel gifted us with a pen from their country. In addition, he shared with us that his experience in Samoa for MES-19 taught a critical lesson to him—to always begin their daily briefings by worshipping God for all the emergency response efforts they are involved in. It was inspiring to hear this feedback from an international medical professional who has responded to medical emergencies worldwide and how Samoa has taught him to begin the day by seeking God's guidance and direction.

In a conversation that followed the formalities, we responded that the London Missionary Society missionaries introduced God, whom we worship in Samoa. These servants of God shared stories about Israel, and how Christ lived and moved around their part of the world. We further responded that we are happy that Samoa's response to the measles epidemic had reminded him and his team to always place God first in responding to a tragedy.

CONCLUSION

The opportunity to become frontline *faifeau* and *faletua* during MES-19 aligned the work of the clergy with the global and local efforts of medical professionals to respond to and contain the measles outbreak that crippled Samoa. The combined efforts of all frontline workers, EMT teams, behind-the-scenes administrators and staff, and professional medical staff demonstrated how the church and state could collectively respond to tragedy. Such efforts adopted a holistic approach to the care provided in body, mind, and soul for caregivers, individuals, and bereaved families impacted by the measles outbreak.

As observed firsthand, faith in God continues to be the strength that Samoans turn to at times of tragedy, as seen through MES-19. The resilience of the Samoan people lies in its national motto—*E faavae i le Atua Samoa* (Samoa is founded upon God). Having God as the foundation in one's life, such an understanding drives local Samoans and those in diasporic communities abroad to return from being affected by such a tragedy.

The Bible teaches many life lessons to its readers from the contexts and situations of ancient times. When challenged by unforeseen life situations and crises in the world we live in today, translating theory and theology into practice allows faithful believers in the word and sacrament to find comfort and solace in God. Through God's Grace and abounding love, we confess our Risen Christ as Lord in knowing that God is always with us through the challenges and blessings in our lives.

BIBLIOGRAPHY

Government of Samoa Ministry of Health. *Heoc Situation Report No. 65: Measles Outbreak October 2019*. Apia, Samoa: Ministry of Health, 2020.

Havea, Jione, et al. "Dialogues: Anthropology and Theology." *Journal of the Royal Anthropological Institute* 28 (2022) 297–347.

Kola, Benjamin. "New Goreku Community Presentation." Presentation at Gender Equality Theology Conference, Uniting World of Uniting Church of Australia, Nadi, Fiji, 2019.

MacIntyre, Chandini Raina, et al. "The Potential Impact of a Recent Measles Epidemic on COVID-19 in Samoa." *BMC Infectious Diseases* 20 (2020) 1–6. DOI: 10.1186/s12879-020-05469-7.

Pala'amo, Alesana. "Three-Dimensional Triangular Roles of the Samoan Church Minister—*Faife'au* (Church Minister), Social Worker, and Counsellor." *Samoa Journal of Theology* 1 (2022) 112–25. https://www.malua.edu.ws/wp-content/uploads/2022/06/Samoa-Journal-of-Theology-Vol1.-Issue-1-2022-FINAL-22June22.pdf.

Swinton, John, and Harriet Mowat. *Practical Theology and Qualitative Research*. London: SCM, 2006.

3

STRANGER IN A BLUE LAND
Reimagining Theology in Place

Dianne Rayson

QUESTIONS ABOUT THE SIGNIFICANCE of place on the practice of theology are at the heart of this chapter. This is a personal journey, one that reflects my own location and relocation, and the concerns raised about who may do theology, where.

You might not know me. I am an Australian. My father was a Welsh immigrant, moving to Australia to avoid going down the coal mine. Decades later, his youngest daughter would be first in the family to go to university, let alone earn a PhD. Ironic that my father's enduring relationship with coal—he spent much of his life driving trains, first powered by coal, then diesel, and finally electric—would be conversely reflected in my research on climate change and an ecotheology for the Anthropocene. My parents met and married in a tiny village in the Hunter Valley, now the location of massive open cut coal mines that transport coal by rail to Newcastle, the world's largest coal exporting port. Despite living right by this harbor of colliers: giant vessels called capesizers, my relationship is with the water, where the river meets the ocean. I swim in the sea and know that I am home. This is Awabakal country. The ancient meeting place by the harbor, Muloobinda, is now covered by a KFC.

I am also connected to Biripi country. On farmland between the mountains and the sea I raised my children to adulthood, turned the soil and coaxed veggies to feed us all. Here I faced years of drought as the fertile land turned to dust and the river stones turned to bone. Here I faced the bushfires of the Black Winter and Summer and wondered if tomorrow I would die. I have buried cats and dogs—family members—in this soil. Our larger siblings, the horses and Lollypop the milking jersey, are resting at Elephant's Graveyard, the far hill where we take the beasts for their final rest. I will be buried there with them when I die.

Behind our farm, further into the hills, is a cold waterfall and beyond that, a sacred area where men's business took place. That was prior to the massacres by gun, poison, and disease. As I walk the land that I care for, I listen for the voices of those who have gone before and look for the messages that the creatures tell.

I tell you this so you may know me. I am a white person, a settler, invader, *waitskin*, Second Nations person, a woman, a mother, deeply connected to this country now called Australia. I am an ecotheologian and have spent the last decade or so helping the church turn toward creation both theologically and ethically. Climate change and biodiversity loss are my constant conversation partners, and tormentors.

With this background, I now ask you to help me think through what it means to be a non-Indigenous scholar and do theology "in place." What does it mean to move to a foreign county and "do theology" in a different place? How does one navigate learning from local wisdom without reappropriating that knowledge? How do we ensure that our theologies are life giving and contribute to well-being rather than detract from it?

DOING THEOLOGY

I like the phrase "doing theology." It is active, almost energetic, and makes theology itself a process in motion. Theology is not fixed, just as religion and dogma are not fixed. St Anselm of Canterbury's (1033–1109 CE) classic definition of theology as "faith seeking understanding"[1] captures the fluidity of the process: that while faith might be assumed, understanding is not and the two are held together in a tension of "seeking." The seeking continues while faith on one hand, and understanding on the other, fluctuate. Like a seesaw, understanding might increase while faith diminishes, only to be rebalanced as faith increases. The Latin axiom *intellectus quaerens fidem et fides quaerens intellectum*—faith seeking understanding and understanding seeking faith—probably captures this dynamic more accurately.[2] There is a

1. *Proslogion*, in Anselm, *Basic Writings*, 75–78.
2. Muoneme, *Hermeneutics of Jesuit Leadership*, 2.

dialogue between the two, and that transaction sometimes places the seeker in disarray or feeling disorientated until a new equilibrium between faith and understanding is restored.

"Seeking" is a present-continuous verb that has meaning for theological method. Theology is something that is always done in the present. It is ongoing and contextual: always (ideally) responding to the context in which it is situated, in which *I* am situated. Theology is a necessarily creative process, imagining new responses to the questions posed by a changing environment. We draw on tradition, reason, sacred texts and lived experience (the classic sources of theology) to the extent that they are useful in the present context and in addressing contemporary needs. This avoids what Ormerod describes as "intellectual archaeology": a backward-looking theology that prioritizes historical voices over present ones.[3] Given that the majority of those voices are of a different place, time, gender, and social context to me (and most of us), their voices must be treated carefully and with caution. What was once understood in a different time and place needs delicate consideration of its relevance and appropriateness in the Anthropocene and in different locations.

Seeking, as a verb, can be imagined in the metaphor of leaving home, venturing abroad to discover new contexts and new theological responses to the questions that are opened up in a different milieu.[4] As a discipline among many in the academy, theology is necessarily informed by the other arts and sciences, allowing reason to have its place alongside revelation and faith. Neuroscience, for example, points to the innate human drive to seek understanding, to make sense of the world as embodied creatures. As such, theology responds to intellectual, spiritual, and emotional concerns; some have said, the heart and mind. I prefer to think of humans as fully integrated persons: heart, mind, body, community all within the broader, ecological relationality of the biosphere. Theology needs to respond on all these levels. If it fails to do so it fails to truthfully interrogate its context and location.

Lovat and Fleming have proposed a working definition of theology as the "heartbeat of religion."[5] Theology functions to beat lifeblood through individuals, church-communities and institutions. According to these authors, the subject matter of theology is threefold: the spiritual, the human experience of the spiritual, and the way we construct those responses. That is to say, theology attempts to consider God, the transcendent, the numinous, the Other. It considers the nature and meaning of the human response to the

---

3. Ormerod, *Introducing Contemporary Theologies*, 4.
4. See Lovat and Fleming, *What Is This Thing*.
5. Lovat and Fleming, *What Is This Thing*, 42.

Other and the way those experiences develop into beliefs. Finally, theology involves the study and interpretation of the traditions (social, oral, textual, and structural) that capture and convey these experiences through time.

Theology also has responsibilities. Its primary responsibility is to church-communities and institutions to promote self-understanding and their place in the world.[6] It has responsibilities to the other disciplines to both learn from and correct other truth claims. Theology has a place in broader society: to represent religious voices, interrogate social issues, and to promote ethical action. In summary then, in this way of understanding, the practice of "doing" theology is always contextual, best done in community, and always with an eye to the needs of the world. Theology attempts to contribute to individual and community well-being and not detract from it.

THEOLOGY IN PLACE: GROUNDEDNESS

This brings me to being a stranger in a different place. I want to explore some parameters around how a person like me might do theology *well* in the Pacific. I have come to the Pacific to do theology. I am the stranger here. And yet I am not. As someone from the east coast of Australia, our whole shoreline is the edge of the Pacific, embracing *moana* in our arms. Australia is part of the broader setting of Oceania and geopolitically we are variously part of the Indo-Pacific, or Asia, or ASEAN, not to mention our inexorable ties with the US and the UK. Our identity is mixed. Our people are also mixed: more than 96 percent of Australians are not indigenous to this land.[7] We are mostly newcomers, however attached we feel to place. A quarter of a million of us are Pasifika—wayfarers who have come to this long coastline and abided.[8]

What does it mean to be a stranger? In some previous work I utilized Dietrich Bonhoeffer's notion of groundedness, the significance of having one's feet in the soil of the land in which one lives. Bonhoeffer draws on the metaphorical meaning—to be anchored in one's homeland and tradition, and yet to remain sensible or, to use another metaphor, to not lose one's head. It is to be rooted in a firm foundation, to be established within a tradition and be wary of existential challenges to that way of life: to law and order, to political and religious disruptions. In Bonhoeffer's own time it was a challenge to the Nazi co-opting of *Blud und Boden*—the notion

---

6. Ford, *Shaping Theology*.

7. Australian Bureau of Statistics, "Religious Affiliation in Australia," under "Migration and Religious Affiliation."

8. Ravulo, "Pacific Communities in Australia"; Howes and Liu, "How Many People."

of the blood and soil of the fatherland—for extremist political purposes. In prison, reflecting on ten years of opposing the Third Reich, Bonhoeffer asked, "Have there ever been people in history, who in their time, like us, had so little ground under their feet? . . . Who stands firm?"[9]

In addition to the metaphor of being grounded in a firm foundation, there is something literal to the notion of having one's feet in the soil that Bonhoeffer is also referencing. He describes this as "remaining wholly children of the earth." He wondered whether Christians who "venture to stand on earth on only one leg will stand in heaven on only one leg too."[10] An earthly ontology and a Christian ethic are inexplicably linked:

> Only those standing with both feet on the ground, who are and remain wholly children of the earth, who do not undertake hopeless attempts to flee to unreachable heights, who make do with what they have and gratefully hold fast to it, who have the full strength of human existence—those are the ones who serve time and thus also eternity.[11]

Bonhoeffer describes the Greek myth of Antaeus,[12] the giant who draws his strength and healing from his Mother Earth. If he is wounded in a fight, overnight he sleeps naked on the earth and is restored to full health. The hero Heracles (Hercules) can overcome Antaeus only when he identifies earth as the source of Antaeus's strength. Heracles clasps Antaeus in a bear hug and raises him from the earth until he is spent.

Gandhi also influenced Bonhoeffer's thinking about groundedness. In Gandhi's Jain and Hindu traditions, the earth itself is sensate, being aware of the footfall of the creatures that walk upon and within it. To walk lightly on the earth then is both a metaphor for leaving no pollution or damage as well as the literal idea that walking heavily affects the face of earth. Theologians from Luther to McFague have described earth as the very face, or body, of God.

I have used the term *Earthly Christianity* to draw together the ecological aspect of this literal understanding of *groundedness* with the ethical, outward facing mission of the church that embraces the reality of the physical world. Earthly Christianity recognizes the kingdom of God among us, not only among the human portion, let alone only among the converted Christian portion of humans. It recognizes the complete work of Christ's

---

9. Bonhoeffer, *Letters and Papers*, 38, 40.
10. Bonhoeffer and Wedemeyer, *Love Letters*, 64.
11. Bonhoeffer, *Barcelona, Berlin, New York*, 531.
12. Bonhoeffer, *Barcelona, Berlin, New York*, 377.

redemption throughout the world.[13] Redemption and reconciliation contribute to well-being.

Moreover, Earthly Christianity involves that very created space which is the world—the planet of ocean and soil, teeming with the life of the biota. It is strange to me that Earth is named such when it is predominantly ocean (71 percent of the surface of the globe is ocean) and the greatest expanse of that is the Pacific. Strange, but understandable given the anthropocentric, land-based worldview of Western Enlightenment scientists. Earthly Christianity recognizes that land, ocean, atmosphere, and crust all contribute to what it means to be embedded in this world. Our Earth itself is "the small blue dot" in our galaxy, just one among the two trillion in the universe. Earthly Christianity recognizes these theological truths, derived from ancient wisdoms, highlighted by Bonhoeffer, affirmed in my own experience and that of others, in community.

Bonhoeffer's view of eternity is limited to those who are fully grounded on earth. Ethics, for Bonhoeffer, are anchored in the present, addressing contemporary concerns with real-time responses. This contrasts with traditional philosophical ethics that preceded Bonhoeffer, that largely sought universal principals based on intellectual logic. Bonhoeffer rejected this, recognizing that often the ethical choice is not between good and evil, but finding the way that embodies Christ. The question is not the sloganized "What would Jesus do?" but rather "Where is Christ?" in the way forward.

This brings me to my own situation. For over a decade I have "done theology" on the oldest lands on earth, curated and cared for by the oldest Indigenous groups on the planet. This ancient continent is among the world's younger nation states, a place now called Australia. In that place, the few but important Indigenous theologians repeatedly invite the church and theology into a space of deep listening and recognition of the wisdom of this place—people like Aunty Dr. Miriam-Rose Ungunmerr Baumann and Aunty Rev. Denise Champion. They speak of the wisdom that emerges from the landscape and how there is reciprocity between land and creatures and people: reciprocity of obligation, care, and wisdom.

Champion describes the parable of the lost coin (Luke 15:8–10) as not simply being a story of the one lost coin that was found, but also about the other nine who are not complete without the lost one. The *oikos* is not complete if one is missing. According to Champion, the story is also about a single coin that was always in the house all along. God sweeps the house, but the coin was always there. Indigenous wisdom, housed in people and landscape, has always been the wisdom of Creator God, held by Christ.

13. Rayson, "Earthly Christianity."

Indeed, Champion states that:

> As Aboriginal peoples we bring things to this community. We bring knowledge. We bring understanding. We bring wisdom. But the community is not complete until it is there. If the western church thinks they can get along without us, they will never be complete.[14]

This is testament to the extraordinary grace of Indigenous Australian theologians that they invite others into that space, to share the wisdom. Indigenous leader Brooke Prentis describes this as the obligation that her people have to care for country.[15] Caring for country includes caring for the creatures and people in that country, even if those people are uninvited, like myself, and even if my (quite recent) ancestors might have been complicit in genocide. Such generosity in the *oikos*, such grace despite unconscionable treatment, is again based in a deeply ecotheological thinking that emerges as ethic. In turn, this has fed into my own theology of place and belonging, because it resonates with an ecotheological understanding of Christ being in and through all things and speaking wisdom to those who inhabit that place. It has sustained me through drought and bushfires, through mouse plagues, floods, and hailstorms. It informs the way I relate to the land on which I lived, a land that has been stolen and cleared of forest and species and yet continues to speak its wisdom.

A NEW BLUE PLACE

I tell this story because I now find myself in a new place, somewhere I have ironically labeled Blue Land. This is a fluid place, connected by sweat of wayfarers and the saltwater tears from the sorrow of colonization, indentured labor, and climate crisis. But there is much joy here, too, and I'm reminded that Bonhoeffer says that even tears of bliss are salty.[16]

The questions that confront me relate to doing theology here in this new place. How does one do theology without colonizing it? As an ecotheologian I am drawn to the Pacific, to live in a place that is warm, to be close to the ocean. Bonhoeffer wondered when he was locked in a prison cell whether proximity to the sun doesn't lead to richer creativity: "The hot

---

14. Champion and Dewerse, *Anaditj*, 15.
15. Prentis, "Learning to Be Guests."
16. Bonhoeffer, *Barcelona, Berlin, New York*, 546.

countries, from the Mediterranean to India to Central America, have really been essentially the intellectually creative countries."[17] In contrast, he said:

> The colder countries have lived and been nourished by the intellectual [*geistig*] creativity of others, and their own original contribution, technology, basically serves the material needs of life and not the life of the spirit. Could this be the reason why we keep being drawn to the hot countries? And could such a thought perhaps reconcile one to the discomforts of the heat?[18]

There's something about being browned by the sun, taking light from the moon, that makes us more human, just as the English poet Gerard Manley Hopkins described that when our feet are always covered, or shod, we don't feel the connection with earth, in the poem "God's Grandeur":

> And all is seared with trade; bleared, smeared with toil;
> And wears man's smudge and shares man's smell: the soil
> Is bare now, nor can foot feel, being shod.[19]

This week I have worshipped in chapel with my feet in dust, the sea air blowing through me, my hair drinking in humidity and dancing, surrounded by voices of Pasifika in song, and I worship more fully. Returning to the tropics after too long away has been like a slow thawing out, a slow rebirth.

I'm even more drawn to the *vanua-* and *moana-*based theology in the Blue Land. Here, as I see it, is an ecotheology that speaks both of ancient wisdom and cutting-edge theology, consistent with neuroscience and ecology. It is an integrated theology that speaks both of connection and to ethics. As such, it has much to offer the well-being of the broader church and theological community. It speaks of the intrinsic spirituality and love of nature, *biophilia* as Wilson has called it,[20] that deeply resonates with that group of people in Australia and elsewhere who call themselves "spiritual but not religious."[21]

My real question is, where is the line drawn between resonating with and responding to Indigenous, contextual, and public theologies, and co-opting that theology in a post-postcolonial recolonizing manner? How far

17. Bonhoeffer, *Letters and Papers*, 448.
18. Bonhoeffer, *Letters and Papers*, 448.
19. Hopkins, *Poems and Prose*, 27.
20. Wilson, *Biophilia*.
21. Australian Bureau of Statistics, "Religious Affiliation in Australia"; Rayson et al., "Report."

does the invitation go from Indigenous people for we non-Indigenous to learn the wisdom of the ancients? How do we safely negotiate the space between learning and re- or misappropriating that which is not our own? Speaking just before the World Council of Churches gathering in Germany in 2022, Pattel-Gray stated:

> The solutions to the growing concern of global climate change must include the ancient wisdom and knowledge of First Nations people as we have, and continue to, live with the whole of creation since time began. This is a resource that has not been recognised or embraced.[22]

How does one "recognise" and "embrace" without appropriating that knowledge? Worse, how does one avoid "trading off" of Indigenous and traditional knowledge, not an unknown problem in the academy. Stories of anthropologists and other social scientists making a career off Indigenous peoples was a common story and probably still is. At least, it concerns me enough, as someone wishing to do theology in a strange place, to be cautious and concerned to *not* appropriate Indigenous knowledge for my own benefit.

INTEGRATION

One way forward, I think, might be to remember that much knowledge is built upon ancient wisdom from many sources. I've already noted Bonhoeffer referring to and drawing on the knowledge within a Greek myth—but this is recent wisdom compared to the most ancient of all peoples in the land now called Australia. Aunty Rev. Denise Champion has humorously noted: "Walter Brueggemann draws on the Hebrew Scriptures to find guidance for contemporary issues. For him, they had credibility because they are from an old wisdom. When I read that I thought, 'Well you obviously haven't sat with Aboriginal people!'"[23]

The Christian faith is built on the wisdom of ancient peoples and their interpretations of the Transcendent and the world around them. Theology as a discipline is built on the interpretation of the texts that contain these stories, and their reinterpretation in new and changing contexts. As Cliff Bird has helpfully said to me, "It is a rare theologian who has an original idea,"[24] and this reflects that our discipline is one of standing on the shoul-

22. World Council of Churches, "Prof. Anne Pattel-Gray," para. 3.
23. Champion and Dewerse, *Anaditj*, 23.
24. Cliff Bird, email to author, Sept. 8, 2022.

ders of those who have gone before, or more likely, feasting at the buffet of ideas and creating new menus. The nature of contextual theology requires discernment in theological reflection and praxis in community. When the "community" is increasingly globalized, facing issues common to all of humanity, it seems to me that the only hope for theology is a rich discourse that considers knowledge and wisdom from many sources and the expedition of local responses and solutions.

WHOSE *OIKOS* IS IT ANYWAY?

The idea of *oikos*, our common home, operates at one level to describe problems of global magnitude that require a global response. Indeed, as "wicked" problems, climate change and biodiversity loss require a range of yet untested responses from across sectors, all working together to limit the negative effects, without certainty of success. *Oikos* has appeal, reminding us of our common humanity, common home, common problems. The issues are shared, but so is the potential solution.

The dangers of *oikos* used in this way are many. Romanticism of the natural world can mask inherent and enduring racism, harking back to "the noble savage" and in some places, entrenching casteism. It can also overlook the diversity of peoples and knowledge, smoothing over local understandings and responses. It can suggest we are all equally affected by climate change and equally culpable, sometimes misanthropizing the problems while absolving corporations and industrialized nations.[25]

The burden of climate change is not shared equally. The effects are felt most acutely amongst people who are the least responsible for the problem and who are already vulnerable: individuals regardless of location, and groups within even wealthy countries. Significantly, in places where the social gradient is steepest, that is, where there is the biggest difference between the wealthiest and the poorest, the effects of external stressors are greatest.[26] But by far, the greatest impact of erratic seasons, severe weather events, sea level rise, land and water salination, and food instability are, and will increasingly be, felt by the world's poorest countries.[27]

My hope in doing theology in a different place, a place where I am outsider, foreigner, and I, rather than the place, is the one who is strange, is to learn from the fellow travelers with whom I journey. May I cowrite papers with colleagues from the Pacific? I certainly hope so. May I learn

25. Zachariah, "Whose *Oikos* Is It."
26. Siegrist and Marmot, *Social Inequalities in Health*.
27. IPCC, "Summary for Policymakers."

new ways of thinking, feeling, and being in a new place? That is my intention and I suspect the process has already begun. Will I need to check my subconscious white privilege? I certainly expect so, while at the same time using whatever resources to which I might have access to raise the voices of others.

MOORING AND BELONGING

> We are a wayfaring people. We have always moved between spaces, across oceans, visiting and staying a time, island to island. We trade, we learn, we marry. We don't need to possess, we just need to be. Stay a while, moor your canoe. You don't need to belong, just be. You'll belong when you take responsibility.[28]

I flew across the ocean, unable to read or write in flight, head pressed against the cabin window and watching the waves. Sparkles of sunlight, gusts of wind, ever-changing patterns and colors. Movement everywhere, making my own seem somehow less significant. Landing in torrential rain I was bathed before I arrived at my new home. The next morning, before dawn, I heard the drumbeat that had accompanied my whole life only this time it wasn't in my head. I knew I belonged here. I spent the August day thawing out, returning to the tropics after a decades-long winter.

Being located provides a certain lens on one's theology. It is impossible not to write with urgency about sea level rise when one's own home and neighbors' homes are at direct risk, or to theologize differently when religious anachronisms from a different time and place affect local people, women especially, so directly and significantly. Ecological and gender injustice both have their roots in the colonial past and its enduring effects. However, the words I write are mine and I am responsible for them. I speak only from my own privileged viewpoint, sneaking a peak over a different horizon.

Robin Wall Kimmerer, who so generously shares indigenous wisdom from Turtle Island (that great island swimming between Pacific and Atlantic), invites us all to "become indigenous" to place. She states:

> I want to envision a way that an immigrant society could become indigenous to place . . . Immigrants cannot by definition be indigenous. . . . But if people do not feel "indigenous," can they nevertheless enter into the deep reciprocity that renews

---

28. Fatilua Fatilua, email to author, Sept. 10, 2022.

the world? Is this something that can be learned? Where are the teachers?[29]

Jione Havea pushes back against such generosity lest it obfuscates color. In his chapter "Forgive Us Our Trespasses," Havea discusses otherness and blackness in terms of "People of the land." For Havea, People of the land include Indigenous Australians, laborers and workers, enslaved people as well as biblical tribes who were variously colonized, overrun, and exploited for the purposes of building the "People of God." By extension, the "People of the land" includes victims of missions and "ordinary people in the islands."[30] Havea is concerned that we (and especially black people) "see" blackness, otherness, and pay attention to it. He quotes Spivak, who describes the Pacific as "the 'absent' part of the Asia-Pacific that people fly over."[31] As a white person now living in a decidedly non-absent island, I attempt to confront these tensions: resisting a biblical message that is also colonial; being a member of the People of God but perhaps at the expense of the People of the land; being non-indigenous but with my feet in the sand and my hands in the soil. We are all moored somewhere, those of us who are not People of the land. We balance learning from local knowledge with our history of pillage and ignorance.

My colleagues describe the process of transitioning from guest to local, just as some of them have transitioned from diaspora to returning to place. That process involves a shift in knowing, from etic to emic, as well as shift in responsibility. Part of belonging is taking on increasing responsibility within community and ecology. Permission to explore *moana* theology and learn ancient wisdom involves responsibility to colleagues and to place.[32]

We all have responsibilities: to the land, each other, the other-than-human parts of creation, and to God. As I walk a new land, a fluid, blue land that is more water than soil, I learn new responsibilities just as I learn new wisdoms. Theology can be this way: wise to its context and to its blindspots. Feet grounded in the soil and imagination soaring in the cosmos. Honoring the sources of its knowledge and the heritage of its words. Building new communities, networks, and relationships; being accountable to those around me.

A final comment reflects something similar to what Jonas Edward Salk, creator of the polio vaccine, is attributed as saying, that we revere the wisdom of the ancestors and, in turn, live lives that might have us remembered

---

29. Kimmerer, *Braiding Sweetgrass*, 213.
30. Havea, "Forgive Us Our Trespasses," 212.
31. Havea, "Forgive Us Our Trespasses," 215.
32. Thanks to Faafetai Aiava for ongoing personal communications.

as wise ancestors also. But the climate catastrophe, loaded with existential threat for the survival of many species, including our own, means that instead of being concerned about being *wise* ancestors, we should be more concerned that we will not be ancestors *at all*. If we are to learn anything we need to find a way to learn from the ancient wisdoms held in custodianship by Indigenous and Pasifika people, to write theology that is life-giving to the biosphere and not only to human, colonialist parts of it; to do theology that enriches church communities and assists social and political processes to walk gently and restore justice.

BIBLIOGRAPHY

Anselm. *Basic Writings*. Edited and Translated by Thomas Williams. Hackett Classics. Indianapolis: Hackett, 2007.

Australian Bureau of Statistics. "Religious Affiliation in Australia." Australian Bureau of Statistics, Apr. 7, 2022. https://www.abs.gov.au/articles/religious-affiliation-australia#religious-affiliation-in-2021.

Bonhoeffer, Dietrich. *Barcelona, Berlin, New York*. Edited by Clifford J. Green. Dietrich Bonhoeffer Works 10. Minneapolis: Fortress, 2008.

———. *Letters and Papers from Prison*. Edited by John W. De Gruchy. Dietrich Bonhoeffer Works 8. Minneapolis: Fortress, 2010.

Bonhoeffer, Dietrich, and Maria von Wedemeyer. *Love Letters from Cell 92: The Correspondence between Dietrich Bonhoeffer and Maria von Wedemeyer 1943–45*. Edited by Ruth-Alice von Bismarck and Ulrich Kabitz. Translated by John Brownjohn. Nashville: Abingdon, 1995.

Champion, Denise, and Rosemary Dewerse. *Anaditj*. Adelaide: Self-published, 2021.

Ford, David F. *Shaping Theology: Engagements in a Religious and Secular World*. Oxford: Blackwell, 2007.

Havea, Jione. "Forgive Us Our Trespasses: Black Australia, Peopled Wilderness, Eroding Islands." In *Indigenous Australia and the Unfinished Business of Theology: Cross-Cultural Engagement*, edited by Jione Havea, 207–20. Postcolonialism and Religions. New York: Palgrave Macmillan, 2014.

Hopkins, Gerard Manley. *Poems and Prose*. Edited by W. H. Gardner. Penguin Classics. London: Penguin, 1953.

Howes, Stephen, and Huiyuan Liu. "How Many People with Pacific Island Heritage Live in Australia?" DevPolicyBlog, Dec. 22, 2022. https://devpolicy.org/how-many-people-with-pacific-island-heritage-live-in-australia-20220517/.

IPCC. "Summary for Policymakers." In *Climate Change 2022: Impacts, Adaptation and Vulnerability; Contribution of Working Group II to the Sixth Assessment Report of the Intergovernmental Panel on Climate Change*, 3–33. Cambridge: Cambridge University Press, 2022.

Kimmerer, Robin Wall. *Braiding Sweetgrass: Indigenous Wisdom, Scientific Knowledge and the Teachings of Plants*. Minneapolis: Milkweed, 2013.

Lovat, Terence, and Daniel J. Fleming. *What Is This Thing Called Theology? Considering the Spiritual in the Public Square*. Macksville, Aus.: Barlow, 2014.

Muoneme, Maduabuchi Leo, SJ. *The Hermeneutics of Jesuit Leadership in Higher Education: The Meaning and Culture of Jesuit-Catholic Presidents.* Routledge Research in Educational Leadership. New York: Routledge, 2017. https://doi.org/10.4324/9781315208572.

Ormerod, Neil. *Introducing Contemporary Theologies: The What and the Who of Theology Today.* Enlarged and rev. ed. Maryknoll, NY: Orbis, 1997.

Prentis, Brooke. "Learning to Be Guests of Ancient Hosts on Ancient Lands." *Thought Matters* 7 (2017) 79–86.

Ravulo, Jioji. "Pacific Communities in Australia." University of Wollongong Australia, 2015. https://ro.uow.edu.au/sspapers/3892/.

Rayson, Dianne. "Earthly Christianity: Bonhoeffer's Contribution to Ecotheology and Ecoethics." *The Bonhoeffer Legacy: An International Journal* 6 (2018) 21–34.

Rayson, Dianne, et al. "Report on the 2020 and 2021 Australian Church Life Surveys." NCLS Research Occasional Paper 39, Macquarie Park, Aus., 2022.

Siegrist, Johannes, and M. G. Marmot, eds. *Social Inequalities in Health: New Evidence and Policy Implications.* Oxford: Oxford University Press, 2006.

Wilson, Edward O. *Biophilia: The Human Bond with Other Species.* Cambridge: Harvard University Press, 1984.

World Council of Churches. "Prof. Anne Pattel-Gray Urges: 'Include Ancient Wisdom and Knowledge of First Nations People.'" World Council of Churches, Aug. 30, 2022. https://www.oikoumene.org/news/prof-anne-pattel-gray-urges-include-ancient-wisdom-and-knowledge-of-first-nations-people.

Zachariah, George. "Whose *Oikos* Is It Anyway? Towards a *Poromboke* Eco-Theology of 'Commoning.'" In *Decolonizing Ecotheology: Indigenous and Subaltern Challenges*, edited by S. Lily Mendoza and George Zachariah, 201–18. Intersectionality and Theology. Eugene, OR: Pickwick, 2022.

4

A SIN OF OMISSION
The Sinking Islands

Tioti Timon

KIRIBATI AND FOUR OTHER small island nation countries—Maldives, Marshall, Tokelau, and Tuvalu—are made up of low-lying islands. The Maldives is in the Indian Ocean, while the other four are all in the Pacific Ocean. These small island nations are located in different oceans, but they share the same fate: facing the rising sea level, these nations are on the brink of disappearing from the face of this planet.

On these low-lying islands, all people live in coastal areas where they witness extensive coastal erosions, of the beach as well as of the (is)land, taking place.[1] Such erosion is increasingly displacing people from their ancestral homes. Islanders are exposed to coastal hazards, which are the front line of countries that are vulnerable, and are already suffering from the environmental fallout of climate change. They are facing what seems to be a hopeless future with the threat of losing their lands to the rising sea.

In no time, the low-lying islands will be nothing but a vast ocean.

---

1. William-Raynor, "Earth Today."

MATERIAL DESTRUCTION

The ascent of sea levels has resulted in the deleterious impact of coastal areas, causing significant damage to the vital vegetation upon which local communities depend for their sustenance. The destruction of our lands has rendered it increasingly challenging to rely on indigenous food sources. The most unfortunate consequences of climate change on low lying islands are the impact they have on food sources. With the loss of land and water, vegetations are suffering and are on the decline.

This has given rise to a population that rely heavily on imported and predominantly processed foods. The consequence has been the increased number of noncommunicable diseases including "diabetes, obesity, gout, hypertension, coronary heart disease, stroke, and certain cancers."[2]

Our life is heavily dependent on money, and there are a lot of problems for us in meeting the high cost of living. With the financial challenges of our time, our culture of sharing and supporting one another is no longer practical. Life is becoming very difficult—because of the impacts of climate change, and of health and financial struggles.

These are among the serious challenges against the attempts to save the lives of those living in danger, or impending danger, due to climate change. All of us are meant to exist in an "eco-relational household" where harmony of life is upheld, and resources are meant to be shared.[3] But this is not the case for the islanders in Kiribati.

Destruction of the Spirit

Pacific low-lying islands are not just facing the loss of their lands. Their traditional culture is based on a communal lifestyle that is already suffering and will suffer even more in the years to come. This is something of great import to Pacific islanders, which those in the West can hardly imagine. There is an intimate bond between the islanders and the lands, as well as with their material culture.

The sociologist and philosopher Zygmunt Bauman wrote of times past, in which "men and women lived in a time-space with structure; a solid, tough, durable time-space—just the right benchmark against which to plot and monitor the capriciousness and volatility of human will—but also a hard container in which human actions could feel sensible and secure."[4]

---

2. Thomas, "Self-Reliance in Kiribati," 166–67.
3. Bird, "*Pepesa.*"
4. Bauman, *Tourists and Vagabonds*, 8.

Such has been the island way of life, in which people are bound up with their place and situation—in fact, islanders are tied to land and material culture by powerful emotions. By and large, this is no longer known or experienced in the West. Often, in the West, writes Bauman: "Only the shallowest of roots, if any, are struck. Only skin-deep relations, if any, are entered with the locals. Above all, there is no mortgaging of the future, no incurring of long-term obligations, no allowing something that happens today to bind the tomorrow."[5]

Indigenous people of Oceania are connected to their lands and ocean, and thus know every consequence of what they do. This interconnectedness is evident in the way the people in Kiribati regard land as *te aba*, people or nation,[6] and in Fiji the land is "a mother."[7] According to Talia, "The land, sea and sky are the backbones of life and the main resources of religio-cultural heritage. It is like the blood that flows to nurture and maintain life as regarded by people of Oceania."[8]

Understandably, the loss of a mother (as in Fijian understanding of land/*vanua*) is the most hurtful experience to a child, whose life is entirely dependent on the mother. In Kiribati, the loss of a nation (*te aba*) is more than that. *Te aba* is the source of life that gives the meaning of life to all who live on it. "To be cast out from one's *vanua* [land] is to be cut off from one's source of life."[9] The essence of nation-land is fading, as people are being cut off from the source of life. Regarding such impacts, local people appear to have lost their sense of being connected to their environment.

Migration

Moving inland for a more secured place creates problems of overcrowding, because the islands are small in length and narrow in breadth. The internal migration of people has created social-related challenges, especially in capital towns where resettled people experience problems such as domestic violence, land disputes, sex work, pollution, and other consequences of overcrowding.

Migration is a threat to island communities, especially if a whole nation is being relocated. The solution of relocation is not met when you are taken to another (is)land. For example, when the Kiribati population are

5. Bauman, *Tourists and Vagabonds*, 12.
6. Timon, "Theological Reflection of Land."
7. Tuwere, *Vanua*.
8. Talia, "Toward Fatele Theology," 14.
9. Tuwere, *Vanua*, 36.

relocated to Fiji or New Zealand, they are relocated to a land where they find solution for the problem of land erosion and of overcrowding but, in their new home, they encounter more challenges.

Migrants from indigenous land will end up at a meaningless place where, as a new world, people live without their rights as landowners.[10] Instead, they will rent or mortgage the rights that belong to a local landlord, and they must adopt a different, foreign, and strange cultural standard of living. This is evident in the migration of Pacific islanders to other countries. They migrate from the traditional village to a global village, where life is heavily dependent on money. The transition from a traditional subsistence lifestyle to a contemporary market-based economy brings with it key environmental challenges. The Pacific migrants face racism, abuse, injustice, and discrimination, among other challenges.

Therefore, to settle in a new place is the beginning of experiencing new and real problems. Proper planning is needed to ensure that people do not encounter more difficulties during relocation. In developing countries, the failure of resettlement results not just from "inadequate inputs of resources (money, staff, and political will), but from the inherent complexity of resettlement as a social process involving human beings with hopes, dreams, aspirations, and, especially, memories."[11]

This indicates that security approaches focus on the individuals, groups, and communities who are affected by climate change, and insist that they must be given the opportunity to participate effectively in decisions that affect them. The church also needs to seriously consider climate change as a matter of human security, because it undermines people's welfare, well-being, water, food, security, shelter, health, and culture. This unstable situation requires a strong politics of security, that migration should be constructed as a positive policy solution in the context of climate change. In other words, migration is part of the problem, not part of a solution.

MANEABA

In response to migration as problem, I take the design of the *maneaba* (name for the community or village meetinghouse in Kiribati) as an approach to be taken in the interconnection of care and responsibility for planet Earth and victims of climate change. The self-expression and self-definition of the main role of this community building comes from its name.

---

10. Wright, "Indigenous Elders."
11. Burson, *Climate Change and Migration*, 78.

Maneaba comes from *mwaneaba*, which is made up of two Kiribati words—*mwanea* and (*te*) *aba-manea*, meaning "to accommodate or take care." This care is rendered toward *te aba* (lit.: "people" and "land") so the purpose of the *maneaba* (and what happen in it, as a meetinghouse) is to accommodate or to take care of the land and people.

The meaning of the word *mwaneaba* is embodied, therefore, in two categories of existence: "The people who live on the land and the land on which people live."[12] Thus, the Kiribati word *mwaneaba* reminds the people of their cultural existence being recognized in their role to *mwanea te aba* (lit.: "to care for both the land and the people"). This approach is based on the inclusiveness of the effort, skill, and knowledge of the community.

Spiritual Goal

Maneaba requires the community's involvement to contribute and work together as a group. The design and purpose of *maneaba* is to strengthen the traditional culture of inclusiveness and care for every member of the community. No one is to be excluded.

A positive feature of this model is that it brings the community to participate and be responsible for the common good of the community. Under this system, individualism is not encouraged, but rather communal ways of living, where sharing and hospitality is practiced within the community. If this system is employed for the future security of our planet, people, and the environment, then no one will be left behind.

In order to maintain the life of every species on earth, it will be necessary to live alongside and integrate with other living communities; not to live in separation as a superior being or ruler, but to serve and preserve everyone involved. As the theologian and intellectual historian Alister McGrath insists: "There is thus no theological ground for asserting that humanity has the 'right' to do what it pleases with the natural order. The creation is God's, and has been entrusted to humanity, which is to act as its steward, not its exploiter."[13] When we preserve the life of low-lying islands, we also preserve the life of all creation, and thus glorify and honor the Creator. Moreover, when we destroy the life of the land and ocean, at the same time we destroy God the Creator.

There is a responsibility that is relational between human beings, and towards the environment, and vice versa. Lacking an understanding of this

---

12. Timon, "Theological Reflection of Land," 6.
13. McGrath, *Re-Enchantment of Nature*, 29.

relational responsibility, people will never realize and acknowledge that their destructive activities to their environment is a sin against the Creator.

VICTIMS' TRAJECTORY

Unfortunately, at present, the trajectory is toward the destruction of our island home, and the tearing apart of our fabric of life. The former president of Kiribati, Anote Tong, explained that, in the next century, our country will be under water, and that the country is already suffering because of severe weather problems. One of the actions Tong took was to request a moratorium on investments in new coal mines. He stressed that if we do not survive, it will be due to the international community not coming to our assistance.[14]

This reality creates lot of fear and uncertainty about the future among the Kiribati people. Tong advocated around the world for bold action to address climate change. For the government, the future of Kiribati will be in the collective concern of the international community to do something about reducing carbon emissions.[15]

Even though the islands are sinking due to rising sea levels, the courage of the people is resilient. In Kiribati, the government addressed the nation on the issue of climate change, and the need to continue to work on the following: "a) to keep citizens informed, b) to consolidate a national shared hope and vision for a better future of the people of Kiribati while c) adapting to the impacts of climate."[16] Climate change has brought the nation of Kiribati together to renew their commitment to serve their islands and the planet as a whole. The positive aim for this gathering was to call upon all nations to unite with them to save their island and the home planet.

Climate change is a pressing global issue that affects all of us, and as responsible citizens, we have a crucial role to play in complementing government efforts to address its impacts. It is essential for the public to understand the seriousness of climate change and the need for proactive measures to adapt to its effects.

By acknowledging our responsibilities and acting at individual and community levels, we can support and strengthen government-led adaptation programs. Encouraging national leaders to collaborate and work together is crucial in preparing communities to cope with the challenges

---

14. Timon, "Theological Reflection of Land," 9–11.
15. Worland, "Meet the President."
16. Office te Beretitenti Press Release, "Wet Weather," para. 12.

of climate change. Together, as a united front, we can build resilience and create a sustainable future for generations to come.

MATTERS OF JUSTICE

If, therefore, the indigenous peoples have been living with a deep connection to a land as their only home on earth, then any dislocation and/or disconnection from their homeland by powerful external, imperial forces constitutes a violation of their human rights.

Climate change is a reality that is not only so obvious but also, with more destructive power and acceleration, boosted by "the greed and selfishness of the few people and industrialized countries who treasure their comfort no matter what."[17] Teuatabo has stressed the spiritual and cultural devastation that comes when indigenous people are forced to leave their land, because it is a matter of people with both land and culture. The land and the people go together. You cannot exist without your country, so the question of displacement becomes a question of existence as human beings.

Citing the voices of government leaders in low-lying atolls, the former president of Kiribati lamented: "For those of us whose very survival is at stake, our plea is very simple, let us pay no lip service to this critical issue that demands immediate and urgent action." However, the former president said that not many political leaders were willing to listen. A president from Tuvalu extended the same lamentation: "We cannot just sit back and watch our homeland slowly disappear . . . time is running out fast. Climate change could well be the greatest challenge that humanity has ever known. I make a very strong plea to all to act quickly and responsibly, to ensure that countries like Tuvalu do not disappear."[18]

These voices are concerned with the well-being, security, and future of the land and people, calling upon the international community to work together for the victims of climate change. Because there is much uncertainty and insecurity among people living on low-lying islands, I argue that injustice and selfishness are the main causes that must be addressed for the survival of climate change victims. It is, ultimately, a problem of the heart—and here not only the church, but the God of creation also, have a pivotal role. The first task of the Holy Spirit, "when he comes, will [be to] convict the world concerning sin, and righteousness, and judgement" (John 16:8 author's translation).

17. Teuatabo, "Climate Change in Kiribati," 12–13.
18. Nunn, "End of the Pacific," 157–58.

Small island nations have often been the most outspoken in the world in calling for action to address climate change. However, it is rare to hear leaders from powerful countries publicly discussing worst-case scenarios where sea levels rise to the point where low-lying islands become uninhabitable and entire nations need to relocate.

As the world moves into the technological age, what future is there for the powerless, innocent people struggling to get on with life? Whom shall we blame, and would the perpetrator accept their *being* blamed? Or is blame even necessary to motivate compassion?

Parliamentarians speak easily of justice, peace, security, and a higher standard of living in their campaigns. Is it bringing justice to the lowly and powerless who have no say? Everything in this world is a race to be seen and to be ranked at the top of human powers.

United to Fight

The situation that low-lying atolls are facing is not so much the end of their world, but the beginning of a new life in a new creation. The climate change crisis has resulted in the coming together of Pacific countries, and churches, as a united voice against injustice in the world and at the same time a challenge to their own people to assess their way of living that has also contributed to the destruction of their environment.[19] Each country may not be able to save their own country entirely, but they nevertheless have a responsibility to do their part to live in solidarity with creation that will be a living message for later generations.

To unite as one nation is an initial step, to fight against the challenges of global warming related to sea level rise. The next challenge is for different nations to work together. Therefore, all nations need to engage and work together for effective solutions to save the planet.

In response to this concern, the government of Kiribati held a national discussion for the first time in Kiribati history, where the entire nation, including the Kiribati people living in diaspora, were brought together to discuss the critical issue of climate change (2015). The theme of this national discussion was: "Let's work together to build national resilience against climate change impacts." The public must declare where they stand on the issue of climate change, because climate change is a social issue caused by human interference (which is ongoing, thus adding fuel to the climate crises).

The churches should be faithful in their moral and theological teachings, so that people understand what constitutes justice in the relationship

---

19. Conradie and Ayre, "Ecclesiology and Ecology."

between human beings and creation. The people are to be encouraged to understand what justice is, and to live with justice in order to stand against injustice. Moreover, churches should empower their prayer for world leaders to be filled with compassion and consideration for the victims of global warming.

Political Responsibility

The challenge of sea level rise is a wake-up call to people living on this planet, to act and do something to save this planet. Climate change is not only destroying lives on low-lying atolls; it is also destroying the lives of millions of vulnerable people who are struggling for life across the world.

In a resilient response to climate change, the Kiribati government agencies and churches held workshops to educate the population on how to mitigate and adapt to climate challenges and crises. People were informed and encouraged to plant mangroves and coconut trees for protection of their lands from soil erosion. However, more steps should be undertaken, because climate change has created a global ecological crisis that needs a global plan of action for the life of the whole planet.

Therefore, all nations are challenged to work together to fight against the injustice that is oppressing and destroying all forms of life. In addition, the challenge of climate change is the missional responsibility of the church, because it is also a spiritual issue. This is specifically recognized by Pope Francis in his 2015 *Laudato Si'*, where he states: "If you know what is wrong and you are able to fix it, but for some reason lack the will or imagination to go ahead and fix it, then you have a spiritual problem."[20] There are strong Christian roots to environmental degradation, which lays the blame on Christianity for its part in the crisis, both in general terms, as leaders in the industrial revolution, and in the development of capitalism and consumerism. In specific terms, Christian countries are among those that contribute the most to climate change,[21] irrespective of the reality that many of the smaller and poorer Christian countries are the ones that suffer the most.

While Christians in some contexts contribute disproportionally to carbon emissions, Christians in other contexts are or will increasingly become the victims of climate change. Capitalism, consumerism, and the prosperity message are aspects of Christian Western cultures and churches. Christians, in defending their own interests in the context of climate change, have done so without caring for the victims of climate change. Therefore, instead of

20. Francis, "*Laudato Si'*," §6.
21. Conradie, "Ecology and Mission," 104.

merely confessing their faith, I propose that these Christian nations and churches must declare their confession of guilt.[22]

The Church's Vocation

While climate change represents the most urgent threat to the future well-being of poor and vulnerable communities around the world, it nevertheless occupies a low priority in the church's ministry and mission. Although this scenario has affected the inhabitants of millions living in poor countries, pastors have not taken climate change seriously in their preaching or other pastoral responsibilities within their communities.

LenkaBula has highlighted the church's silence in its prophetic role as well as its failure to take responsibility to address the issue of injustice and discrimination that threatens the life of vulnerable communities.[23] In the Accra Confession, churches are called to be transformed in order to "promote God's household of life and reflect on the ways God gives life and protects justice in creation and human society" to care for the earth for present and future generations.[24]

The church in its prophetic role should not remain passive, but rise and tell the truth, demonstrate and protest against wealthier countries and industrial injustice that do not care for the future of this planet. As Steven Chu, the US Secretary of Energy and Nobel Prize winner has said, "from here on in, every day has to be Earth Day."[25]

What does this—every day has to be Earth Day—mean when five countries on this planet are sinking? How can we celebrate Earth Day every day when low-lying countries are vanishing from the face of this planet? How can we praise God for the beautiful creation when five sinking countries are ignored?

Even though climate change is a global struggle that dominates all other agendas, and is prominent in the public imagination, it is also a challenge that can be addressed only through a collective, indeed a global, effort. As we live in one world where we share—the same air that we breathe, the same water that we drink, and the same land on which we live—a unified international fight against ecological destruction is the most effective approach to deal with the problem. If one part of the same body is injured, the whole body will also be affected. This is a challenge by the church, to all

22. Conradie, "Ecology and Mission," 108.
23. LenkaBula, *Choose Life*, 128.
24. Conradie, "Theological Resources," 38.
25. Miller, *God, Creation*, 23.

governments, to call upon the powerful nations to work together to save the planet. Each nation can act to make a difference. To unite as one nation is an initial step to fight against the challenges of global warming. Therefore, all nations need to be engaged and work together for effective solutions to save the planet.

The Creator gave humankind a way of life which has been abused by people who do not have due regard for the welfare of the future of the earth. Let's work together to build national resilience against climate change and consolidate an international shared hope and vision for a better future.

BIBLIOGRAPHY

Bauman, Zygmunt. *Tourists and Vagabonds: Heroes and Victims of Postmodernity*. Political Science Series 30. Vienna: Institute for Higher Studies, 1996.

Bird, Cliff. "*Pepesa*—The Household of Life: A Theological Exploration of Land in the Context of Change in Solomon Islands." PhD diss., Charles Sturt University, 2008.

Burson, Bruce, ed. *Climate Change and Migration: South Pacific Perspectives*. Wellington: Institute of Policy Studies, 2010.

Conradie, Ernst M. "Ecology and Mission (Marturia): The Church in God's Householding." In *The Church in God's Household: Protestant Perspectives on Ecclesiology and Ecology*, edited by Clive W. Ayre and Ernst M. Conradie, 94–115. Pietermaritzburg: Cluster, 2016.

———. "Theological Resources for Responding to Climate Change: An Overview. Missionalia." *Southern African Journal of Mission Studies* 37 (2009) 33–52.

Conradie, Ernst M., and Clive W. Ayre. "Ecclesiology and Ecology in Ecumenical Perspective." In *The Church in God's Household: Protestant Perspectives on Ecclesiology and Ecology*, edited by Clive W. Ayre and Ernst M. Conradie, 1–9. Pietermaritzburg: Cluster, 2016.

Francis, Pope. "*Laudato Si'*: On Care for Our Common Home." Vatican, May 24, 2015. https://www.vatican.va/content/francesco/en/encyclicals/documents/papa-francesco_20150524_enciclica-laudato-si.html.

LenkaBula, Puleng. *Choose Life, Act in Hope: African Churches Living Out the Accra Confession; A Study Resource on the Accra Confession; Covenanting for Justice in the Economy and Earth*. Geneva: World Alliance of Reformed Churches, 2009.

McGrath, Alister. *The Re-Enchantment of Nature: Science, Religion and the Human Sense of Wonder*. Sydney: Hodder & Stoughton, 2003.

Miller, Richard W., ed. *God, Creation, and Climate Change: A Catholic Response to the Environmental Crisis*. Maryknoll, NY: Orbis, 2010.

Nunn, Patrick D. "The End of the Pacific? Effect of the Sea Level Rise on Pacific Island Livelihoods." *Singapore Journal of Tropical Geography* 134 (2013) 143–71.

Office te Beretitenti Press Release. "Wet Weather Fails to Dampen Public Hearing Spirit." Climate, 2004. http://www.climate.gov.ki/tag/president.anote.tong. Link discontinued.

Talia, Maina. "Toward Fatele Theology: A Contextual Theological Response in Addressing Threats of Global Warming in Tuvalu." MTh thesis, Tainan Theological College, 2009.

Teuatabo, Nakibae. "Climate Change in Kiribati: Report to the Sustainable Development." *Kiribati National Report to World Summit on Sustainable Development* 3 (2002) 12–20.

Thomas, Frank R. "Self-Reliance in Kiribati: Contrasting Views of Agricultural and Fisheries Production." *Geographical Journal* 168 (2002) 163–77.

Timon, Tioti. "A Theological Reflection of Land in the Context of Climate." MTh thesis, Charles Sturt University, 2013.

Tuwere, I. Sevati. *Vanua: Towards a Fijian Theology of Place*. Suva, Fiji: Institute of Pacific Studies of the University of the South Pacific, 2002.

William-Raynor, Petre. "Earth Today: Small Islands to Shape Priorities at Upcoming Climate Talks." *Jamaica Gleaner*, Aug. 16, 2017. http://jamaica-gleaner.com/article/news/20170817/earth-today-small-islands-shape-priorities-upcoming-climate-talks/.

Worland, Justin. "Meet the President Trying to Save His Island Nation from Climate Change." *TIME*, Oct. 9, 2015. https://time.com/4058851/kiribati-cliamte-change/.

Wright, Robin M. "Indigenous Elders and Medicine Peoples Council Statement United Nations Convention on Climate Change COP21 Paris, France, 30 November–11 December 2015." *Journal for the Study of Religion Nature and Culture* 10 (2016) 255–59.

5

REIMAGINING CLIMATE CHANGE EDUCATION IN THE PACIFIC

'Elisapesi Hepi Havea and Lynley Tulloch

CLIMATE CHANGE IS HAVING serious impacts on Pacific Island ecosystems, biodiversity, and livelihoods, putting the well-being of people and nonhuman animals at risk.[1] The uncertainty and complexity of climate change is of critical concern for ecological and social well-being and survival. Climate change is causing an increase in the number and frequency of extreme weather events, rising sea levels and an increase in disease and ill-health.

Climate change education (CCE) is one response to these challenges. CCE aims to prepare students for the impact of climate change—now and in the future. This aim is met by building knowledge and awareness of climate change and supporting students in problem-solving and decision-making. The action component of climate change is perhaps the most crucial in empowering students to make a difference in addressing climate change. While climate change education (CCE) is of critical importance, if it is based within sustainable development discourse (SDD) then its relevance to Pacific Island communities is questionable. This is because CCE is often

---

1. Hills et al., "Social and Ecological Imperative."

situated within the field of education for sustainable development (EfSD),[2] which is dominantly framed through a Euro-Western lens.[3]

Sustainable development discourse (SDD) is currently the dominant environmental discourse globally and is embedded within United Nations interglobal governmental policy contexts.[4] This UN-led discourse of SDD is based on free-market neoliberal capitalistic premises.[5] For CCE to be meaningful for Pacific peoples we need to reimagine what it can look like in Pacific contexts.

This chapter addresses the challenge of reimagining CCE in the Pacific. We explore the issue of climate change and what it means in the Pacific before exploring the dominant UN response. Following this we discuss approaches to CCE and identify the features that are relevant to Pacific contexts. Finally, the *talanoa* approach to CCE is discussed and highlights its relational, dialogic and transformative potential. This discussion is based on research done in Tonga, but the findings can be transferred to other Pacific Island contexts.[6]

CLIMATE CHANGE AND THE PACIFIC REGION

Since the last ice age twelve thousand years ago the Earth has enjoyed a relatively stable and warm climate, ideal for life to flourish. This epoch is known as the Haloacene.[7] However, in the more recent past, human activity—including industrialization, agriculture and the technological systems that sustain them—has caused large-scale global environmental change. This includes climate change, ocean acidification, pollution of airways and waterways, and biodiversity loss.[8]

Scientists claim we have now entered the Anthropocene, a period when human activity is changing weather patterns.[9] The climate is changing due to carbon emissions as a result of industrial activity and use of fossil fuels. As a result, we are experiencing an increasing number of extreme

   2. Banjay and Blum, "Education Responses"; Mochizuki and Bryan, "Climate Change Education."
   3. Tulloch and Neilson, "Neoliberalisation of Sustainablity."
   4. Tulloch and Neilson, "Neoliberalisation of Sustainablity."
   5. Kothari et al., "Buen Vivir"; Tulloch and Neilson, "Neoliberalisation of Sustainablity."
   6. Havea, "Climate Change Education."
   7. Kress and Stine, *Living in the Anthropocene*.
   8. Kopnina and Shoreman-Ouimet, *Sustainability*; Kress and Stine, *Living in the Anthropocene*.
   9. Kress and Stine, *Living in the Anthropocene*.

weather events. The sixth assessment report by the Intergovernmental Panel on Climate Change (IPCC) details a range of devastating observed impacts and projected risks of climate change for small islands including those in the Pacific: "Small islands are increasingly affected by increases in temperature, a larger proportion of the most intense tropical cyclones (TCs), storm surges, droughts, changing precipitation patterns, sea-level rise (SLR), coral bleaching, and invasive species, all of which are already detectable across both natural and human systems."[10]

The IPCC report states that the ongoing impact of humans on the degradation of terrestrial and marine ecosystems means that small islands are increasingly vulnerable to climate change. They draw on studies to suggest an extinction risk of 100 percent for endemic species within Pacific regions by 2100 for > 3°C warming. The IPCC also addresses coral bleaching, which is severe in the Pacific regions. Future climate scenarios predict: "Above 1.5°C, globally inclusive of small islands, it is projected there will be further loss of 70–90% of reef-building corals, with 99% of corals being lost under warming of 2°C or more above the preindustrial period."[11]

Loss of coral reefs and the degradation of terrestrial and marine ecosystems are having (and will increasingly have) serious consequences for food and water security, health and well-being, economies, human displacement, and culture. By the end of this century sea levels are predicted to rise by one meter. Low-lying islands such as the Marshall Islands, Tuvalu, and Kiribati face becoming uninhabitable.[12]

From the above discussion it is evident that the environmental crisis we face is multifaceted and felt unevenly across the globe. The Pacific region is particularly vulnerable to the impacts of climate change due to its reliance on local ecosystems for subsistence, small land area, and high population density.[13]

UN RESPONSE TO CLIMATE CHANGE

At the global level, the United Nations (UN) call for capping temperature rise at 1.5°C through net-zero strategies and for all nations to adopt the seventeen UN Sustainable Development Goals (SDGs). These were promulgated at the Twenty-Sixth Conference of the Parties (COP26), and O'Riordan has

---

10. IPCC, *Small Islands*, 1.
11. IPCC, *Small Islands*, 1.
12. Kim et al., "Climate Change and Health."
13. Kim et al., "Climate Change and Health."

argued that addressing climate change through these measures is a daunting and unrealistic goal.[14]

COP26 called for education to be a key part of climate strategies. Teaching climate change issues and environmental education should be introduced to the curriculum. Education was regarded as having transformative role in addressing the climate crisis.[15]

The UN narratives of climate change and SDGs are dominantly viewed through the lens of neoliberal capitalism and Euro-Western science and worldviews.[16] Euro-Western worldviews are based on anthropocentrism, individualism, and economic growth as progress.[17]

Such approaches are based on a human-ecology dichotomy that is at odds with indigenous epistemologies. Accordingly, mainstream discourses of climate change often miss (or misrepresent) the perspectives, realities, and approaches in the Pacific. Pacific Island relational ontologies and knowledge systems are holistic and often incommensurable with Western ecological science.[18] While there has been a concerted attempt by the UN since the 1990s to articulate traditional ecological knowledge (TEK) with Western ecological science, this has resulted in a misalignment and simplification of indigenous knowledge systems.

Too often Euro-Western education approaches (including EfSD) relegate indigenous knowledge systems to the margins; drawing upon them only as they are regarded as providing "cultural insight" or "specialized ecological and traditional knowledge."[19] The core business or backbone of CCE is assumed to be Western climate science and solutions are framed in terms of "behavior change" and "green technologies" and, most worrying, "economic growth." This is not to say that climate science is not imperative to draw on, or that behavior change and technology are not important in tackling climate change. Rather, we argue that it is important to shift the orientation for CCE to the Pacific so that it is grounded in Pacific ontologies and epistemologies. Accordingly, this chapter questions CCE based on SDD, arguing that the underpinning Western neoliberal assumptions are inadequate bases for CCE in the Pacific region. Instead, we propose a socio-ecological approach to CCE that is grounded in *talanoa* as a pedagogy. This approach draws on Pacific Island narratives, epistemologies, value systems, and realities.

14. O'Riordan, "COP 26."
15. Steer, *COP26*.
16. Tulloch and Neilson, "Neoliberalisation of Sustainablity."
17. Gruenewald, "Foucauldian Analysis."
18. Fache and Pauwels, "Tackling Coastal 'Overfishing.'"
19. Mochizuki and Bryan, "Climate Change Education."

SOCIO-ECOLOGICAL THEORY AND CLIMATE CHANGE EDUCATION

Socio-ecological theories focus on the interaction between people and their environment. They consider the systems within which people are embedded, including local and global political and economic contexts.[20] A socio-ecological worldview looks at how economic and social systems contribute to our ecological crisis. The relationship between capitalist economic growth, the global economy and ecological concerns is pivotal to foreground in a socially critical CCE. In times of severe ecological crises such as we are currently experiencing, education needs to prioritize conscientization and to privilege ecological worldviews.[21]

Banjay and Blum have argued that education is a "critical element in the response to the challenges of climate change."[22] In linking climate change to EfSD, they argue that it aims to engage students in authentic, inquiry-based pedagogy and critical thinking. We agree that these are core qualities to transformative CCE. However, these approaches are also often deeply Euro-Western in orientation and approach and are hence unfamiliar and alienating for students in the Pacific.

We argue for a form of CCE that is socio ecological and focuses on connections "between children, families, communities and the natural environment."[23] Such an education is based on a vision of healthy, sustainable, and resilient communities where human and environmental wellbeing are interconnected. Such societies can form good decisions based on sound socio-ecological understandings. CCE is integral to achieving such a society.

Reimagining CCE in the Pacific region within a socio-ecological position involves basing it on Pacific Island peoples' cultures. While these are diverse, Corcoran argues that there are some common values and practices:

> The predominant values are trust, deep respect for elders, creativity, restraint, reciprocity, compassion, awareness of interdependence with the environment, and an abiding faith in God . . . and there is a deep spirit of heritage that includes intense consciousness of land and sea. It embraces and permeates all that we do there, all that we know, all that we are.[24]

---

20. Stanger, "Moving 'Eco' Back."
21. Gruenewald, "Foucauldian Analysis."
22. Banjay and Blum, "Education Responses," 5 (PDF).
23. Lehtonen et al., "Climate Change Education."
24. Corcoran and Koshy, "Pacific Way," 130.

Through reconceptualizing core sustainability concepts and values (e.g., intergenerational equity, social justice, ecological integrity) in terms of a relational ontology, CCE can be transformative, meaningful, and responsive to Pacific contexts. Relationships between people and people and the environment are central to responsibilities and community identity and so need to be foregrounded.[25]

Thaman demonstrates how core Pacific values of peace and relationships are essential to understanding sustainable development from a Pacific ontology:

> peace is something that is the outward expression of appropriate interpersonal and inter-group relationships, known in Polynesian societies as vaa/wah. Today positive vaa or its equivalent, is often seen as a pre-condition to peaceful co-existence and sustainable development.[26]

A socio-ecological position to CCE is based on relationships which are at the heart of Pacific lives. Positive *vā* fosters meaningful connections between people and develops an ethic of care for sustainability.

TALANOA AS A CLIMATE CHANGE EDUCATION APPROACH: A CASE STUDY

In this section we outline *talanoa* as a transformative approach to CCE. This discussion is based on research by one of the authors ('Elisapesi Havea) who undertook a *talanoa* approach to CCE within Tonga.[27] Although this research was based in Tonga, the findings can be extended more widely to other Pacific islands.

We identify several characteristics within *talanoa* that align with a socio-ecological model and make it particularly suitable for the Pacific region. The characteristics are:

- Meaningful (culturally relevant)
- Relational (with people, nature, and place)
- Dialogic/interactive
- Ecocentric (intense consciousness of land and sea)
- Place based (local knowledge/involving community and elders)

---

25. Tulloch, "Embedding Education for Sustainability."
26. Thaman, "Ako and Faiako," 354.
27. Havea, "Climate Change Education."

- Transformational (for students, teachers, and wider community)
- Socially critical
- Values based

These themes will now be outlined through a discussion of *talanoa* as a methodology for CCE in the Pacific. We begin with the assertion that using a *talanoa* approach to CCE ensures that it is meaningful to Pacific students through being culturally relevant.

Talanoa is an appropriate pedagogy for teaching and learning about climate change in Tonga and the wider Pacific region because it is culturally relevant and hence meaningful to students. Thompson et al. highlight that Pacific students' lack of engagement in classroom discussions and with the school curriculum are due to factors such as unfamiliar educational pedagogies and curriculum content.[28] Therefore, appropriate teaching methodologies and contextualization and customization of teaching will enhance Pacific learner's engagement in classroom discussion and with the class curriculum.

Talanoa is dialogic as it is an oral form of communication which enables people in the Pacific to learn, relate to each other, narrate, and tell stories.[29] It is an activity used for creating and transferring knowledge,[30] and it also allows people to talk from their hearts, meaning that it is values based.[31] The Tongan system of supporting thinking, teaching, and learning occurs through the verbal expression of *talanoa*.[32] *Talanoa* is a process used in many ways to obtain information and to find out people's feelings.[33]

Traditional education in the Pacific was carried out through oral forms and the key means of learning about behavior, traditions, the past and the present include myths, legends, song, dance, poetry, proverbs, and rituals.[34] People of the Pacific were trained and educated in informal ways in which learning occurred through observing, listening, memorizing, and practical application, and children learned by observing their parents and relatives.[35] Traditionally, the teacher had possession of knowledge and skills and was

28. Thompson et al., "Training Manual."
29. Tavola, *Secondary Education in Fiji*.
30. Vaioleti, "Differentiating Talanoa Research Methodology."
31. Halapua, "Talanoa, Talking from Heart."
32. Halapua, "Talanoa, Talking from Heart."
33. Otsuka, "*Talanoa* Research"; Tavola, *Secondary Education in Fiji*.
34. Pasikale, *Seen, but Not Heard*.
35. Cummins, "School and Society"; Coxon et al., *Politics of Learning*; Paongo, "Nature of Education."

viewed as superior to the learner. Therefore, the learner was expected to have a relationship of respect and deference towards the teacher.[36]

Talanoa is based on relationality and can bring about a sense of *maheni* (familiarity) and *feʻilongaki* (knowing each other's identity and place) among Tongan people. When a group of Tongan people gather they usually engage in different types of *talanoa*, including *fakatalanoa* (to encourage discussion when they do not know each other), *pō talanoa* (when they already know each other), or *talatalanoa* (in which they talk about selected topics or talk endlessly). Tongan people come together to *talanoa* about their experiences, express their aspirations, voice their issues, and speak their perspectives in forums, meetings, seminars, and radio programs.[37]

Vaioleti argues that *talanoa* will produce relevant knowledge and possibilities for addressing Pacific issues, and this is the transformational aspect of CCE.[38] *Talanoa* and its pedagogical and philosophical stances are an essential element of *ako*. *Talanoa* can be used constructively by a teacher and learner to make meaning and reach understanding, and in this way, it is dialogic and interactive. In *talanoa*, there is a possibility that both teacher and learners can use diagnostic and formative assessment simultaneously to stay within a learning engagement in order to scaffold one another to a mutual understanding or reach shared meaning.[39] This approach may ensure the learner understands concepts being learned and for the teacher to know that the learning has taken place. *Talanoa* is at its most powerful when used formatively to scaffold learners' current understanding to another level desired by the *faiako* (teacher).[40]

Talanoa is a pedagogy that explores the knowledge, strengths, and merits of using the Tongan language and cultural practices in teaching and learning.[41] Moser and Dilling recommend that teaching climate change has to be effective, concrete, and doable; otherwise, a message of fear will not produce reasonable responses to danger, but instead it will produce denial. In *talanoa*, participants share power and the responsibility for the process and discussion at hand.[42] If it is used for teaching, learning will be the *fatongia* (responsibility) of both teacher and student and are likely to stay

---

36. Coxon et al., *Politics of Learning*.
37. Manuʻatu, "Tuli ke maʻu hono ngaahi mālie."
38. Vaioleti, "Talanoa Research Methodology."
39. Prescott and Johansson Fua, "Enhancing Educational Success"; Thaman, "Ako and Faiako"; Vaioleti, "Talanoa, Manulua."
40. Thaman, "Ako and Faiako"; Vaioleti, "Talanoa, Manulua."
41. Lātū, "Talanoa."
42. Moser and Dilling, "Making Climate Hot."

engaged in the learning relationship until the desired outcome is achieved. Therefore, if used for CCE, a good *talanoa* can be a platform for participants to co-construct new solutions or knowledge.[43]

Moreover, *talanoa* is an established framework for generating discussion about complex topics throughout the Pacific.[44] For instance, *talanoa* dialogue was brought into the COP24 held in Katowice, Poland, with the purpose to "share stories, build empathy and generate trust."[45] *Talanoa* dialogue was acknowledged as an inclusive and participatory process that incentivized exchanges between parties and nonparty stakeholders. It was also highlighted in the UNFCCC report that *talanoa* dialogue had the potential to generate greater confidence, courage, enhanced ambition, and climate action.

TALANOA AS POSITIONED IN WESTERN PERSPECTIVES

Talanoa, as positioned in Western perspectives, can either be referred to as talk, dialogue, or conversation. Vygotsky acknowledges the role of talk in organizing our understanding of the world.[46] Posner et al. explored the link between classroom talk, meaning construction, and learning. They found that meaning making and understanding are dialogic processes. They noted that, "if the aim of the teaching is for students to develop an understanding of some topic, then those students must engage in some form of dialogic activity."[47] This is concurred by a statement by Driver et al. emphasizing talk or dialogue as a social activity and that helps individuals construct knowledge and understanding:

> Knowledge and understandings, including scientific understandings, are constructed when individuals engage socially in talk and activity about shared problems or tasks. Making meaning is thus a dialogic process involving persons-in-conversation, and learning is seen as the process by which individuals are introduced to a culture by more skilled members.[48]

---

43. Vaioleti, "Differentiating Talanoa Research Methodology."
44. Vaka et al., "Getting to the Heart."
45. UNFCCC, *Report of the Conference*, 6.
46. Vygotsky, *Mind in Society*.
47. Posner et al., "Accommodation of Scientific Conception," 211.
48. Driver et al., "Constructing Scientific Knowledge," 7.

Spoken word is discussed by Alexander as an emerging pedagogy that exploits the power of talk to shape children's thinking and to secure their engagement, learning and understanding.[49] Noddings stresses the significance of open-ended dialogue between teachers and students, where real dialogue is a seeking for understanding, empathy, or appreciation.[50] Mercer and Alexander support that children learn through conversation that explore their thinking and understanding and children need scaffolding and support in the classroom to interact in ways that optimize learning.[51] Cazden explored many ways teachers use discourse as scaffold.[52] Teachers use talk to introduce students into new perspectives and new ways of thinking about, reconceptualizing, or recontextualizing whatever issues or phenomena are being discussed. Executing scaffolding in the context of CCE, teachers need to provide scaffolding that builds not only students' understanding of how climate systems work or the causes and effects of climate change but how we know what we know. For instance, what is the evidence for anthropogenic climate change and how sure are scientists about their claims?[53]

Brown and Kennedy think that this places interaction and dialogue at the center of the learning process, with the teacher in a pivotal role to enhance the interactive learning experience. They also argue that supporting teachers in reflecting on their interactional style with regards to the nature of the interactive context and the way conversations engage with children's ideas, can impact positively on children's participation and learning.[54] Brown and Kennedy also believe that as children participated more in conversations, there was evidence of children connecting their ideas together giving more of a genuine dialogue.

IMPLEMENTING *TALANOA* IN CCE

The development of *talanoa* as a learning and teaching approach is in line with recommendations from Pacific scholars and from Western perspectives. Thompson et al. suggest that Pacific learners' engagement in classroom discussion and with the classroom curriculum can be enhanced by adopting an appropriate teaching methodology, with cultural contextualization and

---

49. Alexander, *Towards Dialogic Teaching*.
50. Noddings, *Challenge to Care*.
51. Mercer, *Words and Minds*; Alexander, *Towards Dialogic Teaching*.
52. Cazden, *Classroom Discourse*.
53. Holthuis et al., "Stanford Global Climate Change."
54. Brown and Kennedy, "Learning through Conversation."

customization.[55] For instance, Pacific students have the potential to learn best in a group and from discussion. When students participate in activities and talk, they create meaning together and can find ways of going about things that are important to their social environment, to their families, and to the groups to which they belong.[56] The use of *talanoa* aligns with the process of scaffolding—this is when students build their understanding of causes and effects of climate change and also about how scientists support their claims.[57]

Talanoa is an oral form of communication which enables people in the Pacific to learn and relate to each other through narration and storytelling,[58] and *talanoa* is used for creating and transferring knowledge.[59] Therefore, *talanoa* is a vehicle for students to co-construct ideas about climate change. This chapter presents three main elements of *talanoa* that may enhance students' and teacher's knowledge and awareness of climate change as well as motivate them to act in response.

The three elements of *talanoa* that will be further explored in this chapter are: *talanoa fakatoka, talanoa felāfoaki,* and *talanoa kavekavehoko.*[60] These three elements aim to make the learning about climate change more effective and at the same time empower the students and teachers with knowledge and skills to act upon climate change.

Talanoa fakatoka

Talanoa fakatoka explores students' existing knowledge and attitudes about climate. It could help students express their feelings about climate change. This is in line with Otsuka and Tavola who believed that *talanoa* is a way to obtain information and to find out people's feelings about things.[61] This would help the teacher decide what she or he may need to address in the classroom. *Talanoa fakatoka* is also intended to build positive relationships among group members so they can work harmoniously within groups.

---

55. Thompson et al., "Training Manual."
56. Vygotsky, *Mind in Society.*
57. Holthuis et al., "Stanford Global Climate Change."
58. Tavola, *Secondary Education in Fiji.*
59. Vaioleti, "Differentiating Talanoa Research Methodology."
60. Havea, "Climate Change Education."
61. Otsuka, "*Talanoa* Research"; Tavola, *Secondary Education in Fiji.*

Talanoa felāfoaki

Talanoa felāfoaki allows a space for students to co-construct new solutions or knowledge about climate change.[62] *Talanoa felāfoaki* aligns with the concept of social constructivism where students' thinking and meaning-making were socially constructed.[63] *Talanoa felāfoaki* also provides a platform for students to scaffold. Scaffolding introduces students into new perspectives and new ways of thinking about reconceptualizing climate change issues.[64] *Talanoa felāfoaki* as a social constructivist approach is consequential in CCE because it emphasizes collaborative learning and social interactions. Vygotsky highlights that learning is a social activity and through interactions, learners can create meaning and can grow into the intellectual life of those around them. *Talanoa* is also identified by the UNFCCC as an inclusive and participatory process.

Mercer and Alexander argue that children learn through conversation which explores their thinking and understanding.[65] In the classroom, the conversation needs to be scaffolded and children need to interact in ways that improve the process of learning. *Talanoa*'s dialogic and interactive nature could allow students to scaffold from where they are in terms of their climate change knowledge toward the scientific knowledge.

Talanoa kavekavehoko

Talanoa kavekavehoko is the part of learning where students share their new knowledge with others and voice their concerns about the impacts they have already experienced or heard, and impacts that are projected to happen in the future. *Talanoa kavekavehoko* give students an opportunity to discuss the possible action plans to deal with climate change in their settings particularly in the Pacific Island countries. During *talanoa kavekavehoko*, students express how they feel empowered and motivated to address climate change in their local context. This correlates with the UNFCCC report, which stated that *talanoa* had the potential to generate greater confidence, courage, and enhanced ambition to address climate change.[66]

---

62. Vaioleti, "Differentiating Talanoa Research Methodology."
63. Vygotsky, *Mind in Society*.
64. Holthuis et al., "Stanford Global Climate Change."
65. Mercer, *Words and Minds*; Alexander, *Towards Dialogic Teaching*.
66. UNFCCC, *Report of the Conference*, 6.

EFFECTIVENESS OF *TALANOA* FOR CCE

A study conducted in Tonga indicates that using *talanoa* as an approach to teach and learn about climate change has positive impacts both on students and on teachers.[67] This chapter also presents the effectiveness of using the three elements of *talanoa fakatoka*, *talanoa felāfoaki*, and *talanoa kavekavehoko* in regard to the study that was conducted in Tonga.

Talanoa fakatoka was successful in breaking down the barriers within the group members and helped them rebuild confidence so they could be able to communicate freely and openly. *Talanoa fakatoka* strengthens the relationships between students as well as between students and teachers. *Talanoa fakatoka* helps to explore the students' and teachers' existing understanding about climate change. Students and teachers were open to express what they knew or felt about the issue through *talanoa fakatoka*.

Talanoa felāfoaki allowed the process of co-construction and scaffolding to enhance students' learning about climate change. Students believed that *talanoa felāfoaki* provided a platform for them to build their knowledge together and to reconceptualise climate change. Conducting *talanoa felāfoaki* helped the students' interpretation and critical skills. *Talanoa felāfoaki* was effective in allowing students to show-case what they already knew about climate change, and it also helped them shape and enhance their understanding about climate change. Students believed that *talanoa felāfoaki* was effective in allowing them to appreciate and acknowledge other people's ideas and helped them embrace the importance of listening to others.

Talanoa kavekavehoko played a part in empowering students to voice their concerns about climate change and their willingness to help fight against the detrimental impacts of climate change. *Talanoa kavekavehoko* provides an opportunity for the students to show-case what they have co-constructed during the *talanoa felāfoaki*. Students appeared to gain confidence when they conducted *talanoa kavekavehoko*. One of the students stated:

> Havea highlights that using talanoa can align to what Thaman (2010) stresses to integrate Tongan values and beliefs into global education initiatives. Values such as *'ofa* (compassion), *faka'apa'apa* (respect), *feveitokai'aki* (reciprocity) and *tauhivaha'a* (nurturing inter-personal relations) are crucial to be instilled in young people, and they could learn these values through listening and participation.[68]

---

67. Havea, "Climate Change Education."
68. Johansson Fua et al., "Sustainable Livelihood and Education," 15.

CONCLUSION

The case study on the use of *talanoa* to teach and learn about climate change in Tonga illustrates the importance of culturally relevant CCE. *Talanoa* as CCE has a positive impact both on the students and the teacher(s). *Talanoa* was instrumental in eliciting student interaction and meaning-making. *Talanoa* provided an intellectual space for students to explore what they knew and what they didn't know about climate change. *Talanoa* also helped students to explore broadly how impacts of climate change may affect themselves, their families, and society in general. Importantly, *talanoa* was successful in engendering interest and developing sufficient climate change knowledge for students to be able to develop action plans to mitigate and to adapt to climate change. *Talanoa* is a culturally relevant approach because it instills cultural values and knowledge to make teaching and learning relevant and meaningful. *Talanoa* helped enhance the vā or relationship among students and between the students and the teacher(s).

This chapter highlighted the need to reimagine CCE through a socio-ecological approach and a Pacific Island lens. *Talanoa* as pedagogy for CCE is based on educational theory from both Pacific and Western perspectives. At the core of this approach is dialogue and relationships. The students are active participants in their own learning, which is situated in relevant and meaningful cultural knowledge, values, and norms. Such an approach is transformative in that it supports students in social change for living sustainably with the earth. It takes an ecocentric lens rather than an anthropocentric worldview. It is argued that the *talanoa* approach is a relevant pedagogy for Pacific peoples, empowering them to address climate change in ways that are meaningful for them. The *talanoa* approach is place based (local knowledge/involving community and elders), and it is socially critical and based on Pacific values.

BIBLIOGRAPHY

Alexander, Robin. *Towards Dialogic Teaching: Rethinking Classroom Talk*. 3rd ed. Thirsk, UK: Dialogos, 2006.

Banjay, B., and N. Blum. "Education Responses to Climate Change and Quality: Two Parts of the Same Agenda?" *International Journal of Educational Development* 30 (2010) 335–450. https://discovery.ucl.ac.uk/id/eprint/1526915/1/Bangay2010 Education359.pdf.

Brown, Kirsty, and Hilary Kennedy. "Learning through Conversation: Exploring and Extending Teacher and Children's Involvement in Classroom Talk." *School Psychology International* 32 (2011) 377–96. https://doi.org/10.1177/0143034311406813.

Cazden, Courtney B. *Classroom Discourse: The Language of Teaching and Learning*. 2nd ed. Portsmouth, NH: Heinemann, 2001.

Corcoran, Peter, and Kanayathu Koshy. "The Pacific Way: Sustainability in Higher Education in the South Pacific Island Nations." *International Journal of Sustainability in Higher Education* 11 (2010) 130–40.

Coxon, Eve, et al., eds. *The Politics of Learning and Teaching in Aotearoa-New Zealand*. Palmerston North, NZ: Dunmore, 1994.

Cummins, H. G. "School and Society in Tonga, 1826 to 1854." MA thesis, Australian National University, 1977.

Driver, Rosalind, et al. "Constructing Scientific Knowledge in the Classroom." *Educational Researcher* 23 (1994) 5–12. https://doi.org/10.3102/0013189X023007005.

Fache, Elodie, and Simonne Pauwels. "Tackling Coastal 'Overfishing' in Fiji: Advocating for Indigenous Worldview, Knowledge, and Values to Be the Backbone of Fisheries Management Strategies." *Maritime Studies* 19 (2020) 41–52. https://doi.org/10.1007/s40152-020-00162-6.

Gruenewald, David A. "A Foucauldian Analysis of Environmental Education: Toward the Socioecological Challenge of the Earth Charter." *Curriculum Inquiry* 34 (2004) 71–107. https://www.jstor.org/stable/3202115.

Halapua, Sitiveni. "Talanoa, Talking from the Heart." *Matangi: Tonga Online*, Dec. 22, 2005; updated Apr. 27, 2014. https://matangitonga.to/2005/12/22/talanoa-talking-heart.

Havea, 'Elisapesi H. "Climate Change Education in Tongan Secondary Schools." PhD diss., University of Waikato, 2020.

Hills, T., et al. "A Social and Ecological Imperative for Ecosystem-Based Adaptation to Climate Change in the Pacific Islands." *Sustainability Science* 8 (2013) 455–67. DOI: /10.1007/s11625-013-0217-5.

Holthuis, N., et al. "The Stanford Global Climate Change Education Project: Classroom Implementation, Student Achievement, and Project Evaluation." Paper presented at the American Educational Research Association annual meeting, Vancouver, Can., 2012.

IPCC [International Panel on Climate Change]. *Fact Sheet: Small Islands*. IPCC, 2022. https://www.ipcc.ch/report/ar6/wg2/downloads/outreach/IPCC_AR6_WGII_FactSheet_SmallIslands.pdf.

Johansson Fua, Seu'ula, et al. "Sustainable Livelihood and Education in the Pacific: Tonga Pilot Report." University of the South Pacific, 2008. http://repository.usp.ac.fj/5383/1/SLEP_TO_Jan_07.pdf.

Kim, Rokho, et al. "Climate Change and Health in Pacific Island States." *Bulletin of the World Health Organization* 93 (2015) 819.

Kopnina, Helen, and Eleanor Shoreman-Ouimet, eds. *Sustainability: Key Issues*. Key Issues in Environment and Sustainability. London: Routledge, 2015.

Kothari, Ashish, et al. "Buen Vivir, Degrowth and Ecological Swaraj: Alternatives to Sustainable Development and the Green Economy." *Development* 57 (2014) 362–75.

Kress, W. John, and Jeffrey K. Stine, eds. *Living in the Anthropocene: Earth in the Age of Humans*. Washington, DC: Smithsonian, 2017.

Lātū, M. "Talanoa: A Contribution to the Teaching and Learning of Tongan Primary School Children in New Zealand." MEd thesis, Auckland University of Technology, 2009.

Lehtonen, Anna, et al. "Climate Change Education: A New Approach for a World of Wicked Problems." In *Sustainability, Human Well-Being, and the Future of Education*, edited by J. W. Cook, 339-74. Cham, Switzerland: Palgrave Macmillan, 2019. DOI: /10.1007/978-3-319-78580-6_11.

Manu'atu, Linitā. "Tuli ke ma'u hono ngaahi mālie: Pedagogical Possibilities for Tongan Students in New Zealand Secondary Schooling." PhD diss., University of Auckland, 2000.

Mercer, Neil. *Words and Minds: How We Use Language to Think Together.* London: Routledge, 2000.

Mochizuki, Yoko, and Audrey Bryan. "Climate Change Education in the Context of Education for Sustainable Development: Rationale and Principles." *Journal of Education for Sustainable Development* 9 (2015) 4-26. https://doi.org/10.1177/0973408215569109.

Moser, Susanne C., and Lisa Dilling. "Making Climate Hot: Communicating the Urgency and Challenge of Global Climate Change." *Environment Science and Policy for Sustainable Development* 46 (2004) 32-46.

Noddings, Nel. *The Challenge to Care in Schools: An Alternative Approach to Education.* 2nd ed. Advances in Contemporary Educational Thought. New York: Teachers College Press, 2015.

O'Riordan, Tim. "COP 26 and Sustainability Science." *Environment: Science and Policy for Sustainable Development* 64 (2022) 2-3. https://doi.org/10.1080/00139157.2022.1999748.

Otsuka, Setsuo. "*Talanoa* Research: Culturally Appropriate Research Design in Fiji." Paper presented at the Australian Association for Research in Education annual conference, Parramatta, Aus., 2005. https://www.aare.edu.au/data/publications/2005/otso5506.pdf.

Paongo, Kalapou. "The Nature of Education in Pre-European to Modern Tongan Culture and History." Paper presented at Tongan History Conference, Australian National University, Canberra, Jan. 14-17, 1987.

Pasikale, A. *Seen, but Not Heard: Voices of Pacific Islands Learners: A Qualitative Study of Pacific Islands Learners in Second-Chance Education, and the Cultural Differences Impacting on Their Aspirations, Opportunities and Participation.* Wellington: Pacific Islands Education Unit, Education and Training Support Agency, 1996.

Posner, George J., et al. "Accommodation of a Scientific Conception: Toward a Theory of Conceptual Change." *Science Education* 66 (1982) 211-27.

Prescott, S. M., and S. Johansson Fua. "Enhancing Educational Success through Talanoa: A Framework for the Pacific." Unitec, 2016. https://unitec.researchbank.ac.nz/bitstream/handle/10652/3676/Enhancing_Educational_Success_through_Talanoa.pdf?sequence=1&isAllowed=y.

Stanger, Nick. "Moving 'Eco' Back into Socio-Ecological Models: A Proposal to Reorient Ecological Literacy into Human Developmental Models and School Systems." *Human Ecology Review* 18 (2011) 167-73. https://www.jstor.org/stable/24707472.

Steer, Liesbet. *COP26: A Turning Point for Education as a Key Solution for Climate Challenges?* Global Center on Adaptation, Nov. 24, 2021. https://gca.org/cop26-a-turning-point-for-education-as-a-key-solution-for-climate-challenges/.

Tavola, Helen Goodwill. *Secondary Education in Fiji: A Key to the Future.* Suva, Fiji: Institute of Pacific Studies of the University of the South Pacific, 1991.

Thaman, K. H. "Ako and Faiako: Cultural Values, Educational Ideas and Teachers' Role Perceptions in Tonga." PhD diss., University of the South Pacific, 1988.

Thaman, Konai Helu. "Teacher Capacities for Working towards Peace and Sustainable Development." *International Journal of Sustainability in Higher Education* 11 (2010) 353–64. DOI: 10.1108/14676371011077577.

Thompson, Sandy, et al. "Training Manual for Teaching Working with Pacific Students: Engaging Pacific Learners." ResearchGate, June 2009. https://www.researchgate.net/profile/Aue_Te_Ava2/publication/263929238_Training_manual_for_teaching_working_with_pacific_students_Engaging_pacific_learners_Authors/links/0a85e53c5f6a358abf000000.pdf.

Tulloch, Lynley. "Embedding Education for Sustainability (EfS) into Teacher Education in the South Pacific, Challenges and Opportunities." University of the South Pacific, 2019. http://repository.usp.ac.fj/12085/1/Lynley_Tulloch_embedding_sustainability_into_teacher_education_in_the_South_Pacific_(1)_(1).pdf.

Tulloch, Lynley, and David Neilson. "The Neoliberalisation of Sustainablity." *Citizenship, Social and Economics Education* 13 (2014) 26–38. https://doi.org/10.2304%2Fcsee.2014.13.1.26.

UNFCCC [United Nations Framework Convention on Climate Change]. *Report of the Conference of the Parties on Its Twenty-Fourth Session, Held in Katowice from 2 to 15 December 2018*. UNFCCC, Mar. 19, 2019. https://unfccc.int/sites/default/files/resource/10a1.pdf.

Vaioleti, T. M. "Talanoa: Differentiating the Talanoa Research Methodology from Phenomenology, Narrative, Kaupapa Maori and Feminist Methodologies." *Te Reo* 56/57 (2013) 192–212.

———. "Talanoa, Manulua and Founga Ako: Frameworks for Using Enduring Tongan Educational Ideas for Education in Aotearoa/New Zealand." PhD diss., University of Waikato, 2011. http://hdl.handle.net/10289/5179.

———. "Talanoa Research Methodology: A Developing Position on Pacific Research." *Waikato Journal of Education* 12 (2006) 21–34.

Vaka, Sione, et al. "Getting to the Heart of the Story: Using Talanoa to Explore Pacific Mental Health." *Issues in Mental Health Nursing* 37 (2016) 537–44. DOI: 10.1080/01612840.2016.1186253.

Vygotsky, L. S. *Mind in Society: The Development of Higher Psychological Processes*. Edited by Michael Cole et al. Cambridge, MA: Harvard University Press, 1978.

Part Two

WELL-BEING OF TRADITIONS AND THEOLOGIES

6

LOTU-NOA
Impact of Delusional Religiosity on Well-Being

Nāsili Vaka'uta

RELIGION CAN BE BOTH a balm and a blight. It can offer solace and hope to some but fuel division and intolerance among others.

When practiced with care and respect for others, religion is a positive life-affirming force. It shapes a person's identity, it provides a sense of belonging, it offers something to hope for, and it can make life worth living. Contrariwise, it becomes life-negating when driven by self-centered agendas, strict dogmatic truth claims, visions of supremacy, cultures of intolerance (see appendix, table 4), and violent urges to control. I give this latter religious orientation a Tongan name and frame, *lotu-noa*, which shares the same semantic domain with what is known in the field of mental health as *delusional religiosity* (DR).

My primary aim in this essay is to establish a working definition of DR as a basis for further conversations at the intersection of religion and health care. It should also be clear from the outset that this work is not a scientific analysis nor am I pretending to be an expert in the science of the mind and mental health. I am simply seeking meaningful explanations for certain outlooks and actions within religious circles that from my perspective would be detrimental to communal well-being if not given urgent attention.

"Lotu fakalelei na'a lavea ha taha!"[1] goes a Tongan saying about beliefs that are theoretically bizarre and practically antagonistic. At times it is uttered lightheartedly, but it also carries a very important warning: *one's faith has the propensity to cause harm if it is not observed with due consideration for the well-being of others.*[2]

WHY DELUSIONAL RELIGIOSITY?

During the COVID-19 pandemic, there were cases in which religious groups or individuals exhibited behaviors that could be considered delusional or extreme (see appendix, table 1). The following are examples:

- *Defiance of lockdown measures*: In Aotearoa New Zealand, but also in other parts of the world, some faith communities (especially churches) held in-person services despite restrictions on group gatherings.

- *Conspiracy theories and misinformation*: Throughout the pandemic, various conspiracy theories emerged, linking COVID-19 to religious or political agendas. Some groups propagated unfounded claims, such as the virus being a deliberate creation or a punishment from a higher power. The influence of misinformation on social media platforms has contributed to the spread of these beliefs. Online communities and individuals have circulated baseless theories, often intertwining them with religious narratives.

- *Faith-based healing and rejection of medical treatment*: In some cases, individuals or religious groups exhibited delusional religiosity by relying solely on faith-based healing or rejecting medical treatment for COVID-19. They believed that prayer, religious rituals, or spiritual practices alone can cure the illness, leading to a refusal to seek appropriate medical care. Instances of individuals or families opting for religious rituals or practices instead of medical intervention have been reported in various countries. These cases often involve severe illness or even deaths that could have been preventable with proper medical attention.

- *End-times prophecies and apocalyptic beliefs*: The COVID-19 pandemic has fueled a sense of fear and uncertainty, leading some religious groups or individuals to interpret it through the lens of apocalyptic

---

1. Literally: "Be careful with your faith, it might harm someone else!"
2. Responses from faith communities to COVID-19 vaccinations and health advice especially during lockdowns in New Zealand brought to the fore some disturbing aspects of religion.

beliefs or end-times prophecies. They claim that the pandemic signifies the fulfillment of prophetic events or the imminent arrival of a religious figure or divine judgment. These beliefs manifested in various ways, such as the promotion of doomsday scenarios, urging followers to prepare for the end times, or interpreting the pandemic as a sign of divine intervention.[3]

DR is, however, not a new phenomenon. It is as old as religion itself, and history is littered with incidences of faith-motivated violence.[4] In 1978, Jim Jones led the Peoples Temple, a religious group that moved from the United States to Guyana in South America. Jones exhibited delusional religiosity, proclaiming himself as a messiah and exerting an immense influence over his followers. In a tragic turn of events, Jones orchestrated a mass murder-suicide known as the Jonestown Massacre, where over nine hundred members of the group died by drinking poisoned punch. This event serves as a harrowing example of the destructive consequences that can arise from delusional religiosity and charismatic leadership.[5]

These events are typically driven by a vision of society that is inspired by *a fictitious faith-based narrative* of supremacy and domination.[6] No religion is immune from this ailment.

LOTU-NOA: A TONGAN FRAME

Lotu in Tongan cultural context refers to any religion, religious tradition, belief system, faith community, and everything related to religious views and practices. It is a very wide concept that is central to Moana (Pacific, Oceanic) cultures. *Lotu* plays a significant role in the lives and worldviews of Moana islanders.

The term *noa* is a particle of *negation* and *diversion*. It negates or tones down the meaning of what it is attached to. It encompasses "aimlessness,"

---

3. It's critical to emphasize that these examples represent the actions and beliefs of a minority and should not be generalized to all religious groups or individuals. The majority of religious communities adhered to public health guidelines and worked to promote the well-being and safety of their members during the COVID-19 pandemic.

4. Runciman, *History of the Crusades*.

5. Scheeres, *Thousand Lives*.

6. Religion for the most part is not a physical or biological entity, nor is it a heavenly institution as it is portrayed to be. Any religion and/or faith is a constructed narrative, a myth that on the one hand helps people make sense of themselves and the world around them, and on the other hand, when taken as absolute, divinely revealed truth, serves as motivation for religious tensions and violence. I refer to the latter orientation as *lotu-noa*.

"meaninglessness," "formlessness," "lack of direction," and in some cases "vanity." Numerically, it has the zero value. *Noa* dilutes meanings of words to the extent that words no longer carry their usual sense. The following are examples:

First, *anga-noa*: this refers to a person who is hardly affected by what is going on—due to lack of information or lack of attention given to the situation. Such a person does not see the need to change or adapt; one simply lives. An *anga-noa* person is carefree and worries about nothing. At times, such a person fails to acknowledge one's responsibility.

Second, *lau-noa*: this term can mean talking nonsense, irrational utterance, meaningless conversation, or silly behavior. *Lau-noa* is used with reference to someone whose speech has no relation to the occasion; one who acts in a manner that makes no sense. Those exhibiting *lau-noa* behavior are more interested in demanding attention while irritating others.

Third, *mū-noa*: this refers to someone who is in a state of ignorance, and who acts with a lack of understanding or knowledge. The act may appear malicious but, in most cases, this is not intentional due to the person's unawareness of the implications of one's action. This kind of behavior does not happen because one ignores the information provided. Rather, it happens because the person is either incapable of rational thinking or does not have access to relevant information.

Fourth, *hē-noa*: this refers to one who goes astray or is being misled. To *hē* is to deviate from the intended route or the expected destination. *Hē-noa* denotes going astray because others are flocking in the same direction, or one thinks that it is the right direction. Like *mū-noa*, there is no malicious intention. One just goes with the flow. This is synonymous with the term *fāi-noa*, to follow or act blindly without proper knowledge basis.

Fifth and final, *tuē-noa*: this refers to someone who is being ignored, isolated; attracting no attention and/or care. *Tuē* is about applauding someone or paying attention to someone or something. *Tuē-noa* refers to lack of consideration. A person who is *tuē-noa* is likely to suffer from loneliness and emotional withdrawal. *Tuē-noa* affects one's life to an extent that one follows or attaches to whoever shows up and pays attention. A *tuē-noa* person is in a state of vulnerability.

These *noa* terms provide a semantic domain for *lotu-noa*. *Lotu-noa* can mean:

- A belief or practice that is *anga-noa*; *lotu* that does not take responsibility for the well-being of others and could not care less about critical issues
- A belief or practice that is *lau-noa*; *lotu* that is meaningless and useless

- A belief or practice that is *hē-noa*: *lotu* that is misleading and lacks directions
- A belief or practice that is *mū-noa*: *lotu* that is ignorant and lacks understanding
- A belief or practice that is *fāi-noa*: *lotu* that is blind and uncritical
- A belief or practice that creates a sense of *tuē-noa*: *lotu* that cultivates isolation, loneliness, and insecurity in order to dominate and control

I opted for *lotu-noa* instead of the commonly used Tongan concepts for delusion—*'āvanga, 'āvea, vale, fakasesele*—to avoid stigmatizing those who exhibit characteristics of DR, and to indicate that it is not just a problem of the mind but also a spiritual one. To tackle DR requires both psychological and theological interventions, mental and spiritual engagements.

DELUSIONAL RELIGIOSITY: PERSPECTIVES

The meanings of *lotu-noa* presented above resonate with the following perspectives on delusional religiosity (see also appendix, tables 1–4). First, in the context of mental health, DR refers to the presence of *fixed and false beliefs or convictions* related to religious or spiritual themes that are not consistent with the individual's cultural or religious background. These delusions may involve grandiose religious ideas, religious persecution or conspiracy theories, or religiously themed hallucinations.[7]

Second, Daniel Freeman uses the term *religious delusions* (RD) to refer to false beliefs or convictions that involve religious or spiritual themes.[8] These delusions may include beliefs in being a religious figure, possessing special powers or abilities, receiving divine messages, or experiencing religious persecution. This is common among cult leaders.[9]

Third, the American Psychiatric Association employs the concept of *delusional disorder* (DD) to explain a diagnostic category in psychiatry characterized by the presence of delusions exclusively related to religious or spiritual themes. Individuals with this disorder exhibit firm, non-bizarre religious beliefs that are not widely accepted within their cultural or religious context.[10]

Fourth, the term *pathological religious beliefs* (PRBs) refers to rigid, fixed, and often irrational religious convictions that significantly deviate

7. Iyassu et al., "Psychological Characteristics."
8. Freeman et al., *Persecutory Delusions*.
9. Sofou et al., "Religious Delusions."
10. Tamminga, "Psychotic Disorder."

from the mainstream religious beliefs and practices. These beliefs may cause distress, impair daily functioning, and be resistant to rational argumentation or evidence. This is usually found among new religious movements and breakaway groups from mainline faith communities.[11]

Fifth, DR can mean *religious obsessions* (ROs). These are intrusive and distressing thoughts, ideas, or images that are of a religious or spiritual nature and cause significant anxiety or discomfort. These obsessions may involve fears of committing sacrilegious acts, concerns about moral purity, or excessive preoccupation with religious rituals.[12]

Sixth, another term that is synonymous with DR is *spiritual delusions* (SDs). These involve false beliefs or ideas that pertain to spiritual or transcendent realms. These delusions may include beliefs in communicating with divine beings, possessing supernatural abilities, or being chosen for a special mission by a higher power. Some leaders of charismatic religious movements and evangelical churches often make this claim.[13]

Seventh, some forms of DR are known as *messianic delusions* (MDs). They are characterized by the belief that one is a messiah, a savior, or a chosen divine figure with a mission to bring about significant religious or spiritual change. These delusions often involve grandiose and megalomaniacal ideas of personal importance and power.[14]

Eighth, Freeman also mentions the term *religious persecution delusions* (RPDs)—also known as persecutory delusions (PDs).[15] This refers to false beliefs of being targeted or persecuted because of one's religious or spiritual beliefs. These delusions may involve the perception of being monitored, conspired against, or victimized by individuals or organizations because of one's religious affiliations. Some opponents of COVID-19 vaccinations and health advice in general exhibit these kinds of belief.[16]

Ninth, DR obsesses with *miracles*. This refers to fixed and false convictions that one has witnessed or will experience extraordinary supernatural events or interventions. These beliefs may involve claims of personal healing, divine interventions, or extraordinary abilities attributed to religious or spiritual experiences. Such obsessions often lead to detrimental consequences.[17]

11. Mohr and Huguelet, "Schizophrenia and Religion."
12. Tek and Ulug, "Religiosity and Religious Obsessions."
13. Rankin, *Religious and Spiritual Experience*.
14. Grover et al., "Religion, Spirituality, and Schizophrenia."
15. Freeman et al., *Persecutory Delusions*.
16. Akyildirim Cor and Akcay, "COVID-19 Related Delusional Beliefs."
17. Everitt, "Alternative Therapies."

Tenth, and finally, DR involves *religious conspiracy delusions* (RCDs). These carry the false belief that there is a hidden or secret agenda by religious or political organizations to control or manipulate individuals through religious doctrines or practices. These delusions often involve suspicions of religious and government institutions being involved in conspiracies or manipulative actions. A lot of RCDs emerged during COVID-19 lockdowns, and they manifested themselves in different shapes and forms.[18] The worst and most influential of all conspiracies is the QAnon conspiracy that affected the United States politically and socially.[19]

CHRISTIAN MANIFESTATIONS OF DELUSIONAL RELIGIOSITY

In Christianity, generally speaking, DR manifests in various ways, and it is important to note that not all Christians or Christian denominations exhibit these characteristics. Notwithstanding, the common characteristics include:

Grandiose beliefs: Individuals hold grandiose beliefs about their own importance or divine mission. They believe that they are a chosen one, a prophet, or even the second coming of Christ. In the nineteenth century, John Nichols Thom claimed to be the Messiah and founded a religious sect known as the "New and Latter House of Israel."[20]

Divine messages and revelations: Individuals claim to receive direct messages from God or other divine beings. They believe that they have exclusive access to divine knowledge or that they are the sole interpreters of Scripture. In the nineteenth century, Joseph Smith, the founder of Mormonism, claimed to have received divine revelations and translated the Book of Mormon through the use of seer stones.[21]

Persecution complex: Individuals with delusional religiosity perceive themselves as being persecuted or targeted due to their religious beliefs. They interpret everyday conflicts or criticisms as evidence of persecution or spiritual warfare. The Branch Davidians, led by David Koresh, believed they were being persecuted by the government and interpreted the 1993 raid on their compound in Waco, Texas, as an act of persecution and the fulfillment of biblical prophecies.[22]

18. Kosarkova et al., "Religious Conspiracy Theories."
19. Rothschild, *Storm Is upon Us*. See also Bloom and Moskalenko, *Pastels and Pedophiles*.
20. Isham et al., "Understanding, Treating, and Renaming."
21. O'Connor and Vandenberg, "Psychosis or Faith?"
22. Tabor and Gallagher, *Why Waco?*

Overemphasis on signs and symbols: Delusional religiosity can involve an intense focus on signs, symbols, and coincidences as divine messages or proof of their beliefs. They may interpret everyday occurrences as divine interventions or specific signs meant only for them. Take for example, Harold Camping, a Christian radio broadcaster, who predicted the end of the world based on his interpretation of biblical numerology and the occurrence of specific signs and symbols.[23]

Rigidity and exclusivity: Individuals have rigid and exclusive interpretations of religious doctrine. They reject alternative perspectives or religious diversity, believing that only their specific interpretation is correct. The Westboro Baptist Church in the United States, known for its extreme beliefs and provocative protests, promotes a highly exclusive interpretation of Christianity, condemning various groups, including LGBTQ+ individuals and the military.[24]

Loss of critical thinking: Delusional religiosity can lead to a loss of critical thinking and a diminished ability to question or evaluate beliefs objectively. Individuals may disregard contradictory evidence or logical inconsistencies, holding on to their delusions despite rational arguments. The Heaven's Gate cult is a good example. Led by Marshall Applewhite, they believed that a spaceship was trailing the Hale-Bopp comet and that they needed to commit suicide to reach a higher level of existence.[25]

Withdrawal from mainstream Christianity: Individuals with delusional religiosity may withdraw from mainstream Christian communities or reject established church authorities. They form or join splinter groups or create their own religious movements based on their unique beliefs. The True Russian Orthodox Church, founded by Pyotr Kuznetsov, broke away from the mainstream Russian Orthodox Church, claiming that the ROC had lost its true teachings and authority.[26]

HEALTHY RELIGIOUS BELIEFS (HRBS) VS. DELUSIONAL RELIGIOSITY (DR)

Not all religious beliefs are delusional. There are clear differences between HRBs and DR that deserve a brief discussion here.

First, the difference between *subjective experience* and *fixed delusions*. HRBs are subjective and personal experiences of faith, spirituality, and

23. Sarno and Shoemaker, "Church, Sect, or Cult?"
24. Barrett-Fox, *God Hates*.
25. Zeller, "Extraterrestial Biblical Hermeneutics."
26. Halpin, "Cult Leader Pyotr Kuznetsov."

meaning. They provide individuals with a framework for understanding and finding purpose in life. A person who finds personal solace and meaning in their prayer practices, connecting with a higher power, and experiencing a sense of peace and guidance, is a good example. DR, on the other hand, involves fixed and rigid beliefs that are impervious to contrary evidence, often disconnected from reality, and resistant to logical reasoning. An example is an individual who believes they are the sole recipient of divine messages and interprets everyday events, such as hearing the wind blow, as direct communication from God. They insist on the absolute truth of their interpretations despite contradictory evidence. Christians in fundamentalist and evangelical folds may exhibit this kind of DR.[27]

Second, the difference between *integration with daily life* and *impairment*: Individuals with HRBs inspire them to engage in charitable acts, cultivate compassion, and treat others with kindness, leading to positive interactions and enhanced well-being. Those with DR become so extreme that they withdraw from social relationships, neglect personal responsibilities, or engage in harmful behaviors, causing impairment in their daily life.[28]

A third difference between HRBs and DR is in terms of *openness to interpretation* and *absolute certainty*. Those with HRBs hold varying interpretations of religious texts or theological concepts while still finding common ground and respect for each other's perspectives. Individuals with DR typically claim to have exclusive and absolute understanding of religious truth, dismissing all other interpretations and rejecting any form of critical examination or dialogue.[29]

Fourth, *flexibility* and *rigid dogmatism*. An individual with HRBs has the ability to evolve and adapt over time as they engage in ongoing learning, reflection, and dialogue with others. They remain open to new insights and are willing to reevaluate their beliefs. DR persons, on the contrary, strictly adhere to rigid dogmas and doctrines, rejecting any form of critical inquiry or examination of their beliefs, and refusing to consider alternative viewpoints.[30]

Fifth, and finally, difference between HRBs and DR lies in *emotional well-being* and *distress*. A person's religious belief is healthy when it provides comfort, hope, and a sense of purpose during challenging times. They experience positive emotions such as gratitude, peace, and joy in their religious practices. On the other hand, one is delusional when religious beliefs cause

27. Koenig, *Religious and Spiritual Issues*.
28. Pargament, *Spiritually Integrated Psychotherapy*.
29. Hood et al., *Psychology of Religion*.
30. Paloutzian and Park, *Handbook of the Psychology*.

significant distress, anxiety, or fear due to an extreme focus on apocalyptic scenarios or belief in divine punishment, leading to a constant state of worry or unease.[31]

SOME PRACTICAL EXAMPLES

Case 1

Sione, a forty-five-year-old man, firmly believed that his local religious community was conspiring against him because he had questioned certain traditional practices. He reported experiencing frequent episodes of fear and paranoia, firmly convinced that he was being followed and that his life was in danger. Despite reassurances from family and friends, he held steadfastly to his delusional belief of religious persecution.

This is a good example of what is known as religious persecution delusion (RPD),[32] where individuals believe that they are being targeted or persecuted due to their religious beliefs or affiliation. They also believe that they are constantly under surveillance by a religious sect that aims to harm them because they have deviated from their religious teachings.

Case 2

Mele, a thirty-year-old woman, firmly believed that she was the reincarnation of a revered spiritual leader. She claimed to receive divine revelations and considered herself responsible for leading a spiritual revolution. Her delusion of messianic identity led her to engage in proselytizing activities and display erratic behavior, including renouncing material possessions and adopting an ascetic lifestyle.

Mele here displays messianic delusion (MD) which involves a belief that one is a divine or chosen figure with a special mission or role in relation to religious or spiritual matters. The individual may perceive herself as a savior, prophet, or the embodiment of a religious figure.[33]

---

31. Koenig et al., *Handbook of Religion and Health*.
32. Freeman et al., *Persecutory Delusions*.
33. Ellison and Lee, "Religious Delusions and Hallucinations."

Case 3

Viliami, a fifty-year-old man, developed a religious conviction in which he believed he had direct communication with God. He claimed to have been selected to lead a spiritual movement that would bring enlightenment to humanity. He displayed a condescending attitude towards others, considering himself intellectually and spiritually superior.

Viliami's case is known as grandiose religious delusion (GRD). That involves an exaggerated sense of self-importance and superiority in religious matters. Individuals with this delusion believe they possess special knowledge, are chosen by a higher power, or have a unique divine mission.[34]

Case 4

'Ana, a thirty-five-year-old woman, suffered from a religious guilt delusion. She firmly believed that she had committed unforgivable sins and that she was condemned to eternal damnation. Despite reassurances from religious authorities and loved ones, she continued to experience extreme distress and self-loathing due to her delusional belief.

This final case resembles what is known as religious guilt or sin delusion (RGD/SD). In this type of delusion, individuals experience an intense and unwarranted sense of guilt, feeling convinced that they have committed grave sins or transgressions against their religious beliefs. They may believe that they are damned or destined for punishment.

Overall

The above cases constitute only a tip of the delusional iceberg. They manifest themselves in various forms and expressions. It is of utmost importance for leaders of faith communities and other sectors of society as well to gain a better understanding of DR to be able to detect and intervene when it gets out of hand.

FACTORS INFLUENCING DEVELOPMENT OF DR

The spread of DR can be influenced by various societal factors. While the specific factors may vary across different contexts, here are some common societal influences:

34. Freeman and Garety, "Advances in Understanding."

1. *Cultural and religious context*: The cultural and religious context in which an individual grows up can influence their beliefs and perceptions. If an individual is raised in an environment where religious beliefs are strongly emphasized and rigidly enforced, they may be more susceptible to developing DR. Cultural or religious practices that discourage critical thinking or discourage questioning of beliefs can contribute to the development and maintenance of DR.[35]

2. *Social isolation*: Social isolation and lack of social support can play a role in the development of DR. When individuals are socially isolated or lack meaningful connections, they may seek solace and validation in religious or spiritual beliefs. In some cases, this isolation can contribute to the intensification of DR, as the individual lacks alternative perspectives or feedback that could challenge or counterbalance their delusional beliefs.[36]

3. *Psychological vulnerability*: Individuals with preexisting psychological vulnerabilities, such as a history of trauma, emotional instability, or personality disorders, may be more prone to developing DR. These vulnerabilities can be exacerbated by societal factors, such as societal stressors, stigmatization, or marginalization, which can increase the risk of developing delusional beliefs as a coping mechanism or means of finding meaning and purpose.[37]

4. *Religious extremism*: Extreme religious ideologies or fundamentalism (see appendix, table 3) can contribute to the development of DR. When individuals adopt rigid and absolutist interpretations of religious doctrines, they become more susceptible to developing delusions that align with these beliefs. Religious extremist groups or charismatic leaders who promote conspiracy theories or engage in manipulation tactics can also influence vulnerable individuals and contribute to the development of delusions.[38]

5. *Media influence*: Media, including online platforms and social media, can play a role in shaping and reinforcing DR. Misinformation, conspiracy theories, and echo chambers in certain media environments can amplify existing delusions or lead individuals to adopt new delusions. The availability of these platforms allows delusional beliefs to

---

35. Gaines, "Culture-Specific Delusions."
36. Jetten et al., *Social Cure*.
37. Satici, "Psychological Vulnerability, Resilience."
38. Richardson, "Religion, Delusions, and Violence."

spread rapidly and find support from like-minded individuals, further reinforcing the delusions.[39]

It is important to note that these societal factors do not necessarily cause DR on their own but can contribute to its emergence and spread. Understanding these influences can help inform strategies for prevention, intervention, and support for individuals who may be at risk or already affected by DR.

IMPACT OF DR ON WELL-BEING

DR can have a significant impact on an individual's or a community's well-being, affecting various aspects of life. Here are some ways in which DR can impact well-being:

1. *Emotional distress*: Delusional beliefs that are strongly held, despite being irrational or inconsistent with reality, can cause emotional distress. Individuals may experience anxiety, fear, confusion, or frustration due to the conflict between their delusions and the outside world. The intensity of these emotions can vary depending on the content and nature of the delusions.

2. *Social isolation*: DR can lead to social isolation and strained relationships. Individuals may struggle to relate to others who do not share their beliefs or who challenge their delusions. This isolation can result in a sense of alienation, loneliness, and reduced social support, which can further impact mental well-being.

3. *Occupational and educational impairment*: Delusions can interfere with an individual's ability to perform effectively in their work or educational settings. Difficulty concentrating, preoccupation with religious ideas, and conflicts with colleagues or supervisors can lead to impaired job performance, reduced productivity, and educational setbacks.

4. *Family and relationship challenges*: The presence of DR can strain family relationships. Loved ones may struggle to understand or accept the individual's delusions, leading to conflicts, misunderstandings, and strained communication. This can result in increased tension, emotional strain, and challenges in maintaining healthy relationships.

5. *Safety risks*: In some cases, DR can pose safety risks for individuals or others. If the delusions involve harmful or violent beliefs or if

---

39. Siddiqui et al., "Social Media Misinformation."

individuals engage in risky behaviors based on their delusions, there is an increased potential for harm to themselves or others.

6. *Reduced quality of life*: DR can significantly impact an individual's overall quality of life. The persistent preoccupation with delusions and the associated distress can limit one's ability to engage in activities, pursue personal goals, and experience a sense of fulfillment and contentment.

7. *Impact on self-identity*: DR can significantly impact an individual's self-identity and sense of self. The delusions may become central to their identity, influencing their beliefs, values, and behaviors. This can create internal conflicts, a loss of personal autonomy, and a diminished sense of self-worth.

It is important to recognize that the impact of DR on well-being can vary among individuals. Some individuals may experience significant distress and impairment, while others may maintain a functional and relatively stable life despite their delusions. However, addressing and managing DR is crucial for promoting overall well-being, reducing distress, and improving the individual's quality of life. This often requires a combination of psychotherapy, social support, and, in some cases, medication to address associated symptoms.

IN CLOSING: THE NEED FOR BETTER UNDERSTANDING

It is important to understand that DR can have profound effects on individuals and communities, leading to social and interpersonal challenges, religious extremism (see appendix, table 2), and even violence. Understanding the underlying factors, manifestations, and consequences of DR is crucial for mental health professionals, religious leaders, and policymakers in addressing the needs of affected individuals and promoting healthier religious engagement. Understanding the phenomenon and manifestations of DR is of utmost importance for several reasons:

First, *mental health support*. Recognizing and understanding DR allows mental health professionals to provide appropriate support and interventions for individuals experiencing this condition. It helps in distinguishing between religious beliefs that are within the realm of personal spirituality and those that may require therapeutic intervention. By understanding the underlying psychological processes, professionals can devise effective treatment plans tailored to the individual's specific needs.

Second, *avoiding of stigmatization*. Without proper understanding, individuals exhibiting signs of DR may face stigmatization and judgment from their communities or society at large. Education and awareness about this phenomenon help reduce prejudice and foster empathy. By understanding that DR is a psychological condition rather than a deliberate choice, we can promote acceptance and support for those affected.

Third, *protecting of vulnerable individuals*. DR may be more prevalent among individuals who are already vulnerable due to mental health issues or cognitive biases. By understanding the risk factors and causes, we can identify those who are more susceptible and provide early intervention and support to prevent the development or worsening of delusions. This understanding also helps in safeguarding individuals from potential exploitation or harm that may arise from their extreme beliefs.

Fourth, *promoting of interfaith dialogue*. Understanding DR encourages engagement in interfaith dialogue. By engaging with individuals who hold distorted religious beliefs, we can promote healthy discussions, challenge irrational thinking, and foster understanding across different faiths. This dialogue can contribute to breaking down stereotypes, reducing prejudice, and building bridges of empathy and respect.

Fifth, *strengthening of societal cohesion*. DR sometimes lead to extreme behaviors that may disrupt social cohesion and harmony. Understanding this potential allows communities to address potential conflicts, support affected individuals, and mitigate any negative consequences that may arise from their beliefs. It helps in creating inclusive spaces that promote healthy religious expression while ensuring the well-being and safety of all members.

Sixth, *advancing of research and knowledge*. Studying DR contributes to the advancement of psychological research and understanding of the human mind. By exploring the causes, mechanisms, and potential treatments, researchers can deepen their understanding of the complexities of belief systems and their impact on mental health. This knowledge can inform future studies and interventions in the field of psychology.

Understanding DR is essential for providing appropriate mental health support, promoting empathy, reducing stigma, protecting vulnerable individuals, fostering interfaith dialogue, strengthening societal cohesion, and advancing our knowledge of human psychology. By engaging the DR phenomenon and potential, we can contribute to the well-being and inclusivity of individuals and communities.

APPENDIX: RELIGIOSITY ASSESSMENT TOOLS

Table 1. Delusional Religiosity

For each indicator, evaluate whether it is "not present," "somewhat present," or "clearly present" within the religious group or community. After completing the assessment, consider the overall pattern and severity of indicators to form a holistic view of the group's toxic religiosity. This rubric is a tool to guide your assessment, but professional guidance and multiple perspectives are recommended for a comprehensive evaluation.

Indicators	Not Present	Somewhat Present	Clearly Present
Excessive Control	Members have personal autonomy	Some restrictions on personal choices	High degree of control
Isolation	Members interact freely outside	Limited interaction with outsiders	Members isolated from others
Fear and Guilt	Minimal use of fear or guilt	Some manipulation through fear/guilt	Heavy reliance on fear/guilt
Intolerance	Tolerant of diverse beliefs	Some intolerance of differing views	Strong "us versus them" mentality
Lack of Autonomy	Encourages critical thinking	Some discouragement of questioning	Questioning is highly discouraged
Financial Exploitation	Transparent financial practices	Pressure for excessive financial giving	Financial exploitation present
Emotional Manipulation	Emotional well-being supported	Some emotional manipulation present	Heavy emotional dependency
Rejection of Science	Acceptance of scientific knowledge	Some skepticism towards science	Complete rejection of science
Cult of Personality	Leader not idolized, free thinking	Some leader-focused mindset	Leader revered without question
Violence or Harm	No harm or violence towards members	Emotional/psychological harm present	Physical or emotional harm evident

1. *Excessive control*: This indicator refers to situations where the religious group or leaders exert a high degree of control over members' lives, decisions, and choices. Members may be restricted in their activities, relationships, and personal freedoms.
2. *Isolation*: Isolation involves keeping members away from nonmembers, preventing them from interacting with friends, family, or communities outside the religious group. This isolation can create dependency on the group and hinder critical thinking.

3. *Fear and guilt*: Toxic religiosity may use fear tactics or guilt to manipulate members into compliance. Members might be made to fear consequences or believe they are inherently flawed, creating emotional dependence on the group's teachings.
4. *Intolerance*: A group that demonstrates intolerance towards other beliefs, cultures, or lifestyles promotes an "us versus them" mentality. This can lead to discrimination and hostility towards outsiders.
5. *Lack of autonomy*: In such environments, questioning or independent thinking is discouraged. Members are expected to conform unquestioningly to the teachings of the group without room for personal exploration or growth.
6. *Financial exploitation*: Members may be pressured to donate money, give up their possessions, or contribute beyond their means. Financial exploitation can lead to financial instability and dependency on the group.
7. *Emotional manipulation*: Emotional manipulation involves controlling members' emotions and fostering dependency on the group for emotional well-being. This can lead to psychological vulnerability.
8. *Rejection of science*: When critical thinking is discouraged and scientific facts are dismissed in favor of dogma, members might become disconnected from mainstream knowledge and rational thought.
9. *Cult of personality*: A charismatic leader may be elevated to a near-divine status, leading to uncritical devotion. This can inhibit independent thought and create an environment of blind loyalty.
10. *Violence or harm*: This is the most severe indicator, involving the use of violence, abuse, or harm. It signifies a high level of toxic religiosity.

It is important to remember that the presence of one or more indicators doesn't necessarily mean a group is entirely toxic. The severity and combination of indicators, as well as their impact on members' well-being, should be considered when assessing the situation. If you suspect toxic religiosity, consider seeking advice from professionals or support networks that specialize in religious cults or harmful groups.

Table 2. Religious Extremism

This diagnostic grid provides an overview of different elements that contribute to religious extremism. It is essential to approach discussions about religious extremism with a comprehensive understanding of the complexities involved, while actively working towards promoting open dialogue, tolerance, and peaceful coexistence among diverse religious groups.

Aspects of Religious Extremism	Descriptions/Examples	Observations/Notes
Intolerance of Other Beliefs	Refusing to accept or respect beliefs different from one's own and considering them as invalid or harmful	
Use of Violence	Advocating or employing violent actions to advance religious or political agendas, often targeting those with differing belief.	
Rejection of Pluralism	Rejecting the coexistence of different religious beliefs and advocating for the dominance of one's own belief system	
Fundamentalism	Adhering strictly to a particular interpretation of religious texts or teachings, often excluding alternative viewpoints	
Us versus Them Mentality	Dividing the world into "believers" and "nonbelievers," often promoting hostility and demonization of those outside the group	
Supremacy and Exclusivity	Believing that one's religious group is superior to all others and should have exclusive control or influence	
Recruitment and Radicalization	Actively seeking to recruit individuals into extremist beliefs and actions, often exploiting vulnerabilities or grievances	
Opposition to Modernity	Rejecting modern values, technologies, and social norms, often in favor of strict adherence to traditional religious teachings	
Persecution of Dissent	Silencing or punishing those within the same religious group who question or deviate from extremist beliefs	
Justification of Violence	Rationalizing violent actions as necessary for religious or ideological purposes, often citing religious texts as support	

Table 3. Religious Fundamentalism

This diagnostic grid provides an overview of different elements that contribute to religious fundamentalism. It is important to approach discussions about religious fundamentalism with an understanding of its variations and impacts, recognizing that not all fundamentalist beliefs lead to harmful actions. Engaging in respectful conversations and promoting critical thinking can help foster understanding and empathy among individuals with diverse perspectives.

Aspects of Religious Fundamentalism	Descriptions/Examples	Observations/Notes
Literal Interpretation	Adhering strictly to the literal meanings of religious texts or teachings, often rejecting metaphorical or contextual understandings	
Rejection of Modernity	Rejecting or being skeptical of modern values, technologies, and cultural norms in favor of traditional religious teachings	
Resistance to Change	Resisting changes within the religious doctrine, rituals, or practices, often preserving historical traditions at all costs	
Exclusivity and Separatism	Believing that one's religious group is the sole truth and distancing from other beliefs or groups that do not align	
Moral Absolutism	Believing in a single set of moral principles based on religious teachings, often with limited room for ethical grey areas	
Opposition to Secularism	Rejecting the separation of religious and secular institutions, aiming for religious influence on governance and society	
Gender Roles and Conservatism	Upholding traditional gender roles and family structures based on religious teachings, often restricting women's roles and autonomy	

Cultural Homogenization	Advocating for the dominance of a particular religious culture within society, sometimes suppressing diversity and pluralism
Inerrancy of Religious Texts	Believing that religious texts are infallible and without error, leading to unwavering adherence to every statement
Evangelism and Conversion	Actively promoting and seeking to convert others to the same religious beliefs, often with an urgent sense of mission

Table 4. Religious Intolerance

This diagnostic grid offers a starting point for understanding various aspects of religious intolerance. It is crucial to approach discussions about religious intolerance with respect for diversity, a willingness to learn, and a commitment to foster religious freedom, respect, and understanding.

Aspects of Religious Intolerance	Descriptions/Examples	Observations/Notes
Discrimination Based on Religion	Treating individuals unfairly or denying them opportunities due to their religious beliefs. This can manifest in education, employment, housing, and public services.	
Stereotyping and Stigmatization	Assigning negative attributes or making assumptions about individuals based on their religious affiliation. This can lead to biases and misconceptions.	
Hate Speech and Incitement	Using derogatory language or promoting violence against individuals or groups based on their religious beliefs	
Violence and Persecution	Physically or verbally attacking individuals or groups due to their religion, often leading to displacement, harm, or loss of life	

Cultural Insensitivity	Disregarding or disrespecting the practices, customs, and beliefs of different religions, often out of ignorance or ethnocentrism	
Religious Exclusion	Excluding individuals or groups from social, political, or economic activities due to their religious affiliation	
Legal Discrimination	Implementing laws or policies that favor or disadvantage specific religious groups, often leading to unequal treatment	
Social Media and Online Hate	Using digital platforms to spread hate speech and incite violence against individuals of certain religious backgrounds	
Religious Symbolism	Targeting religious symbols or places of worship for vandalism or destruction. This can be a form of expressing intolerance.	
Lack of Interfaith Dialogue	Failing to engage in conversations and interactions between different religious groups to promote understanding and cooperation	

BIBLIOGRAPHY

Akyildirim Cor, S., and B. D. Akcay. "COVID-19 Related Delusional Beliefs: A Case Report." *European Psychiatry* 66 (July 2023) S809–10. DOI: 10.1192/j.eurpsy.2023.1715.

Barrett-Fox, Rebecca. *God Hates: Westboro Baptist Church, American Nationalism, and the Religious Right*. Lawrence: University Press of Kansas Press, 2016.

Bloom, Mia, and Sophia Moskalenko. *Pastels and Pedophiles: Inside the Mind of QAnon*. Stanford, CA: Redwood, 2021.

Ellison, Nicole B., and J. Lee. "Religious Delusions and Hallucinations in Mental Disorder: Clinical Characteristics and Psychological Mechanisms." *Mental Health, Religion & Culture* 13 (2010) 237–51.

Everitt, Brian S. "Alternative Therapies: Magic, Miracles and Delusions." ResearchGate, 2016. From *Health and Lifestyle*, 125–45. DOI: 10.1007/978-3-319-42565-8_6.

Freeman, Daniel, and Philippa A. Garety. "Advances in Understanding and Treating Persecutory Delusions: A Review." *Social Psychiatry and Psychiatric Epidemiology* 49 (2014) 1179–89.

Freeman, Daniel, et al., eds. *Persecutory Delusions: Assessment, Theory, and Treatment*. Oxford: Oxford University Press, 2008.

Gaines, A. D. "Culture-Specific Delusions: Sense and Nonsense in Cultural Context." *Psychiatric Clinic North America* 18 (1995) 281–301.

Grover, Sandeep, et al. "Religion, Spirituality, and Schizophrenia: A Review." *Indian Journal Psychological Medicine* 36 (2014) 119–24.

Haplin, Tony. "Cult Leader Pyotr Kuznetsov Tries Suicide after Realising He Was Wrong about Doomsday." *Times*, Apr. 4, 2008.

Hood, Ralph W., et al. *The Psychology of Religion: An Empirical Approach*. New York: Guilford, 2009.

Isham, Louise, et al. "Understanding, Treating, and Renaming Grandiose Delusions: A Qualitative Study." *Psychology and Psychotherapy Theory, Research and Practice* 94 (2021) 119–40. https://doi.org/10.1111/papt.12260.

Iyassu, Robel, et al. "Psychological Characteristics of Religious Delusions." *Social Psychiatry and Psychiatric Epidemiology* 49 (2014) 1051–61. DOI: 10.1007/s00127-013-0811-y.

Jetten, Jolanda et al. *The Social Cure: Identity, Health and Well-Being*. New York: Psychology, 2012.

Koenig, Harold. *Religious and Spiritual Issues in Psychiatry*. Washington, DC: American Psychiatric, 2008.

Koenig, Harold G., et al. *Handbook of Religion and Health*. Oxford: Oxford University Press, 2001.

Kosarkova, Alice, et al. "Religious Conspiracy Theories about the COVID-19 Pandemic Are Associated with Negative Mental Health." *International Journal of Public Health* 12 (2023). DOI: 10.3389/ijph.2022.1604324.

Mohr, Sylvia, and Philippe Huguelet. "The Relationship between Schizophrenia and Religion and Its Implications for Care." *Swiss Med Weekly* 134 (2004) 369–76.

O'Connor, Shawn, and Brian Vandenberg. "Psychosis or Faith? Clinicians' Assessment of Religious Beliefs." *Journal of Consulting and Clinical Psychology* 73 (2005) 610–16. DOI: 10.1037/0022-006X.73.4.610.

Paloutzian, Raymond F., and Crystal L. Park. *Handbook of the Psychology of Religion and Spirituality*. New York: Guilford, 2013.

Pargament, K. I. *Spiritually Integrated Psychotherapy: Understanding and Addressing the Sacred*. New York: Guilford, 2007.

Rankin, Marianne. *An Introduction to Religious and Spiritual Experience*. London: Bloomsbury, 2009.

Richardson, J. T. "Religion, Delusions, and Violence: An Empirical Critique of the NRM Violence Literature." *Terrorism and Political Violence* 25 (2013) 201–21.

Rothschild, Mike. *The Storm Is upon Us: How QAnon Became a Movement, Cult, and Conspiracy Theory of Everything*. New York: Melville, 2021.

Runciman, Steven. *A History of the Crusades*. 3 vols. Cambridge: Cambridge University Press, 1987.

Sarno, Charles, and Helen Shoemaker. "Church, Sect, or Cult?" *Nova Religio: The Journal of Alternative and Emergent Religions* 19 (2016) 6–30.

Satici, Seydi Ahmet. "Psychological Vulnerability, Resilience, and Subjective Well-Being: The Mediating Role of Hope." *Personality and Individual Differences* 102 (2016) 68–73.

Scheeres, Julia. *A Thousand Lives: The Untold Story of Hope, Deception and Survival at Jonestown*. New York: Simon & Schuster, 2011.

Siddiqui, Mohammed Yaseen Ahmed, et al. "'Social Media Misinformation': An Epidemic within the COVID-19 Pandemic." *The American Journal of Tropical Medicine and Hygiene* 103 (2020) 920–21. DOI: 10.4269/ajtmh.20-0592.

Sofou, Natasha, et al. "Religious Delusions: Definition, Diagnosis and Clinical Implications." *Psychiatriki* 32 (2021) 224–31. DOI: 10.22365/jpsych.2021.014.

Tabor, James D., and Eugene V. Gallagher. *Why Waco? Cults and the Battle for Religious Freedom in America*. Berkeley: University of California Press, 1997.

Tamminga, Carol. "Psychotic Disorder Due to Another Medical Condition." MSD Manuals, Apr. 2022; modified Sept. 2022. https://www.msdmanuals.com/en-au/home/mental-health-disorders/schizophrenia-and-related-disorders/psychotic-disorder-due-to-another-medical-condition.

Tek, Cenk, and Berna Ulug. "Religiosity and Religious Obsessions in Obsessive-Compulsive Disorder." *Psychiatry Research* 104 (2001) 99–108.

Zeller, Benjamin E. "Extraterrestial Biblical Hermeneutics and the Making of Heaven's Gate." *Nova Religio: The Journal of Alternative and Emergent Religions* 14 (2010) 34–60.

7

AGASALA
Reimagining the Theology of Sin

Rene Sau Maiava

SIN IS A BIG theological topic, and reconstructing a theology of sin is an even bigger challenge. Nonetheless, reconstructing allows me to offer, from my Samoan context, *agasala* as part of what Pacific and Māori theologies are developing as we consider Christian faith from our locations, contexts, and worldviews.

    A lot of what I had been taught on sin had to do with humanity's offenses and insults toward God, specifically an individual's attitudes and actions that damaged or broke her/his/their relationship with God. With this "vertical" view, one that focuses on the relationship between a person and God (assumed to be above creation), the negative impact upon those harmed on earth has less attention. Yet, the way Christians treat each other matters to God; how we spend our time and money matters to God; how we care for creation matters to God. To worship God as the Creator and dismiss the ways we think and behave towards creation is a problem that Western Christian theology has not grasped in the same ways as Pacific and Māori theologies have. I make this statement having received formal theological education in Auckland, Aotearoa New Zealand for seven years, where the curriculum was based largely on Western Christian theological developments and reflections.

As a New Zealand–born Samoan woman, raised and residing in Aotearoa, Western Christian theology could only partially help me understand the destructive impact of sin. As I sought out Pacific and Māori theological reflections, it became clearer that the private and personal nature of the Western theology of sin and its vertical view was only part of the ways in which humanity damages and breaks relationships with God. The ways in which we interact within our families, places of worship, communities and as part of God's creation on our shared planet, impacts our relationship with God. In doing so, it also damages our own sense of well-being.

AGASALA AND COLONIZATION

There are many ways that sin causes damage, through greed and pride in our relationships with each other and with creation, and spreads like a disease infecting all those involved. This systemic nature of sin, that takes into account how problem attitudes and actions affect more than just an individual and their worship of God, is the core of *agasala*. It takes the horizontal view of damaging and breaking relationships on earth as we do, at the same time, toward heaven.

The *agasala* of colonization is an example of how attitudes and actions cause harm and destruction of life, that damages and breaks relationships systemically and personally. Colonization has all the elements of *agasala* in pride and greed with attitudes of *me and my people are better and deserve to get everything we want in any way we can*. It shamelessly drains the lives and livelihoods of the vulnerable, poor, and powerless. The *agasala* of colonization does not care about *how* (the imperial) "we" get rich and powerful, it only cares that "we" are and that "we" stay that way.

Samoan theologian Upolu Luma Vaai describes the *agasala* of colonization as

> one reality swallowing and digesting another. It is when one dominant culture digest the many cultures, when male rights digest female rights or vice versa, when the powerful digest the resources of the powerless, governments digest the land that belong to the people, religious organisations digest money that belongs to the poor, and the list of imbalances goes on.[1]

As we consider Pacific well-being, the *agasala* of colonization is important to recognize and address, as it takes on many forms and exists on many levels. Māori theologian Jenny Te Paa Daniel's work engages with the

---

1. Vaai, "Tino Theology," 229.

"digesting" *agasala* in her experiences as an Anglican and academic in Aotearoa. She writes, "I am intimately acquainted with the operating principles of colonization—those legendary and tiresome sinful derivatives of imperialism, sexism, classism, racism and clericalism."[2] These "isms" of domination from governmental forces, one gender over another, rich over poor, one ethnicity over others, and religious leaders over their congregations show how widespread the *agasala* of colonization can be.

AGASALA—HORIZONTAL VIEW AND SYSTEMIC NATURE

The term *agasala* was an addition to the *gagana* Samoa (Samoan language) by early Christian missionaries and represents "sin" in the biblical Samoan translation of the *Tusi Paia* (Holy Bible). It is made up of two words: *aga*, meaning "behavior" or "moving towards," and *sala*, which can be understood as damaging and breaking the harmonious relationships we have with ourselves, with others, with creation, and with God.

In reconstructing the theology/topic of sin from the perspective of *agasala*, it includes those thoughts and actions "towards" (towards here is also from the word *aga*) another person or creation that may damage life for that person or creation. This "towards" (*aga*) idea highlights how humans can drift into *sala*.

The societal structure within *fa'aSamoa* (Samoan culture) enables an awareness of wrong behavior that damages relationships. Each member within the *aiga* (nuclear and extended family) has a role, taught to them by their parents and elders, that formulates a way of knowing and being in the world. Some people have several roles, but the point I make here is that each person within the *aiga* understands their roles and how these impacts the family unit, village, and wider community. This way of knowing is the basis for understanding *agasala* as systemic rather than privatized, horizontal rather than vertical. It is both the outside forces that influence behavior and that towards which one moves (motivated by human traits on the inside) that results in *agasala*.

Attitudes and actions that are destructive towards one's neighbor and to the creation impact one's relationship with and towards God. While this may seem overly cultural in its emphasis, it does not oppose the Christian biblical understanding that also values relationships to the extent that humanity's interactions with one another hinder their worship of God. In the Sermon on the Mount, for example, Jesus explicitly advised that if "our

---

2. Te Paa Daniel, "Bible and Colonization," 200.

neighbor" has any issue against "us" we need to care for that relationship first *before* we come to worship God (Matt 5:22–24 NRSV).

SAMOAN THEOLOGIANS' ENGAGEMENT WITH *AGASALA*

In reviewing selected works of Upolu Luma Vaai, Mercy Ah-Siu Maliko, Fa'afetai Aiava, Feiloaiga Taule'ale'ausumai, and Terry Pouono what stood out was the single definition for *agasala* offered by Vaai's *tino* theology. Vaai explains that *tino* is used symbolically in many parts of the Pacific to refer to "individuals, connections, relations, community, genealogies, birth, experience, truth and motherhood."[3]

Vaai reconstructs a theology of personhood in *tino* theology that provides a basis for understanding *agasala*:

> Sin is therefore not so much about missing the mark of a personal relationship with God, but rather about the "I" contributing to the disfiguring of the tino. Sin is when the "I" becomes obsessed with "resource grabbing," extracting the minimal resources upon which "we" wholly depend, or when "we" accept their imposed status as the passive invisible face of the tino.[4]

What *tino* theology offers is a view of *agasala*, which turns our attention to its systemic nature demonstrated in colonization with its horizontal perspective. *Tino* theology assumes God already has an intimate union with the *tino* through Christ in the Spirit resulting in the *tino* being both theological and spiritual.[5] From a *tino* theology perspective, to *agasala* against creation through nuclear testing, dumping plastic rubbish into the ocean, destroying forestry to make way for building complexes, or mass burning of industrial waste polluting the atmosphere miss the mark in one's personal relationship with God.

Ah-Siu Maliko in her work in public theology addresses domestic violence in Samoan families as *agasala*:

> The church is called to break the silence on the issue of family violence. Breaking the silence means to speak openly about violence, naming it for what it is and naming it as a sin before God.[6]

3. Vaai, "Tino Theology," 223–24.
4. Vaai, "Tino Theology," 236.
5. Vaai, "Tino Theology," 233.
6. Ah Siu-Maliko, *Christian Faith*, 12.

In her report for Samoan communities in New Zealand—*Christian Faith and Family Violence* (2016)—Ah-Siu Maliko refers to "sin" twice.[7] Ah-Siu Maliko's intervention has consistently been for Samoan churches to openly oppose all forms of family violence thus communicating a message of support for families dealing with violence. She also advocates for openness from families to seek help. Ah-Siu Maliko is strong in her message for the victims to not keep it private, but to find the courage to stand against cultural norms that dictate silence and to keep up appearances to "save face."[8] Privatization, in keeping *agasala* a secret or a private matter, finds a tragic illustration in Samoan's acceptance of domestic violence as norm(al). Additionally, privatization in this context, with its narrow heavenward focus that ignores destructions occurring horizontally, makes a vertical view of *agasala* problematic.

Vaai and Ah-Siu Maliko engage with *agasala* as systemic rather than privatized, seeing it through the horizontal lens instead of the vertical one. Vaai's *tino* theology challenges Christians to expand our horizons, inviting us to appreciate God's presence in ourselves as part of creation. This view of personhood is vital for Christian theology as climate change impacts the Earth more drastically with every passing season. In like manner, Ah-Siu Maliko's public theology addressing domestic violence articulates a Christian faith from a Samoan woman's perspective that challenges the church, in particular the way that Samoan Church leaders have been dealing with families struggling with the *agasala* (or social problem) of domestic violence.

In their respective disciplines of theology, Vaai and Ah-Siu Maliko establish a systemic definition of *agasala*. They not only see pride and greed as causing *agasala*, but they also identify the outside forces or stressors that press upon a person such as financial hardship within a capitalist economic system where the wealthy and elite "grab" and "extract" from the poor and vulnerable. Nonetheless, colonization cannot bear full responsibility for a person or the community's *agasala*. While the outside stressors place pressure on a person, family, and communities, bearing *agasala* is within the support of family and/or community. *Tino* theology offers this perspective with its relational nature. Ah-Siu Maliko's public theology also places the recovery from domestic violence within the healing of the church and community. *Tino* theology allows a way of considering and seeing oneself in the world as relationally interconnected within different and diverse dimensions, while Ah-Siu Maliko's public theology (also based upon Samoan-Christian values) offers a way of actualizing one's faith in situations of crisis.

---

7. Ah Siu-Maliko, *Christian Faith*, 12, 16.

8. Ah Siu-Maliko, *Christian Faith*, 57; Ah-Siu-Maliko, *Embodying Aga Tausili*, 193.

The horizontal view of *agasala* is evident within *tino* theology, with the act of greed in resource grabbing and extraction. These are human behaviors that Vaai firmly associates with *agasala*, the gigantic "I" at the expense of the "we." Similarly, Maliko's use of "sin" as *agasala* orients as systemic and horizontal, placing the act of domestic violence as *agasala* before God. Taken from that perspective, coupled with her emphasis in the same work that domestic violence should not be treated as an insignificant *sala*, strengthens her horizontal view of *agasala*. In so doing, neither theologian negated God's place in their theological construction; on the other hand, God is indeed fundamental within their theologies.

Aiava's use of *agasala* provides a relational Samoan Christian theological perspective in line with the privatized and vertical views. His use of the term *sin* in his chapter "Taking Selfies: Honouring Faces (*Alo*) in Theology and Hermeneutics" is brief while uncomplicated. Like Ah-Siu Maliko, *agasala* emphasizes the break down in relationships—in Aiava's case, the emphasis is on the vertical relationship between God and people.

> If it is true that God's face is hidden from the unrighteous, then we are given a clue as to why God chose not to reveal Godself to the Israelites after they had sinned in case they were consumed (Ex 33:2, 23). . . . When Israel turns its face toward sin, it has dishonoured God's face.[9]

Aiava has a different scope and intention. What is of interest is the emphasis and view of *agasala* that Aiava brings alongside those of Vaai and Ah-Siu Maliko. What Aiava offers is a Samoan Christian theology that holds on to a Western Christian traditional understanding of *sala* within a relational context. He presents *agasala* explicitly with the Western categories of theology, such as a systematic theology of the *imago Dei* and theological hermeneutics.

Vaai's definition and use of *agasala* in *tino* theology alongside Ah-Siu Maliko and Aiava's references are serious considerations of how Samoan Christian theology conceptualizes *agasala*. The relational nature of each theologian's work is an important common aspect that is founded upon their Samoan Christian culture. Unified, their work reflects a view of *agasala* that allows for a systemic and privatized approach. This view of *agasala* as systemic and personal affords a balance that builds upon the Western Christian theological tradition that is also part of our Samoan Christian theological heritage.

---

9. Aiava, "Taking Selfies," 261.

Samoan Theologians in Diaspora

In the works of Samoan theologians living in Aotearoa New Zealand, the explicit use of *agasala* is absent. What is of note in the following analysis is the raising of social justice issues, as Ah-Siu Maliko does in addressing domestic violence, without an explicit reference to sin/*agasala*.

Feiloaiga Taule'ale'ausumai and Terry Pouono, both New Zealand–born Samoan theologians who critique the practices of the church that are discriminatory and abusive, refrain from naming the destructive actions and attitudes of the church as *agasala*. While there is no firm definition for *agasala* in the works by Taule'ale'ausumai and Pouono, the following discussion makes obvious connections.

Taule'ale'ausumai pastorally and theologically reflects on the negative impact of colonization, discrimination, and abuse on herself and those alongside whom she has ministered. While she does not refer to *agasala* specifically, the damaging characteristics are described in her work.

Drawing from Vaai's *tino* theology that defines *agasala* as colonization, that of grabbing and extracting resources for one's own gain without considering the needs of others, discrimination as Taule'ale'ausumai describes it would come under the frames as *agasala*. Not simply because discrimination is a misuse of power to ensure the benefit of one people group over another, but more importantly, as Taule'ale'ausumai makes clear, it acts to hinder answering God's call on one's life, which is to act against God: "God calls all people to be involved in mission and when we begin to separate and exclude we fail to fulfil and live out the mission of God."[10] This exclusionary practice alludes to cause and experience. It is not just what oppresses, but also how oppression is experienced. In this regard, Taule'ale'ausumai points to *agasala* (as understood in this reflection), where life—the life God gives, and which Jesus Christ came to affirm—is stunted by not being able to answer God's call and fulfil the design God has for one's life.

> More and more women are being called and are considering the call to enter the ordained ministry, whereas in the past the thought would never have entered their minds.[11]

Taule'ale'ausumai encountered a great deal of criticism as a Samoan woman in ordained ministry. The comparisons to her male counterparts and the questioning of the legitimacy of her ministry led her to doubt God's calling and her vocation: "I didn't believe that God could call me and then

---

10. Taule'ale'ausumai, "Herstory," 32.
11. Taule'ale'ausumai, "Herstory," 34.

make life so miserable."[12] In her judgment, the misery was brought about by the *agasala* against her through oppressive opinions of her calling.[13]

The absence of using an explicit term for *agasala* in her publications is difficult to determine as her theology directly addresses social injustice. Yet, I cannot formulate a direct definition of *agasala* from her works. What can be drawn from her theological reflections is the negative impact of colonization, discrimination, and abuse on herself and those with whom she has ministered alongside.[14] These negative impacts, which stunt if not destroy life, point to *agasala*. The last paragraph of her latest work makes a strong case for this:

> Samoa needs to be liberated from the colonial history and trappings of British society. The church needs to become vulnerable and listen to the voice of the marginalized, the voices of the poor, the women and the abused, the LGBTQ communities as well as the voiceless. The church continues to have a superior status and patriarchy continues to dominate while the women of the church have grown to believe that it is their place to remain as *fautua* (advisors to their husbands without rocking the boat). There are bits of small progress with women being able to study theology, but still cannot be ordained into the Christian ministry; so much more needs to happen for Samoa to truly become an egalitarian society.[15]

Two of Pouono's works discuss the characteristics of *agasala*, without naming them as such: that of greed and pride,[16] evident among dominant groups and colonial mindsets.[17] Pouono's article "Teu le Vā" establishes his relational outlook as a New Zealand–born Samoan Christian leader and theologian. He explains that *vā* is a Samoan term meaning "space" or "interval" that is not empty or divisive, but rather a space that relates. As such, it is also a space/interval where rivalry takes place, which Pouono argues evidences the *vā* as relational, as it "explicitly presupposes an engagement between two parties in a state of competition or variance of some sort."[18]

---

12. Taule'ale'ausumai, "Herstory," 34.

13. Taule'ale'ausumai, "Herstory," 32.

14. In Taule'ale'ausumai's doctoral thesis the subsection "Disagreement with Church Practice" gives detailed accounts of the negative affects upon the congregation and herself ("Samoan Diaspora Church," 138–48).

15. Taule'ale'ausumai, "Pasifika Churches Trapped," 150.

16. Pouono, "Teu Le Vā."

17. Pouono, "Indigenous Language Loss."

18. Pouono, "Teu Le Vā," 90.

Despite this latter characteristic, *teu le vā* (care for the relational space) within the Samoan context is usually attributed to preserving harmony in relationships.

The normal tensions that are present in relationships, that of conflict and disagreements, are realistically considered with *vā*. Rivalry, competition, or variance from harmonious relations is not seen as *agasala*. The movement towards *sala* surfaces when political influence and economic affluence is ambitiously sought compromising the harmonious relationships that *teu le vā* upholds.

Additionally, Pouono lists social and political injustices as contributing factors to the compromise of *teu le vā*, the compounded consequences being a division of "haves" and "have nots" with the former aligning with oppressive and exploitative behaviors against the "have nots."[19] This behavior shows similar traits to Vaai's *tino* theology's definition of *agasala*, the gigantic "I" grabbing and extracting resources at the expense of the "we." In contrast, *teu le vā* requires respect for existing boundaries and relations. Pouono's conceptualization of the *vā* affords a view of how *agasala* can act against relationships from a Samoan Christian context. Greed and pride are personal *sala* with social and political injustices systemic *sala*.

Pouono's *vā* exists in a Christian context, rooted in the biblical principle of love. Specifically, he notes the Scriptural text to love God and neighbor from Matt 22:37 and 39.[20] Pouono decisively positions *vā* from being a framework or a mechanical way of operation, to "an ethic of love stemming from the belief that God is love."[21] In so doing, Pouono's *teu le vā*, like *tino* theology, opposes *agasala*.

In a later work, "Indigenous Language Loss" (2017), Pouono writes from a postcolonial perspective with a focus on the *gagana* Samoa (Samoan language). He makes the case that the issue of language makes for a converging point for new acts of colonization but also resistance. The former is the Congregational Christian Church of Samoa in Aotearoa taking on a "colonial mindset" in strictly adhering to Samoan language use in preaching, teaching and leadership within the church. The resistance is the domination of the English language as the lingua franca of education, economy, and politics in Aotearoa.

Postcolonial views give voice to the marginalized and those who have been given no voice by the colonizers and oppressive regimes. These demonstrations of activism, particularly through literature, are proving effective

---

19. Pouono, "Teu Le Vā," 97.
20. Pouono, "Teu Le Vā," 101.
21. Pouono, "Teu Le Vā," 99.

in decolonizing mindsets where more diverse voices are being heard and read. Postcolonial literature, such as Edward Said's seminal work *Orientalism*, exposes the colonizing of minds through literature and images (1978).[22] The volume in which Pouono's chapter appears, *Postcolonial Voices from Downunder*, provides another more recent, local and Christian theological example.

With the rectifying nature of postcolonial literature against oppressive regimes, it could be presumed that it also raises the readers awareness of what has been previously discussed as *agasala*. However, the connection is difficult to make if the reader is unaware of what *agasala* is in its systemic nature. In Pouono's case particularly, where there is no explicit term referred to, does language loss as a deliberate tool to keep a continuation of the status quo automatically fall into the categorization of *agasala*? Unlike domestic violence, restricting language use is not overtly destructive. Hence, the question arises, is withholding indigenous language use or on the other hand, insisting on it, *agasala*? The discussion within Pouono's works invites careful consideration of these questions. Domination and colonization are oppressive terms that represent a definite power over and control of people by the dominating group from their colonial mindsets.

Language loss as a colonial tool designed to assimilate the indigenous and marginalized population to the dominant culture acts against diversity and the value each group holds as God's image bearers. Similarly, to disregard the language of a people within the larger group is also restricting God's design by seeing the minority's language as inferior or insignificant. Both are not obvious destructive acts that are instantly recognizable; however, in the long term it does irreparable damage. Subversively the dominant group are communicating that their language is superior, and so too their culture.

In Pouono's *teu le vā* and postcolonial perspective, the impacts of *agasala* are highlighted through the ways relationships are damaged through greed, pride, social and political injustices, as well as the suppression of cultural diversity through restrictions on language use. He does not use the term *agasala* in his written works; however, the destructive components of which *agasala* is comprised are evident.

---

22. Edward Said, Gayatri Spivak, and Homi Bhabha are notable figures in postcolonial theory. Much of postcolonialism that has been developed is attributed to their pioneering work, although, according to postcolonial biblical scholar R. S. Sugirtharajah, that result was unintended. "It was only when theorizing became an attractive and an indispensable tool, and when these scholars recognized and addressed the central interests of the colonized other, that they came to be seen as originators and proponents of postcolonial theory" (Sugirtharajah, "Postcolonial Biblical Interpretation," 66).

In considering Taule'ale'ausumai's and Pouono's works, the absence of any explicit term for *agasala* raises questions as to the association of *agasala* with those terms used in dealing with social justice issues. When viewed from a *tino* theological perspective, the connection with *agasala* is clear. Discrimination and colonization, with all its dominating tools, would be considered *agasala*, the gigantic "I" that negates the needs of the "we." Despite the clear connection, both theologians do not utilize *agasala* as a term to describe the destructive issues they address. The contexts they share with Vaai, Ah-Siu Maliko, and Aiava are similar, those of the *fa'aSamoa*, Christian church, religion, and social justice, which gives ample reasons for their using *agasala*, as Ah-Siu Maliko had in her report. It causes me to consider how their work might represent other Samoan Christian theologians who address social issues, using terminology that is associated with *sala*, but do not refer to *agasala* explicitly. And, what that might mean in understanding *agasala* in the different locations and contexts where Samoan Christianity is reconstructing theology going forward.

CONCLUSION

My attempt in reconstructing a theology of sin in *agasala* is so that we can better recognize its systemic and private nature that aggressively, passively or progressively damages, breaks and destroys relationships with all of life horizontally and vertically. In my offering of *agasala*, the invitation is to recognize the drifts towards *sala* and to resist. To do so in attitude and action as Mercy Ah-Siu Maliko has done against family violence and Feiloaiga Taule'ale'ausumai against discrimination within the Samoan church. With the rise of Māori and Pacific theologies, written and taught by women and men, the *agasala* of colonization within Christian churches and theologies is being resisted. Our *aga* can be to resist too!

Our resistance builds our well-being, collectively and individually. As Pasifika people we are relationally oriented, and this is not a departure from Gods' design for humanity. The ways we are treated is important to God, so too is the way that we treat Gods' creation. Recognizing *agasala* allows us to take action that preserves or rebuilds our well-being. For instance, family violence and gender-based violence must be recognized as *agasala*; to do otherwise would be to normalize abusive control through violence and model a cycle of oppression within the family that severely damages well-being, for the victim, witnesses, and the perpetrator.

Racism is also abusive and divisive, with the belief of one people group that they are superior to others, thus fueling an attitude of entitlement to power and privilege over those deemed "inferior," in turn damaging the well-being for those involved as well. In addition to prayer and faith practices, we can seek and receive support from others to recover from the trauma and to rebuild. In doing so we resist *agasala* from continuing, while building up well-being, for ourselves, our families, and our communities.

BIBLIOGRAPHY

Ah Siu-Maliko, Mercy. *Christian Faith and Family Violence: A Report for Samoan Communities in New Zealand*. University of Otago, Aug. 2016. https://ourarchive.otago.ac.nz/handle/10523/7050.

———. *Embodying Aga Tausili: A Public Theology from Oceania*. Lanham, MD: Lexington, 2021.

Aiava, Faafetai. "Taking Selfies: Honouring Faces (*Alo*) in Theology and Hermeneutics." In *The Relational Self: Decolonising Personhood in the Pacific*, edited by Upolu Luma Va'ai and Unaisi Nabobo-Baba, 257–70. Suva, Fiji: University of the South Pacific Press, 2017.

Havea, Jione, ed. *Postcolonial Voices from Downunder: Indigenous Matters, Confronting Readings*. Eugene, OR: Pickwick, 2017.

Pouono, Terry. "Indigenous Language Loss: The Future of Gagana Samoa (Samoan Language) in Diaspora." In *Postcolonial Voices from Downunder: Indigenous Matters, Confronting Readings*, edited by Jione Havea, 170–81. Eugene, OR: Pickwick, 2017.

———. "'Teu Le Vā': The Samoan Cosmic-Community in Aotearoa. Preserving Harmonious Relationships...Where Is the Harmony?" *Pacific Journal of Theology*, 2nd ser., vol. 50 (2013) 88–101.

Taule'ale'ausumai, Feiloaiga. "Herstory: The Struggle of Pacific Women in Ministry." *Pacific Journal of Theology* 7 (1992) 31–34.

———. "Pasifika Churches Trapped in the Missionary Era: A Case in Samoa." In *Theologies from the Pacific*, edited by Jione Havea, 139–50. Postcolonialism and Religions. Cham, Switz.: Springer, 2021.

———. "The Samoan Diaspora Church in New Zealand: Patterns of Movement and Dynamics amongst Three Generations of Samoan Families." PhD diss., Auckland University of Technology, 2018.

Said, Edward W. *Orientalism*. 25th anniv. ed. New York: Vintage, 2003.

Sugiritharaja, R. S. "Postcolonial Biblical Interpretation." In *Voices from the Margin: Interpreting the Bible in the Third World*, edited by R. S. Sugirtharajah, 64–84. Rev. and expanded 3rd ed. Maryknoll, NY: Orbis, 2006.

Te Paa Daniel, Jenny. "Bible and Colonization: Aotearoa New Zealand." In *Colonialism and the Bible: Contemporary Reflections from the Global South*, edited by Tat-siong Benny Liew and Fernando F. Segovia, 199–210. Postcolonial and Decolonial Studies in Religion and Theology. Lanham, MD: Lexington, 2018.

Vaai, Upolu Luma. "Tino Theology." In *The Relational Self: Decolonising Personhood in the Pacific*, edited by Upolu Luma Va'ai and Unaisi Nabobo-Baba, 223–41. Suva, Fiji: University of the South Pacific Press, 2017.

8

JUDAS GREETS JESUS WITH A *SOGI*?
A Talanoa of Judas's Kiss (Mark 14), the Lover's Kiss (Song 8:1), and the Sogi of Limaleleima'oloa

Brian Fiu Kolia

WHAT IS IN A kiss? This is a question that I will explore in this *talanoa*. Kissing, in its complexity, expresses love, affection, and intimacy, but also sex, sexuality, and eroticism. Kissing as betrayal, however, goes against these notions, and against the very fabric of what makes a kiss a kiss.

It seems that kissing at Gethsemane in Mark 14 has been flipped to articulate the opposite of what a kiss means. But perhaps, and this is the premise behind this *talanoa*, what we see in the Gethsemane episode is quite the contrary, and perhaps what might be in view is an extension of the kissing themes that are common in other parts of the bible. It may be that interpreters and readers of this story have taken the love, intimacy, affection, sex, and sexuality out of the kiss due to the nature of the events occurring. But what if we (re)insert these themes and reread the Mark 14 story? What if ancient and modern readers are reminded of kissing in the Song of Songs? Why don't we (re)read this story from a Samoan perspective in light of the language used by Samoan translators to explain the story, where the word for "kiss" (φιλήω in Mark 14:44–45) is the word *sogi*? These questions will plot the markers for this *talanoa* as we seek to highlight and liberate the intimacy connotations that have been suppressed (by whom?) in Judas's kiss. By (re) inserting the themes of affection and intimacy into Judas's kiss, we might also envision how kissing could convey a state of well-being, much like how *sogi* once exhibited the well-being of Samoans prior to the colonial period.

The Samoan word *sogi* means "kiss" but it also means "to sniff" or "to smell." The word is relative to the Māori greeting *hongi*, and historically, *sogi* was no different to this familiar Māori act of welcome because *sogi* also denotes a traditional Samoan greeting where two people "rub noses" (the same way that Māori do). To understand the significance of *sogi*, I will explore its origins.

THE *FĀGOGO* OF LIMALELEIMA 'OLOA

I begin our intertextual *talanoa* by bringing a cultural text: a *fāgogo*. *Fāgogo* is "the art of Samoan storytelling that involves a space where spirits roam and animals possess human-like qualities, a space where animals have conversations with humans and, in some stories, have relations with humans."[1]

The root of the *sogi* is best told through an ancient Samoan *fāgogo* of a woman named Limalelei (short for Limaleleima 'oloa), the granddaughter of the creator god, Tagaloa. The story begins with Tagaloa's son Matila (short for Matilafoafoa) who was born inside a canoe. His mother, Sinaalemoana, while pregnant with Matila, desired fish and her husband Tagaloa would often direct servants to fish for her. As he was born in a canoe, Matila grew up to become a master fisherman.

While Matila was out at sea one day, he arrived at Savaii where he met a beautiful woman. Matila desired the young woman and asked for her to go with him on a cruise in his canoe. The woman agreed and they spent the rest of the night together. In the morning, Matila asked the woman to marry him, but she refused, as she did not want a husband who would be out all day on fishing expeditions, and then come back home smelling like the ocean. So they farewelled, but as a parting gift, Matila gave the woman his *ulalei* necklace (made of whale ivory). Later that year, the woman had a daughter simply called Funa (girl). As Funa grew up, she knew she wasn't like the other girls in the village. They all knew who their fathers were, while Funa had never met her father and had no idea why she wasn't given a name.

One day, Funa confronted her mother, who explained who her father was and that her true name was Lima-lelei-ma-'oloa, in memory of the priceless whale tooth necklace (*oloa*)[2] that was given with love (*limalelei*—lit. "gracious hands") by her father. With her mother's blessing—and wearing

---

1. Kolia, "Eve, the Serpent," 156.

2. The word *oloa* denotes "treasure," implying that the necklace was a treasure; the name for the whale tooth is *ulalei*.

her father's *ulalei* necklace—Limalelei set off on an ambitious journey to find her father, Matilafoafoa. Limalelei sailed to 'Upolu and hiked to the top of Mauga Uafato-Malata, where the earth meets the first level of the sky-heaven. If she truly was the granddaughter of Tagaloa, then she would have to climb to the ninth and highest sky-heaven to find her father.

Limalelei hauled herself up into the first heaven, where she was met by an angry *āitu* guardian who threatened to eat her if she was a human. Limalelei tried to remember what her mother had told her, but it was all so new to her! She fumbled and stuttered, forgetting her father's name and mispronouncing her own name. The *āitu* pressed his face against Limalelei's in the manner of *sogi*, trying to sense if she was telling the truth. "If you really are one of the gods," the spirit said, "then you have nothing to fear. But, if you are a mortal, you don't belong here." She did not smell familiar, but the *āitu* noticed the magical *ulalei* around her neck . . . maybe she was divine after all. He did not want to risk being punished by Tagaloa, so he let the girl pass.

This *sogi* interaction was repeated with the various *āitu* of each *lagi* and Limalelei continued until she reached the fifth heaven. By then she was exhausted and thirsty from climbing the clouds and running from spirits. An old, blind woman sitting at the edge of a clear pond offered her a drink, asking what her name was. Limalelei tried to remember what her mother had told her, she fumbled and stuttered . . . and then sat down and cried in frustration. The old woman wiped away the tears and washed Limalelei's hair and face, so when she pressed her face against Limalelei's, trying to sense if she was telling the truth, the girl no longer smelled like sweat and fish and the earth. "You really are one of the gods," the blind woman said. "So you have nothing to fear. You are the daughter of Matilafoafoa, and you belong here."

Limalelei remembered that name! She asked the old, blind woman how she knew what her father's name was. The old lady revealed that she was Matamolali, the midwife who had delivered her father when he was born. She was there when he took his first breath and Limalelei smelled just like her father did. Matamolali reminded Limalelei who she was and practiced pronouncing the names of her father and grandfather. She told the girl to rub her skin with her mother's favorite perfume (coconut oil scented with *seilala* flowers) and to wear her mother's favorite flowers (*moso'oi*) in her hair and wished her luck on her quest.

Limalelei finally reached the highest heaven, where she was met by Tulī, the sacred messenger of Tagaloa. Limalelei remembered what her mother (and Matamolali) had told her, she was confident and spoke clearly, "My father is Matilafoafoa! My grandfather is the great Tagaloa! I am

Limaleleima 'oloa!" Tulī was convinced and quickly brought the girl to the *malae* where Tagaloa's sons were competing in throwing *ti'a* (javelins).

No one recognized Limalelei when she arrived, and she had never seen any of the Tagaloa family before either. Matila recognized that she was wearing his *ulalei* and he demanded to know how she got the necklace that she wore around her neck! She declared, "My father is Matilafoafoa! My grandfather is the great Tagaloa! I am Limaleleima 'oloa!"

Matila pressed his face against Limalelei's, trying to sense if she was telling the truth. As he inhaled, he smelled the scent of *seilala* oil and *moso'oi* flowers. The memories of his lover, and a passionate night on his canoe, all came flooding back to his mind. "You truly are my daughter," he exclaimed, "so you have nothing to fear. I am your father, Matilafoafoa, and I am happy that you are here!"

Limalelei returned to earth with her reputation intact. The other villagers stopped teasing her about not having a father and not having a name. Now they knew who Limalelei was, and they apologized for treating her differently. When Limalelei grew up and had a son of her own, she named him Matilafoafoa. The first thing she did when he was born was to pick him up and hold him face-to-face and share his first breath. From then on, all the people of Sāmoa began greeting each other with the *sogi*, the same way the gods and spirits did in the sky-heavens.[3]

Intriguingly, the act of *sogi* for Samoans has changed over time from the traditional greeting to a peck on the cheek as commonly practiced today. How did this change? The authors of the website *Digital Fagogo* write that

> Prior to the influenza pandemic of 1918 (which wiped out more than 20% of Samoans), the sogi was the universal, everyday greeting in Sāmoa. But the practice was discontinued once it was understood that pressing faces and inhaling respiratory droplets were potent vectors of the disease.[4]

As with a host of other traditional practices Western colonialism had sought to stop, this one was momentarily halted as a result of Westerners bringing diseases to our lands.

However, due to the resilience of Samoans in those times, the *sogi* managed to survive the colonial periods as some families still practice *sogi* today. In fact, my late grandfather would greet his children and grandchildren with the *sogi*. Subsequently, my father would greet his own grandchildren this way too. I still remember my grandfather would rub his nose

---

3. This is a shortened version of the *fāgogo*, which is available at Digital Fāgogo Collective, "Why We Greet."

4. Digital Fāgogo Collective, "Why We Greet," para. 6.

against mine and breathe in (*sogi*) my scent and it would last a few seconds. My grandfather explained that he knew us all by our scent and that our scents represented our souls which he connected to. At the same time, I felt connected to my grandfather as I could smell his scent, with a strong whiff of Samoan tobacco, which made me feel connected to the land from which the tobacco came. The dried-up banana leaves (*lau sului*) that the tobacco was rolled up in also came from the land.

JUDAS KISS

Having set the scene of the Samoan *sogi* and its origin, our *talanoa* drifts to the other *sogi*, that of Judas. Our *talanoa* takes us to the scene of the Gethsemane *sogi*, to which there are significant details and points that warrant our attention. Specifically, I want to *talanoa* about the significance of the Passover, the apostles who desert Jesus, the garden, and the kiss itself.

Passover—Song of Songs

The first verse (Mark 14:1) highlights the time when this kiss will take place, that is, during the Passover. As mentioned earlier, this *talanoa* will bring to light the nuances of kissing as portrayed in the Song of Songs. At this point, it might not be apparent, but the Markan author letting us know that the events in ch. 14 occur during Passover season is intriguing, because the main text that is read during Passover is the Song of Songs. Marvin Sweeney explains the connection:

> Based in part on the traditions in the Prophets, which depict the relationship between YHWH and Israel or Jerusalem as a marital relationship between groom and bride (see Isa 54; Jer 2; Ezek 16; Hos 1–3; Zeph 3:14–20), Jewish tradition reads Song of Songs allegorically as a presentation of the marital relationship between YHWH and the people of Israel. The relationship between the two lovers thereby symbolizes the relationship between YHWH and Israel at the time of the Exodus from Egypt.[5]

It is clear then that the link between the Song of Songs and Passover is through the theme of love, where the Song of Song's human and erotic love is used to articulate the love of God. We may ask, however: Could a less erotic or less provocative text have been used? According to rabbinic traditions, the Song of Songs seems to be the most appropriate, although

---

5. Sweeney, *TANAK*, 426.

not without debate, where the great Rabbi Aqiba contested: "For the whole world is not worthy as the day when the Song of Songs was given to Israel, for all the Writings are holy, but the Song of Songs is Holy of Holies."[6] In this respect, the Song of Songs represents the perfect text for such an important festival on the Jewish calendar. Jewish tradition does not want to do away with the eroticism and sexuality; instead it embraces it, and uses it to (re)define God's love. Perhaps Mark is hinting at us to do the same, because by letting us know that the scene occurs during the Passover, it sets the scene for Jesus's Last Supper with his disciples, where the Passover reminds us of God's love, articulated to Jewish readers through the Song of Songs.

Desert(ers)

During the supper, the words of Jesus in 14:27 sound an eerie tune: "You will *all* become deserters" (NRSV; emphasis added). Not one, but *all* disciples will desert (read: betray) Jesus, which begs the question: Why is Judas being singled out as the one who betrays?

Perhaps the point is not that Judas will be the sole disciple to betray Jesus, but that Judas's betrayal in contrast to the others would be unique or exceptional. So, in what sense would Judas's betrayal be exceptional? This question raises a sense of irony that is heightened through Peter; the irony is that Peter says that he will not desert Jesus but eventually does, while Judas, who never lies about *not* deserting or betraying Jesus, proceeds with his act of betrayal. In this sense, one might argue that Peter's betrayal probably carries the greater sting after he had stated emphatically that he would not desert Jesus.

Garden

I want to highlight the significance of "garden" in this *talanoa*. The events in the Markan account take place at the garden of Gethsemane, while the rendezvous between the two lovers takes place in and around the garden. The garden metaphor in the Song of Songs is utilized heavily insofar that the woman herself is described as a garden (Song 4:12–5:1). Indeed, "the garden is both the ideal place for sexual consummation and a metaphor for the woman's fertility."[7] Intriguingly, the kiss takes place for Judas in a garden space.

---

6. See Moscovitz, "Tractate Yadayim," 948.
7. Weems, "Song of Songs," 5:405.

In light of the garden atmosphere in the Song, it is not hard to associate kissing with the garden. And like the Song of Songs, there is a kiss that takes place in the garden of Gethsemane, which expresses a deep connection between two souls. The garden was a place of solitude for Jesus, who often retreated there to pray. In ancient times, the garden was a meeting place for lovers. In this intertextual *talanoa*, we can see that the garden becomes synonymous with kissing.

Judas's Kiss

Looking closely at the Judas kiss, it is interesting to note other uses of the Greek term φιλήω constitute a kiss of compassion and intimacy. The term is a favorite of Luke's, as he uses the word to describe the woman kissing Jesus's feet (Luke 7:38) and the father kissing his prodigal son after returning (Luke 15:20). Luke also uses the term to describe the scenes of Paul's departure from Ephesus, embracing and kissing the faithful there as he bids them farewell (Acts 20:27). The word itself is a derivative of the Greek word for "friendly love"—φιλέω. To view the kiss as an act of betrayal departs from the usual usage of the word in the New Testament.

The point I want to make is not that the kiss is not an act of betrayal, but to propose a retrieval of the original intimacy associated with the kiss, before we even make a suggestion of disloyalty by Judas. In the next section, I suggest that we observe the kiss more closely, in light of echoes we may hear from the Hebrew Bible, specifically, the Song of Songs.

SONG OF SONGS KISS

Like the waves of the *moana*, our *talanoa* drifts again, taking us to the kissing motif in the Song of Songs. I want to look at three features in the Song of Songs that send ripples into the Mark 14 account.

First is the kiss. There are many instances of kissing in the Hebrew Bible, some that even possess the familiar sense of betrayal as often read of the Judas kiss, such as Prov 27:6 ("profuse are the kisses of an enemy") and 2 Sam 20:9–10, where Joab purports to greet the unsuspecting Amasa with a kiss and then stabs him to death.[8] The kiss in the Song, however, is not a kiss of betrayal but of love. I invite us then to reconsider the kiss from an alternative (alter-native) perspective, through the word *sogi*, because the

---

8. Marcus, *Mark 8–16*, 991.

word *kiss* is translated in the Samoan bible as *sogi*. In this sense we may feel a connection between the Song's kiss and the Judas one.

The *sogi*-kiss is not merely a planting of lips on another person, but it involves the breathing in of one's scent, as mentioned in the Limaleleima 'oloa *fāgogo*. Intriguingly, some scholars have argued that the word *nĕšîqôṯ* (kisses) in Song 1:2 "means not 'kisses' but 'odors,' related to Arabic *našaqa*, 'to smell (a scent or odor)' and thus is an excellent parallel to *rēaḥ* ['fragrant' (NRSV)] in the following verse."[9] In this sense, it may be that the use of *sogi* is not only fitting, but also provides implications for rereading the Judas kiss as I will consider later.

Second is the location. The affair between the two takes place in the garden.[10] In the Song, Renita Weems claims, "The garden, therefore, is both the place to which they escape together and the place mentioned as a 'well of living water' (v. 15), perhaps hinting at the flood of human body fluids that accompany arousal."[11] This sets up the perfect scene for the lovers who long for each other's kiss, anticipating a meeting in a garden, where they can be mischievous and carefree.

This relates to our third ripple: longing. Longing is important in the context of the Song because it builds up to the kiss that would consummate the love between the lovers. In love poetry, yearning is a common motif.[12] Was there yearning between Judas and Jesus? We shall open up the *talanoa* in the next section.

REREADING THE JUDAS KISS

In this *talanoa*, the Judas kiss reminds us of the Song of Songs: a kiss that takes place in the garden, and a kiss between two individuals who long for one another. To think along these lines is to consider the Judas kiss in a different light—and this may be pushing the envelope a bit, but I say: Why not? *Talanoa*, in one imagination, is to *tala* (expand/extend) into the *noa* (void). To cross borders and go beyond what restricts us, into unchartered waters, to venture into new spaces of *talanoa*. Considering the Judas kiss in light of the lovers of Song of Songs, is a *tala* into the *noa*, to re-envisage the kiss differently. The usual reading of the Judas kiss holds that it was a gesture

---

9. Harris H. Hirschberg, cited in Pope, *Song of Songs*, 297.

10. *The garden* is a common term in the Song, found in 4:12, 15, 16; 5:1; 6:2, 11; and 8:13.

11. Weems, "Song of Songs," 5:405.

12. Garrett and House, *Song of Songs/Lamentations*, 153.

disguised as friendly but had severe ramifications for Jesus. But what Song of Songs reminds us of is the build-up to the kiss. Let us *talanoa* about this.

The yearning of the young lovers in the Song for each other would culminate in a meet and greet in the garden—was there longing between Judas and Jesus? I go back to the questions I asked earlier: Why was Judas's betrayal singled out when *all* the disciples were labeled as deserters? What made Judas's betrayal any different than the rest of the twelve who fled, with one even fleeing the garden naked? It may be that like the Song, the garden is the climax of the yearning between Judas and Jesus. Their yearning for one another had been building up to their kiss at Gethsemane.

Perhaps Judas did long for Jesus, and the kiss might have been more than a greeting, but the sign of a strong emotional attachment between disciple and master, Judas and Jesus.[13] I wonder, out of the disciples, Peter seemed to get all the attention from Jesus, so maybe Judas was longing for similar attention from Jesus? What about Jesus? Early in the Markan gospel, Judas is already labeled as the one "who betrayed him" (3:19 NRSV). What hope did Judas even have in the course of the narrative? It may be that Jesus was longing, too, for this condemned soul to be redeemed. What we have here are two individuals, longing for one another, climaxing in the garden scene, with their fates sealed by a kiss. Perhaps this sounds more like the Song of Songs than we are led to believe!

Lastly, I ask the question: What type of kiss did Judas greet Jesus with? Let us *tala* further into the *noa* by asking: Where did Judas plant his lips? The Greek text isn't clear, and neither are the English versions. The Samoan Bible however has done away with the ambiguity and chosen to be specific: a *sogi*. This is not a peck on the cheek, but a salutation, a greeting entailing a rubbing of the noses while breathing in each other's scent. It was the greeting of the gods and *āitu* of the sky-heavens.

Samoans do not have a word for "kiss" in the Western sense, as it has been transliterated as *kisi* in everyday vernacular, but this is not the word being used in the Samoan Bible. Perhaps the Samoan translators saw this meeting between Judas and Jesus as more than an act of betrayal, but as a greeting! Like the *sogi* between Limalelei and her son Matila, the kiss between Judas and Jesus may have been a deed of reminiscence; of two linked souls taking in each other's scent, for the last time. It may be that as Judas breathes in Jesus's scent, he instead sucks out the life of Jesus.

---

13. Cf. Marcus, *Mark 8–16*, 991.

CONCLUSION

This *talanoa* is an alter-native look at the scene at Gethsemane, to pierce the bubble wrap that has our imagination bound up in traditional readings. *Talanoa* allows us to open up, and to venture out (*tala*) into the unknown (*noa*), to probe and poke and ask questions that the European missionaries of the past taught us not to ask. Funnily, it seems that the Samoan translators have left us with some signs, clues or breadcrumbs (the Hansel and Gretel variety) for later generations to pick up and scrutinize. It may be a whisper of the questions that they wanted to ask but could not, and thus relied on the boldness of their descendants for these questions to be taken up and interrogated.

Of course, the cross and the resurrection mark the pinnacle of the Gospel, but perhaps our ancestors who translated the *Tusi Paia* (Samoan Bible) were asking and inviting us to consider this other scene in the same conversation, where Judas and Jesus greeted each other for the last time, the way the sky-heaven gods did. Perhaps the cross and resurrection marked the ninth and final *lagi* (heaven), and Judas was the final *āitu* who would allow Jesus to pass.

There are also implications for rereading Song of Songs, as the Judas kiss highlights the tragedy of two people who long for each other only to meet their deaths—both in tragic circumstances. Love stories ending in tragedy are not a foreign concept, as the tale of Sina and the Eel ends in tragedy, and so too the tale of Romeo and Juliet. In the Song of Songs, there is tragedy also in the final Song, as the lovers who desired each other's company and to share each other's bodies still have to defy social norms to be together. It is not a free love after all despite the free-spirited nature of their engagements.

I end this *talanoa* for now on this note: although the practice of *sogi* has been curtailed to a large extent, it has not been obliterated to extinction. Prior to Samoa's colonial period in the 1800s, the *sogi* was a reflection of the well-being and prosperity of its people, as Samoans were able to connect with each other through *sogi*, in a safe and healthy manner. Some still practice *sogi* today, and perhaps this is time to revive this ancient practice, as a way of reconnecting our scents with our souls to the land and *moana* from which we have been birthed. Such is the resilience of native bodies in the face of colonial forces. In saying that, COVID, in many ways, is the new 1918 influenza epidemic, and COVID therefore is a reminder of the colonial forces that continue to hamper us all, making it hard to revive cultural practices such as the *sogi*. However, Māori have shown that *hongi* can still be practiced, and they may have to remind us how! If COVID has taught us anything, it is that the strength and resolve of native and indigenous peoples make them stubbornly resilient. Their determination and commitment to protecting one another have been a marked distinction against the greed of individualism that continues to harpoon the safety of the greater community. Reintroducing *sogi* could also be an invitation to go back to our native Pasifika ways of well-being prior to colonization. *Sogi*, after all, did not bring influenza to Samoa, nor did it bring COVID. Colonialism did! Going back to *sogi* therefore is going back to being native! It may well be that Samoans should revive *sogi*, to greet each other like the gods and warriors they once were.

BIBLIOGRAPHY

Digital Fāgogo Collective. "The Story of Why We Greet Each Other by Pressing Noses Together." Digital Fāgogo Collective, 2020. https://www.fagogo.org/fagogo/o-le-tala-o-limaleleimaoloa-ma-lona-tamnbsp.

Garrett, Duane, and Paul R. House. *Song of Songs/Lamentations*. Word Biblical Commentary 23B. Dallas: Word, 2004.

Kolia, Brian Fiu. "Eve, the Serpent, and a Samoan Love Story." *Bible & Critical Theory* 15 (2019) 156–63.

Marcus, Joel. *Mark 8–16: A New Translation with Introduction and Commentary*. Anchor Yale Bible 27A. New Haven: Yale University Press, 2009.

Moscovitz, Leib. "Tractate Yadayim." In *The Oxford Annotated Mishnah: A New Translation of the Mishnah with Introductions and Notes*, edited by Shaye J. D. Cohen et al., 937–56. Oxford: Oxford University, 2022.

Pope, Marvin H. *Song of Songs: A New Translation with Introduction and Commentary*. Anchor Yale Bible 7C. Garden City, NY: Doubleday, 1977.

Sweeney, Marvin. *TANAK: A Theological and Critical Introduction to the Jewish Bible*. Minneapolis: Fortress, 2012.

Weems, Renita J. "The Song of Songs." In *New Interpreter's Bible*, edited by Leander E. Keck, 5:361–434. Nashville: Abingdon, 1997.

9

TALANOA SULI O LE MOANA
Re-Stor[e]ying Ishmael's Inheritance

Iatuivai Kioa Latu

So she [Sarah] said to Abraham, "Cast out this slave woman [Hagar] with her son [Ishmael], for the son of this slave woman shall not inherit along with my son Isaac." (Gen 21:10 NRSVue)

If a man has two wives, one of them loved and the other disliked, and if both the loved and the disliked have borne him sons, the firstborn being the son of the one who is disliked, then on the day when he wills his possessions to his sons, he is not permitted to treat the son of the loved as the firstborn in preference to the son of the disliked, who is the firstborn. He must acknowledge as firstborn the son of the one who is disliked, giving him a double portion of all that he has; since he is the first issue of his virility, the right of the firstborn is his. (Deut 21:15–17 NRSVue)

HERMENEUTICS AFFECTS WELL-BEING. ACCORDINGLY, the well-being of hermeneutics contributes to people's happiness, comfort, and health—physically, mentally, spiritually, and socially. This chapter presents "*Suli* hermeneutics" as a Moana[1] way to counter the unhealthy common tendency and practice of taking the tales of the Hebrew Bible (HB) as holy and thus they are to be served as absolute exemplar principles for lifestyle and/or employed as one size fits all (despite their biases and exclusionism).

This essay re-stories (*talanoa/ga*) *tofi* (inheritance) in the HB, by one of the *Suli o le Moana* (a descendant/offspring of Oceania/Pasifika). The essay aims to restore the land rights of legitimate *Suli* whose inheritance have been lost and deprived in the biblical *tala* (story) told and retold by the privileged *Suli* of Patriarch Abraham—Isaac, the son of his first wife, Sarah. Isaac was not the firstborn of Abraham, but he was the favored son—over against Abraham's firstborn—Ishmael, the son of Hagar (Sarah's maidservant).

Thus, I revisit the issue of *tofi* (meaning "one's reasonable share/portion of ancestral land") in the Hagar-Ishmael narrative, particularly where Sarah said to Abraham in Gen 21:10—"Cast out this slave-woman [Hagar] with her son [Ishmael]; for the son of this slave woman shall not inherit along with my son Isaac" (NRSV). This verse is part of the promise narrative, and it serves the "election theology" with respect to Abraham's land; the drive of the verse culminates in Ishmael's loss of inheritance on account of a negative portrayal of his legitimacy. Despite Ishmael's status as Abraham's *Suli* and firstborn son, he received no share of his father's inheritance, had no claim on it, and had no historic rights in the promised land.

The casting out of Ishmael—for the sake of the owners of this expulsion narrative—is considered justified and absolute. But for a Bible reader and interpreter from Samoa[2] and Moana, there is something disturbing about this story that warrants an "unpacking" (the process of *toe sasa'a le fafao*). Hence this *talanoa* suggests that to "cast out" Hagar (surrogate mother) and Ishmael (Abraham's *Suli taumanava* and firstborn) was a breach of both the biblical law (Torah) and surrogacy customs in the Ancient Near East.

In this essay, Gen 21:10 is unjust and it makes one unhappy, uncomfortable, and unhealthy. Consequently, I propose *Suli* hermeneutics (within the frames of Moana hermeneutics), as a remedy for such unjust and unhealthy biblical texts.

---

1. In this essay, *Moana* refers to the Oceania region of Pasifika.
2. Another ancient *tala* (version) by other Samoans of the name Samoa is that it derives from two words—*Sa* (meaning descendants or offspring of) and *Moa* (the first human child born to *Papa* [Rock] and *'Ele'ele* [Soil]). Hence the name Samoa presumed in this *talanoa* refers to voices of the descendants/offspring of Moa.

SULI HERMENEUTICS

Through this *talanoa*, in the spirit of *talalasi* (many tellings/versions—approaches),[3] I propose that a Samoan biblical, theological, and hermeneutical trajectory with a postcolonial interpretive lens encourages rereading and reinterpreting the ancient biblical narrative of "election" and "dis-election." *Talalasi* can help one reread and reinterpret, as well as re/cross-examine ancient stories in order to make those relevant for contemporary contexts. I will undertake this with the inclusive, relational, and indigenous lens of *Suli* hermeneutics, which finds Ishmael's expulsion to be politically motivated, and concludes that theology and practice built on this event is not consistent with the fuller biblical witness. Such dis-election was unwarranted, unfair, unjustified, and unhealthy, and this has implications and threats to Sāmoan *Sulis*' inheritance as protectors of their ancestral sacred land and titles. The interpretive lens of *Suli* and *Tama a le 'Ele'ele* (child/ren of the land/soil in human form) underlines the importance of a careful reading of Scriptures in ways that do justice to non-Western perspectives, and which have implications for contemporary Moana and other indigenous societies today.

Moreover, the casting out of Ishmael is inconsistent with Samoan customary understandings of inheritance under the three categories of *Suli*: (1) *Suli taumanava/tautoto* (descendant by birth/blood), (2) *Suli vaetama* (descendant through adoption); and (3) *Suli tautua* (descendant through service), which are the highest customary and entitlement qualifications of traditional descendants.

To revisit the subject of *tofi* (inheritance) in the Bible requires lifting the caveat (or ban) that prohibits readers or interpreters from interrogating its texts. That caveat is the view that the Bible is the "holy word of God." This view presumes that the Bible is divinely God's and not a human construction (see 2 Tim 3:16). Consequently, any interpretation that challenges the "election theology" is seen as an unholy or ungodly exercise. But as a student of the Christian Bible, I am aware that the Bible is a "book of records" produced by the descendants of Judah for Judahites.

The purpose of this *talanoa* is not to rewrite this witness by biblical writers that has become part of the Judahites' core testimony regarding their own *tala* or version/telling of land claim over Canaan. Rather, this *talanoa* offers a rereading of this witness from and for non-Hebrew readers.

This *talanoa* argues that the expulsion and dis-election of Ishmael from Abraham's inheritance in the Judahites' narrative is a substantial piece

---

3. *Talalasi* as an alternative reading lens through *talanoa* (an open space for stories) is what Ma'ilo calls an apt "Sāmoan device for telling and retelling stories" (Ma'ilo, "Island Prodigals," 24).

of evidence that supports the idea or theology of "election" in the Hebrew Bible. As a *Suli* of the survivors of colonization in Samoa and the Moana, whose ancestors survived colonization and whose compatriots are currently living in a continuous struggle against neocolonialism and globalization, this contextual, biblical, and hermeneutics approach is warranted.

Origin of *Suli*

In Samoa, the word *suli* refers to the suckers or offshoots (*tama'i-fa'i*) of the *fa'i Samoa* (native Samoan banana plant).[4] *Pogai* (banana corm, which is under the ground) is the life, source, root, origin, or foundation to which everything above the ground is attached and from which they spring. *Pogai* contains the stem's tissues and feeds the *tama'i-fa'i*.

Generatively, all *suli* (suckers) sprout out of the *manava o le 'ele'ele* (womb of the ground) and are rooted to the *pogai*, which holds the very life of the banana plant. Although a banana plant bears *fua* (fruit) only once, her *pogai* produces many suckers. Once the parent banana has fruited, it dies (decomposes) back to the *'ele'ele* and allows suckers to grow from the *pogai* underground of the parent banana plant. However, the way to start a new banana stool (*pupufai*) is through two processes for transplanting it into new ground:

(1) *Vavae tama'i-fa'i*: This is the process whereby banana suckers (*suli* or *tama'i-fa'i*) sprout out from the corm of the mother banana; the *tama'i-fa'i* are said to split or separate (*vavae*) from its *pogai*. When the *suli* is separated from the *pogai*, a portion of the *pogai* is detached with the *suli*/sucker. It is this *suli* that is transplanted to another *fanua* or place/land, which later grows roots to allow new suckers to become the new mother (or head/corm) banana of the new banana stool. Though it has become a new stool, it still carries the name or type of its original *fa'i* (as in *fa'i Samoa* or *mamae*).

(2) *Fa'alaufasi* is the process of "splitting up" (*fasi*) the *pogai* into pieces (*fa'alau*), or of propagation corm. Each *laufasi* (the specimens/pieces of the propagation corm) is covered with soil for several weeks until a new mother banana plant sprouts out. Here also, *laufasi* from the corm (*pogai*) carry the name or type of the banana from which the *laufasi* was split. Each *laufasi* of the same *pogai* can spread over and cover the whole land but still retains the cultivar's name, that is, *mamae* or *fa'i Samoa*.

Once *fa'i Samoa* are planted or transplanted, either by *vavae tama'i-fa'i* or by *fa'alaufasi*, the next generation—that is, what follows after the mother

---

4. In this chapter, I distinguish between *suli* (lowercase refers to bananas) and *Suli* (uppercase refers to human descendants).

banana plant has fruited and fallen (in nine to twelve months)—is called *suli*. The process of producing *suli* which stem from the *pogai* is the "*suli* cycle." A variety of bananas are produced in Samoa through this cycle. Every *pogai* has its own unique name (such as *fa'i Samoa, paka Samoa, mamae, 'Ausulasula*, etc.). All *suli* sprout from the *pogai*, are connected to the *pogai*, and are carriers of the cultivar's name. Once a *suli* of a *fa'i Samoa*, always a *suli* of that cultivar. Whether a *laufasi* or *fa'i vavae*, their *suli* will carry their cultivar's family name. The *suli* cycle is about derivation, association, relationship, connection, being rooted, and continuity.

Like bananas elsewhere, *suli o fa'i Sāmoa* are self-replaced from the *pogai* (corm), in connection to the soil/land. Unless the *pogai* is rooted in or connected to the *'ele'ele*, the *suli* cannot be nurtured, fed, or have the capacity to bear fruit. Without connectedness to the land, the *suli* cycle will end. In other words, *suli, pogai*, and *'ele'ele* are interrelated in the *manava o le 'ele'ele*.

The *suli* cycle ensures the continuity of the banana. This continuity is captured in the proverbial expression *E se'i le futi, ae totō suli* (mother banana dies, but her suckers are rooted in the ground): although the mother banana dies, the *suli* continue to carry the name (title) of the mother banana plant. Accordingly, once a *suli*, always a *suli*.

This *talalasi* study of the origin of *suli* raises important issues and insights. We find that *suli* is more than just a concept; it is also a metaphor, which is encapsulated in the expression *E se'i le futi, ae totō suli*. *Suli* is like a bank into which the wealth of indigenous knowledge and references, rituals, *gafa* (genealogy), and *faiā* (relationships) are deposited. *Suli* is one of the most elementary terminologies by which Samoans signify and form intergenerational relationships and solidify their identity and sense of belonging. Indeed, *suli* is a relational term that best describes the relationship of people as the *suli* of the *'ele'ele*. *Suli* is the "flesh, blood, and bones" of the ancestral land.

The origination of *Suli* (descendant) from *suli* (banana sucker/shoot) is a potent interpretive lens through which to understand what *Samoa* implies, in the sense that Sa also means *Suli*, our divine-human descendants, the *Suli* or Sa of Moa—the first human being born to Papa (Rocks) and *'Ele'ele* (Earth). This is my Samoan version of *tofi* (inheritance).

JUDAHITE VERSION OF INHERITANCE

Here, we turn to the biblical story. In Gen 21:10, it is important to highlight that "the Bible ... belongs to and was created by the people of Judah, whose identity may be rendered in English as 'Judahite,' 'Judean' or 'Jewish' for the same Hebrew designation as *yĕhûdî*."[5] The HB was written in the best interests of Judah, as this is transparent in the final framing of the collection. In general, biblical scholars agree that biblical texts are marked by intense editorial activity.[6] In other words, the Bible is itself a composition of *talalasi* (many tellings, many versions).

This composite work was shaped by many contexts and by ancient law codes, cultures, and traditions that impacted the ancient Near East (ANE). It was derived from multiple sources and authors. To borrow Susan Gillingham's words, we can speak of "one Bible, many voices."[7] The Bible is about *talalasi* or many tellings of the historical Israel in antiquity,[8] in particular the Judahites.[9] Daniel Fleming writes:

> The Bible regales us with tales from the world of Egypt, Assyria, and Babylonia, offered from the perspective of the runaways

---

5. Fleming, *Legacy of Israel*, 4. The Nuzi tablets are also of importance because of the continuing discussion as to the origin of the term *Hebrew* (*Habiru*). Genesis 14:13 mentions "Abram the Hebrew," and in Gen 40:15 Joseph tells the Egyptians that he was stolen out of "the land of the Hebrews." "These occurrences make it seem unlikely that the term originally meant simply a descendant of Jacob, or even a descendant of Abraham. Nuzi is only one of various sources in the Near East where ancient documents refer to a people called the Ha-bi-ru, who seem to have been landless wanderers, sometimes entering into voluntary servitude. Although Nuzi material contains a number of such references, they are insufficient to solve the problem, but may form an important link in its examination" (see https://www.biblicaltraining.org/library/nuzi).

6. Fleming, *Legacy of Israel*, 5.

7. Gillingham, *One Bible, Many Voices*. Compare with Stroup and Brueggemann, *Many Voices, One God*.

8. Jacob's twelve sons (in chronological order: Reuben, Sim'ëon, Levi, Judah, Zeb'ŭlun, Is'sachar, Dan, Gad, Ash'er, Naph'talī, Joseph, and Benjamin) are listed in Gen 35:22—29. It is worth noting that when Abraham's inheritance was allotted among Jacob's twelve sons (Josh 14–24), Caleb (from the tribe of Judah) and the people from the tribe of Judah were first to be given lots (14:6—15:63). Douglas Knight notes that "the Josephites comprise the descendants of the two sons of Joseph, Ephraim and Manasseh (Gen 48). Combined, the land allotted to them is smaller in size than that of Judah. The number of twelve tribes is reached by counting Ephraim and Manasseh separately, after excluding the Levites (so Num 12:20–54; 26:5–62) or the Simeonites (Deut 33:6–25) from the original total of Jacob's twelve sons" (Knight, "Joshua," 329).

9. Fleming claims that "in the obscure process of its creation, the Bible joined the stories and the experiences of these two peoples into one, explaining Judah as part of Israel and Israel as belonging to the proper authority of Judah's royal house of David. Historically, Israel and Judah were distinct, and it is the voice of Israel in particular that can be lost in Judah's choir" (Fleming, *Legacy of Israel*, 4). This view is supported in the New Testament, for instance, in Matthew's genealogy of Jesus in 1:1–17, where Jesus was alluded to as a direct descendant of Abraham (Isaac, Jacob, and Judah) through King David. This line clearly suggests that it is the voice of the Judahites (the Zionists), the soloist in the many songs sung in the entire Bible.

and the defeated. It reports the reigns of kings not in the voice of royal propaganda but with distance and capacity for critique. It presents what are cast as the ruminations of men who spoke for God against both the people and the powers that led them. All this writing may date to settings long after the occasions portrayed, yet the literature is patently a patchwork of reused materials, not always well understood, certainly not a straight-forward work of unified fiction.[10]

For contributors to the Jewish Study Bible, the Tanakh "is complete in itself, not just as a part of a larger Bible or as a prelude to the New Testament . . . the 'Tanakh' is 'the Bible.'"[11] The epic narratives of Israel's and Judah's creation, exile, and restoration were told and retold orally through many centuries before the scribes (the "primary producers of texts in the ancient world," transcribers of "oral lore," and inventors of "new texts"[12]) collected these stories, culminating in the production of the written Hebrew Bible as we know it today, in or around the sixth to fifth centuries BCE.[13]

In the Hebrew Bible, the Judahite stories, their *mana*, perspectives, and voices are dominant. In simplest terms, the HB was created by the people of Judah, "with its key stages of formation taking place just before the fall of Judah's kingdom and then, in the generations afterwards, as the Judahite or Jewish people struggled to maintain an identity against various forces of dispersion and assimilation."[14] In other words, each book in the HB is from the same Judahite world, either associated with Jerusalem or composed in settings after the kingdom's end. It is thus possible to assume that the HB's creation and sequence of events are not innocent.

Brueggemann describes the Torah (law)[15] of Yahweh not as "static and totalizing" but as an "ongoing conversation" between God and God's

---

10. Fleming, *Legacy of Israel*, 59.

11. Berlin and Brettler, *Jewish Study Bible*, x.

12. Barreto and Chan, *Exploring the Bible*, 19: "Scribes not only created literature, but they could also expand on texts, integrate them into larger literary compilations, and even transcribe oral texts into written literature."

13. Stavrapoulou, *God*, 10–18.

14. Fleming, *Legacy of Israel*, 5.

15. The words *Torah* and *law* are both translated into Sāmoan as *Tūlāfono*. Tui Atua's view is that "law" means *tūlāfono* in the context of the traditional polity embodied in the *fono a matai a le nu'u*. "*Tula* means head, *fono* means formal meeting, and so *tūlāfono* literally means the 'head(s) of the formal meeting,' [where] the decisions emerge from the coming together and the synthesizing of wisdom from the 'heads' of a *fono*." These *tūlāfono* are subject to change by consensus of the village council after many meetings (Efi, "Samoan Jurisprudence," 203).

people.[16] This allows me to *talanoa* of the importance of "genealogies" in this epic story of the Judahites. In order to do that, let me talk briefly about 'biblical election.'

Election Theology

Election is fundamental to the thought of the Bible in both the Hebrew Bible and New Testament. To the writers of the HB, Israel is the chosen people of God; to the writers of the New Testament, the church is the *suli* of divine election. In both Testaments, individuals are presented as chosen of God for their particular work. Whether we like it or not, the doctrine of election is a biblical doctrine; and whatever our view of its validity, it demands some attention from the student of the Bible.

Election is defined as "the choice by one person of another person out of a range of possible candidates. This choice then establishes a mutual relationship between the elector and the elected, in the biblical terms a 'covenant' (*berit*)."[17] The content of these practical choices is governed by Torah, but there could be no such standards of election without the prior belief in election.

The election of Israel stems from the election of the patriarchs—Abraham, Isaac, Jacob/Israel, Judah, and King David, and, from a Christian perspective, culminates in Jesus Christ's *gafa* (genealogy) in the Gospels of Matt 1 and Luke 3. In this sequence, *gafa* is important. It is the record of one's claims to family inheritance. Intergenerational inheritance is or can be traced through *gafa*.

The election or dis-election of a person or persons to family inheritance is determined through *tala le gafa* (genealogical explanation)—whether one is connected to the *pogai o le suafa*, the "name of the originator" (or *Fa'apogai*, the term used in the Land and Titles Court). Therefore, *gafa* is powerful! *Gafa* includes and excludes people. The *suli*-ship or membership status of a person in one's family or clan depends on the *gafa* one provides through many generations, held orally or kept in some sort of authorized records keeper (for Samoa, it is kept by elders of the family who pass it down from one generation to another, and some families resort to the Land and Titles Court's records; for the Judahites, they resort to the Bible). The Judahites are able to trace land claims by connecting to the biblical *gafa*. Election and dis-election are determined through *gafa*.

---

16. Brueggemann, "Law That Listens," 2:28 and 39:02.
17. Hagelia, "Divine Election," ix.

In Scripture, many texts enumerate *gafa*. These *gafa* are not only lists of names for the sake of historical records. They also serve cultural and theological functions. These *gafa* also serve literary, social, and political functions that enable people to tell their own stories. These genealogies also provide boundaries as to who belongs to Israel (the Northern Kingdom) or Judah (Southern Kingdom), in order to construct their identity as people set apart from others.

In fact, the purpose of *gafa* in the Bible is primarily about destinies, identification, and entitlement to land. *Gafa* controls who belong to the land and who does not.[18] The *gafa* of Abraham, Isaac, Jacob, Judah, and their offspring is central to their ancestral land claims, particularly the promised land called Canaan. However, biblical evidence indicates that this promised land previously belonged to Canaan (the originator, read: *pogai*) and his offspring, the Canaanites (Gen 10:15–20).

In the Judahite witness, God assures Moses that God's intentions are good and trustworthy: "I will bring you into the land that I swore to give to Abraham, Isaac, and Jacob; I will give it to you for a possession" (Exod 6:8). God's proof of the covenant with Israel is the guarantee of the promised land. Unfortunately, "settler colonies were premised on the elimination of the native societies."[19] The settlers' (Israelites') extermination or expulsion of a majority of the indigenous population was followed by the demographic "swamping" of these peoples (the Canaanites) from their land.

Just as familial disputes over ancestral land and titles claims among consanguineal kin are adjudicated by the Lands and Titles Court in Sāmoa, so the HB reveals tales of sibling rivalry, a theme that runs through the book of Genesis. Such unhealthy rivalry occurs due to the unjust election of one and dis-election of others, for example, between Cain and Abel (Gen 4), between Noah's sons (9:20–27), between Abraham and his nephew Lot (13:1–18), between Isaac and his six other brothers (25:5–6), between Jacob and Esau (chs. 25–36), between Judah and his siblings (ch. 49), and, directly related to this *talanoa*, between Ishmael and Isaac (21:8–21).

---

18. Belonging and not belonging in the monarchical system is clearly delineated. The deep sense of *Suli* can be lost in translation when translated as "heir" in the English context. The notion of "heir and spare" despite being blood brothers in the British monarchy could perhaps have certain similarities with brotherhood in biblical cases regarding the issue of inheritance. See Durant and Scobie, *Finding Freedom*, 34, 213, 261.

19. Wolfe, *Settler Colonialism*, 2.

Reading from Samoa

Although the HB is revered as a sacred book wherein Israelite and Judahite testimonies are recorded, and where the Torah is legally binding, in order to make these biblical *tala* (stories) relevant and not absolutist (or imperial) texts, but applicable to other contexts, I propose that the native interpretive lens of *Suli* must apply. *Suli* hermeneutics is a native or indigenous perspective that allows the voices of the colonized who have been historically silenced to be heard as well.

Suli hermeneutic is used as my cross-examination of the issue and credibility of the biblical evidence concerning inheritance, exclusive to Isaac—the elected—in Gen 21:10. The story of Hagar and Ishmael culminates in Sarah persuading Abraham to sever by dis-electing and disinheriting Ishmael from Abraham's gift of promised land (Gen. 12:1, 5–6, 18–21), the land belonging to the Canaanites.

SULI READINGS OF GENESIS 21:10

In Gen 21:10, Hagar, an Egyptian slave woman and surrogate wife, is "cast out," which is a breach of surrogacy customs in the ANE and is regarded as "abhorrent" in Deut 23:7b–8. As a consequence, Ishmael is also "cast out" and "dis-elected." Ishmael needed to be "cast out" in order for Isaac and his descendants (Israelites and Judahites) to assume 100 percent of the inheritance from Abraham (12:5–7; 15:18–21; 17:8). There is always someone who parts company with or is pushed aside from the community of the nearest kinsmen. Ishmael has to play this role in relation to Isaac, as did Esau to Jacob. Furthermore, the idea of separation is prominent. It is obvious that the writer is concerned not just with the historical origin of the Ishmaelites, but also with the theological distinction of Isaac-Israel from Ishmael.

Genesis 21:13, to the contrary, reaffirms that Ishmael's status as Abraham's offspring is never denied. Ishmael was without a doubt Abraham's firstborn. Since he is acknowledged as Abraham's son up to the moment of Abraham's death (Gen 25:9), it cannot be denied that he is the "firstborn" and entitled to Abraham's inheritance. The right of the firstborn in the Torah is very clear. Deut 21:15–17 states:

> If a man has two wives, one of them loved and the other disliked, and if both the loved and the disliked have borne him sons, the firstborn being the son of the one who is disliked, then on the day when he wills his possessions to his sons, he is not permitted to treat the son of the loved as the firstborn in preference to the

son of the disliked, who is the firstborn. He must acknowledge as firstborn the son of the one who is disliked, giving him a double portion of all that he has; since he is the first issue of his virility, the right of the firstborn is his.

As *Suli taumanava* or *tautoto* (descendant by birth and blood), Ishmael deserves a double portion of (or two-thirds of) Abraham's inheritance.

This right of the firstborn is self-explanatory and an incontrovertible practice. It was also widely observed throughout the ANE. For example, #170 of the Code of Hammurabi prescribes: "If the man's wife and maid-servant have borne sons, and the father counts them with the sons of his wife; if then the father die, then the sons of the wife and of the maid-servant shall divide the paternal property in common."[20]

ANE literature also provide rich resources for reflecting on *Suli taetama* (descendant through adoption) as in the process of *vavae tama'i-fa'i* (see discussion above). In Hammurabi's law, if a man had no children, it was customary that he could adopt someone to carry his name and inherit his property. According to the Hammurabi code, a barren woman could give her maidservant to her husband to produce children for him (codes 144–47). In particular, #146 in the Code of Hammurabi prescribes that "If a man take a wife and she give this man a maid-servant as wife and she bear him children, and then this maid assume equality with the wife: because she has borne him children her master shall not sell her for money, but he may keep her as a slave, reckoning her among the maid-servants."[21] Abraham failed to honor this widely accepted ANE law code when he allowed Hagar to be cast out. More aggravatingly, Hagar was cast out alongside Ishmael.

Even though Ishmael was excluded from living with his father Abraham, he was still eligible to receive his share as the firstborn son. Instead, Hagar and Ishmael remain silent throughout the narrative. This suggests that this story was intended to affirm the social interests of those perceived to be the elected or chosen.

Through *Suli* lens, Ishmael is recognized as both *Suli taumanava/tautoto* and *Suli vaetama*. Adoption does not deny right of inheritance in biblical literature. For instance, both Moses and Jesus are portrayed as adopted children. Both the Gospels of Matthew and Luke record Jesus's *gafa*, through the line of Joseph, his adopted father, and not Mary, his natural mother. The apostle Paul employs the idea of "adoption as a description of

---

20. Pinker, "Expulsion of Hagar," 7. It seems that this code was applied to all *Suli* of Jacob's twelve children born to him by Leah and her sister Rachel, and their maidservants Bilhah and Zilpah upon arrival in Canaan. See Gen 29–30; and Josh 13:15—19:48.

21. Pinker, "Expulsion of Hagar," 7.

the way in which believers are brought into fellowship with Christ. He is particularly concerned to show how adoption can bring Gentiles into God's family, where they can join with Jews."[22] The letter of Paul to the Romans applies adoption spiritually, so that all may be accepted as children of God through Jesus, "and if children, then heirs, heirs of God and joint heirs with Christ—if in fact we suffer with him so that we may also be glorified" (Rom 8:17; cf. Gal 4:7). In this context, suffering may be understood as comparable to *tautua* (service) in the Samoan lifeworld.

In relation to *Suli tautua*, the Genesis text prefigures disputes that resonate with issues of inheritance among consanguineal and non-consanguineal *Suli* who come before the Land and Titles Court. In Samoa, succession depends only on who is the rightful *Suli* who has rendered genuine *tautua*. Despite such *tautua*, Hagar's status as a wife or concubine is ignored by Sarah, who continues to refer to Hagar as a "slave woman" (Gen 21:10). Hagar's status is demeaned despite her *tautua* as a surrogate mother for Abraham and Sarah.

In Samoan terms, Sarah's offer of Hagar as a surrogate to provide a *Suli* (Gen 16:3b) for Abraham should suffice for her son Ishmael to claim Abraham's inheritance as a *Suli tautua* (descendant through service). Since Hagar produced a son for Abraham, her *tautua* was recognized by Abraham—who named his son from her, Ishmael. This suggests that Hagar had some value in this surrogacy as a "second-class wife." This status obliged Abraham and Sarah to support and keep her within their household, and not to cast her out with her son Ishmael.

Therefore, the dis-election of Ishmael is unhealthy, and *solitū lāfono* sees it as an unlawful and unjust act, for it breaches the Torah and ANE surrogacy customs. Such treatment is unacceptable in Samoa.

CONCLUSION

In conclusion, this *talanoa* by *Suli o le Moana* unpacks Sarah's proposal to cast out Hagar and Ishmael in Gen 21:10, that "Ishmael shall not inherit along with Isaac," as politically motivated. This proposal confirms the idea that a specific person's name and lineage through *gafa* is to be registered to inherit Abraham's inheritance.

Such biblical texts should be reviewed and reinterpreted through non-imperial methods like *talanoa/talalasi* and must be subject to cross-examination in order to incorporate inclusivity and impartiality. Talanoaga (the act of group *talanoa*) provides equal opportunities and space for all *Suli*

---

22. Bartlett, "Adoption in the Bible," 376.

to determine the flesh, bones, and blood matters of inheritance. Unwanted and unhealthy rivalries among siblings can be resolved in an equitable manner, regardless of social classification, hierarchy, or race. Accordingly, this *talanoa* through (*talalasi*) reStorying enables any *Suli* like Ishmael to restore his/her lost/deprived inheritance.

In closing, with respect to the primary concern of this book with well-being, this essay presented *Suli* hermeneutics as remedy for unwanted rivalries among siblings, families, villages, peoples, and so forth. *Suli* hermeneutics can be employed as a magnifier for problem solvers to identify the reason(s) why the body of Christ is divided; why there are wars between peoples; why racism is deep rooted; why there are discrimination against and mistreatment of women and children; and why there are so many social and political illnesses. Those could be because of unjust and unhealthy biblical texts such as Gen 21:10 in the name of *tofi* or inheritance.

BIBLIOGRAPHY

Barreto, Eric D., and Michael J. Chan. *Exploring the Bible*. Nashville: Abingdon, 2016.

Bartlett, David L. "Adoption in the Bible." In *The Child in the Bible*, edited by Marcia J. Bunge, 375–98. Grand Rapids: Eerdmans, 2008.

Berlin, Adele, and Marc Zvi Brettler, eds. *The Jewish Study Bible: Torah, Nevi'im, Kethuvim*. 2nd ed. New York: Oxford University Press, 2014.

Brueggemann, Walter. "Walter Brueggemann on Law That Listens." "Law: The Summons to Keep Listening." YouTube, July 16, 2020. From Fuller Forum, "Justice, Grace, and Law in the Mission of God," Fuller Theological Seminary, Pasadena, CA, 2015. https://www.youtube.com/watch?v=krNO3iuFCQA.

Durant, Omid, and Carolyn Scobie. *Finding Freedom*. London: HarperCollins, 2020.

Efi, Tui Atua Tupua Tamasese Ta'isi. "Samoan Jurisprudence and the Samoan Land and Titles Court: The Perspective of a Litigant." In *Su'esu'e Manogi: In Search of Fragrance; Tui Atua Tupua Tamasese Ta'isi and the Samoan Indigenous Reference*, edited by Tamasailau M. Suaalii-Sauni et al., 201–26. Wellington: Huia, 2018.

Fleming, Daniel. *The Legacy of Israel in Judah's Bible: History, Politics, and the Reinscribing of Tradition*. New York: Cambridge University Press, 2012.

Gillingham, Susan E. *One Bible, Many Voices: Different Approaches to Biblical Studies*. Grand Rapids: Eerdmans, 1999.

Hagelia, Hallvard. *Divine Election in the Hebrew Bible*. Sheffield: Sheffield Phoenix, 2019.

Knight, Douglas A. "Joshua." In *The New Study Interpreters Study Bible: New Revised Standard Version with Apocrypha*, edited by Walter J. Harrelson et al., 303–41. Nashville: Abingdon, 2003.

Ma'ilo, Mosese. "Island Prodigals: Encircling the Void in Luke 15:11–32 with Albert Wendt." In *Sea of Readings: The Bible in the South Pacific*, edited by Jione Havea, 23–36. Semeia Studies 90. Atlanta: SBL Press, 2018.

Pinker, Aron. "The Expulsion of Hagar and Ishmael (Gen 21:9–21)." *Women in Judaism* 6 (2009) 1–24.

Stavrapoulou, Francesca. *God: An Anatomy*. London: Picador, 2021.
Stroup, George W., and Walter Brueggemann, eds. *Many Voices, One God: Being Faithful in a Pluralistic World*. Louisville: Westminster John Knox, 1998.
Wolfe, Patrick. *Settler Colonialism and the Transformation of Anthropology: The Politics and Poetics of an Ethnographic Event*. Writing Past Colonialism. London: Continuum, 1999.

10

A MOMENT OF *TASI AE FOI*?
The Canaanite Woman Meets Jesus within Samoan Rhetoric

Fatilua Fatilua

THIS ESSAY DRAWS PARALLELS between the Samoan *vaogagana* (rhetoric) and biblical discourse. In particular, the essay seeks to make sense of an otherwise problematic text and an "embarrassing" moment in the Gospel narrative. Utilizing Samoan *vaogagana faafitifiti* (rhetoric of deflection),[1] this endeavor grows out of a predisposition towards the value of language, in this case Samoan language, to our biblical interpretive system. Foremost is a sense that Pacific Island language and rhetoric has much to offer to biblical hermeneutics and vice versa. Moreover, I subscribe to the idea that we can learn much about social interactions and relationships by exploring the use of words and linguistic tendencies. I share in the notion that words and language provide a window to explore social and cultural predispositions in society. While the Bible remains the focal point of analysis, this endeavor finds parallels within the context of the *fa'aSamoa* (Samoan way of life). In particular, the use of rhetoric to nurture and maintain relationships and connections that shape and give form to the *vā* (space in between, betweenness).[2]

---

1. *Faafitifiti* comes from the verb *fiti*—to flick or deflect. Adding the prefix *faa* converts it to the noun, "deflection." Throughout this chapter I will be using the translation "rhetoric of deflection."

2. See Wendt, "Afterword."

The encounter between Jesus and the Canaanite woman in Matt 15:21–28 remains fertile grounds for biblical commentators and critics because of its problematic nature. When a Canaanite woman asks Jesus for help, she is first given the silent treatment, then a blatant rejection, before her wish is granted. Even though she is later praised for her faith, the fact that the narrative is a bit harsh on her is a matter of concern especially in today's liberating context. How then does one make sense of this "misadventure" in the text? Against this backdrop, my aim is to explore alternatives utilizing indigenous leanings and tendencies from my Samoan context.

First, let me digress for a moment. As a Samoan nurtured and weaned within the warm embrace of the *aiga* (family), brought up at the feet[3] of Western teachers and educators, I submit that I am not a *failauga* (orator) nor the authority on Samoan rhetoric, *tasi ae foi atu* (deflecting any such praises)—the "I"[4] in me though speaks only as someone trying to make sense of the biblical text. Therefore, *tulou*! I must say, for I am about to intrude unto the *vā*, "space in between."

This essay is organized as follows: First, I foreground the value of language in the *faʻaSamoa* (Samoan way of life) and in particular the rhetoric of deflection in navigating the nebulous network of relationships and connections which give form to the *vā*. Some scenarios are produced for clarity. This is followed by an attempt at "marrying" the biblical text with the Samoan rhetoric of deflection. The essay concludes with some lessons learned and a few reminders.

GAGANA SAMOA AND THE *VĀ*

Language is one of the four elements that constitute the *tagata*[5] in Samoan philosophy—others comprise of the *faamatai* (chief system), *fanua ma eleʻele* (land), and *tapuaiga* (worship or religion). A poignant reminder of this is captured in the proverbial expression *o tama a manu e fafaga i fuga o laau a o tama a tagata o upu* (animals feed their young with plants but humans with words). Words matter. Words have consequences. Words are relational. Words build as well as destroy.

---

3. The idea is drawn from Acts 22:3. I do submit that I often sympathize with Paul when it comes to his "multi-context" reality.

4. Cf. Havea, "Islander Criticism," 1. My own use of the capital I underlines personal biases and predispositions.

5. In this construction I use *tagata* to refer to "being." *Tagata* can also signal person, people, or individual.

General understanding in the Samoan language can be ordered under four general categories: everyday language, formal language, oratorical language, and written language. *Gagana faakerisiano* (Christian language), *vaoli'a* (double-meaning talk), and *valiata* (figurative) are important aspects of Samoan *talanoa*. Vetting each aspect of the Samoan language is outside the scope of this study. The focus rather is on the oratorical aspects. It is the medium of communication by which orators and chiefs engage at special events such as wedding, funeral, or other formal occasions. It has also become prevalent within the context of church functions and activities even to the extent where oratory is considered a significant element of learning in the local theological colleges.

Exploring the use of oratory helps to shed light on some of the social and cultural tendencies in Samoan society. Used mainly during formal exchange, proficiency in the use of oratorical language enhances individual reputations as well as bringing honor to the family. Yet, a significant aspect of oratorical language is in negotiating and navigating the nebulous network of relationships constituting the *vā tapuia* or sacred space in Samoan society. Maintaining respect for the *vā tapuia* is vital at all times. As words can nurture *fāiā* or relationships, words can also harm intra as well as interfamilial relations. In a society where one's identity is intimately connected to one's *aiga* (family), keeping and maintaining the *vā tapuia* is essential. That Samoan society consider words part of the daily teachings of the young individual is in recognition of the power of speech and the use of words as building blocks of good relations. In other words, oratorical language plays a vital role in keeping order and maintaining stability within society. It holds an important currency in the well-being of the community.

Within this context, the rhetoric of deflection often emerges when orators engage in dialogue (conversation, debate, *talanoa*). The undergirding principle in this rhetoric of deflection is that words reflect a certain respect for the *vā* at all times. Refusing to take credit, the goal is to deflect or redirect praise. It is grounded in the notion that humility is central to nurturing the *vā* in the *fa'aSamoa*. Humility strengthens connections and relationships within society. It does this by elevating the pursuit of a common goal and subsumes individual interests and objectives.

To further illustrate this phenomenon in Samoan language, I am reminded of the words of the late governor of American Samoa, Tauese Sunia, in his keynote speech at the Malua Theological College graduation in 2001. Sunia, a well-known *failauga* (orator) himself, said this about the nature of Samoan culture and rhetoric:

> The Samoan culture is based on praise. . . . The reason we give a lot in a chief bestowal ceremony, funerals and weddings is to receive praise. . . . It is the reward for all that we do in this country [Samoa]. So, when a family gives plenty, the *failauga* [orator] on their behalf says, "Please forgive the inadequacy of our giving." She is engaging in the Samoan rhetoric of deflection. The receiving party or family will also respond accordingly—"Your presence and giving has made us lowly and irreputable family feel like royalty." Although that other family is greater in status than this one, the Samoan *failauga* strives to deflect any praise coming their way. Why? Because in this culture, glory and praise is deflected. If praise comes your way, the Samoan just simply retorts, "I deserve not, we are the same, do not burden yourself." A chief who has lost her way is one who knows not how to deflect praise.[6]

The Samoan rhetoric of deflection therefore refuses to gain leverage or receive praise. Praises and claims to rewards or meritocracy are politely diffused by deflection. It is considered wisdom in Samoan culture to be gifted with the capacity to refrain from any individual obsession for grandiose and superfluous praises. Instead, the pursuit of the common good is important. In that way, praise is to be shared—*tasi ae foi atu*. It is recognizing the interdependency and interconnectedness that is foundational to maintaining respect for each other. Without which, there is no peace and harmony but chaos and constant individual competition for vainglorious praises and honor.

Similarly, in uncompromising situations *tasi ae foi atu* (rhetoric of deflection) is a way of politely deflecting insults and diffusing any negative or embarrassing labels. It is the first step to redemption for fractured relations. The rhetoric of deflection allows for the participants or representatives of the involved parties to seek reconciliation. The aim is to remain respectful and cognizant of connections and relationships no matter the seriousness of infraction. This is not to be a fleeting solution but rather to come to terms with the fact that the relationship is threatened. In turn, respect for the one

---

6. The above quote is a translation of the following speech I transcribed from the YouTube video clip: "O le aganuu a Samoa e faavae i viiga. . . . E ala ona tatou tigaina e fai mea e tele i saofa'i, maliu, faaipoipoga, tasi lava le mea o loo saili o viiga. . . . Pau lava le mea e totogi ai mea a le atunuu nei o viiga. . . . Vaai i ai i le aganuu, a sii mai poo le ā le afe ma afe o mea e aumai ae fai mai le failauga, ia faatōfāmalie, ua lē tagolima. O lā e faafitifiti mai. E avatu viiga ae faafitifiti mai. E tali atu fo'i lea ia, se ua tupu le aiga tufanua, lo outou gafa na tā i tua, i lo outou afifio mai. E tiga ona maualalo le aualii ia e o mai i le aualii ia, ae taumafai lava le Samoa ia alu ifo i lalo o le isi. Aisea? Leaga o le aganuu lenei, e aumai le viiga ae eu, e eu ese. A vivii mai ae fai mai le Samoa, soia ia, tasi ae fo'i atu. Soia ia, a ē lailoa, gasegase. E iloagofie lava le tamalii e leiloa fai lona tamalii, e leiloa eu viiga" (GOODNEWS, "Kolisi i Malua").

victimized as well as the sacred space between the parties is maintained. Justice and harmony are served through words. Words mend, nurture, and maintain relations. Wisdom is in words.

The rhetoric of deflection can also be interpreted as showing resistance.[7] Resistance to dominant narrative and overpowering rhetoric is wisely and politely deflected. This recognizes again the power of speech to incite and to incriminate. By deflecting insults and speech infringements, the purpose is to politely diffuse any escalating situation. In other words, further escalation to violence not only shows a lack of diplomacy. It is also a poor reflection on the orator whose knowledge and wisdom to navigate the intricacies of the *vā* is found wanting.

SCENARIOS/MODELS FOR DOING RHETORIC OF DEFLECTION

For further clarity I provide further observations on different elements of the *fa'aSamoa* that give rise to the use of the Samoan rhetoric of deflection.

Faaaloaloga (Reciprocity of Gifts)

An important element of the *fa'aSamoa* is *faaaloaloga*, the reciprocity of gifts.[8] To understand this practice warrants a closer look at the root word *faaaloalo* (respect) which essentially underpins mutual respect for the *vā* (space in between). In that context, *faaaloaloga* represents the value placed on shared respect. The act of giving and receiving gifts represents a nurturing of and navigating the relations of respect constituting the space between the respective parties. It is within this context that the rhetoric of deflection emerges.

The giver assumes self-debasement and self-depreciation—*faatofamalie ise taumafaiga ua le a'ua'u* (pardon our inadequacy). The gift, no matter the monetary value, is labeled as "inadequate" and "ill fitted" for the dignity warranted of the occasion and of the level of exchange. In that sense, every effort is taken by the giver to opine the imbalance in the relation as it advantageously "favor" the giver. Purposefully, the rhetoric also negates any sense of mal-intent or malfeasance by the giver. On the other hand, it creates a sense of trust and commitment to the sacredness of the space in between.

---

7. *Talanoa* with Vaiao Eteuati, Mtaafa Elia, and author on July 29, 2022 at the Ministry of Education and Culture, Malifa.

8. See Ipiniu, "*Fafaga* Model."

The rhetoric of the receiver on the other hand is to politely refuse any implications that the gift is inadequate—*aua ia, tasi ae foi atu*—that is, to politely negate and revert any notion that the gift given is inadequate or that there was any mal-intent associated with the giving. The purpose of the receiver is to remove any doubt or uncertainty in the giver. Consequentially, it creates a sense of trust and wholeness within the exchange and in the relationship between the two parties. More importantly, the shared trust is maintained within the *vā-tapuia*. This "tactical game" of seeking the grounds diffuses any sense of competition to attain the higher status.

Faalalolaloga (Seeking the Lowest)

Restoring and mending ruptures in relationships is a vital element to the survival of Samoan society. *Faalalolaloga* is the act of seeking the lowest possible level in a *talanoa*—*afai ua i ai se upu ua sala poo se aga ua le tautamalii, malu avea i fale sou finagalo* (if I have misspoken or erred in our conversation, I seek forgiveness from you)—this is similar to the Christian concept of asking for forgiveness. Yet, even in the context of asking for forgiveness, the Samoan rhetoric of *faafitifiti* plays an important role, negating the lowering of the other. When one apologizes by "lowering of the self," her counterpart seeks an even lower position—*tasi ae foi atu* acknowledges the lowering of the other by offering to share in the act. The rhetoric of deflection allows the *failauga* (orator) to seek the lowest position in the *talanoa*. It is in this manner that the *failauga* builds trust and navigates the complexities of the *vā*. In that way, words nurture the *vā*. But words can also hurt the *vā*.

Diffusing Insult/Embarrassment

The rhetoric of deflection also emerges from the context in which an insult or an offense is perceived in a *talanoa*. There is always a chance that in the heat of *talanoa*, a *mis-talanoa* is imminent. The rhetoric of deflection allows the receiver to return the insult in a respectful manner without causing further damage to the *vā*—*tasi ae foi atu lau saunoaga* (I politely give back what was said) seeks to diffuse an otherwise embarrassing moment. In that way, the rhetoric of deflection has a way of diffusing a potentially escalating moment that could further undermine the holistic abundance of the relationship. *Tasi ae foi atu* gives space for the participants in a *talanoa* to avoid an otherwise embarrassing and damaging moment. As such, the use of the rhetoric of deflection sustains the balance warranted to maintain respect for the *vā*.

THE CANAANITE WOMAN IN MATTHEW 15:21-28

> Rhetoric of Matt 15:21-28 (NRSV)
> *Opening*
> 21 Jesus left that place and went away to the district of Tyre and Sidon. 22 Just then a Canaanite woman from that region came out and started shouting, "Have mercy on me, Lord, Son of David; my daughter is tormented by a demon."
> *Middle*
> 23 But he did not answer her at all. And his disciples came and urged him, saying, "Send her away, for she keeps shouting after us." 24 He answered, "I was sent only to the lost sheep of the house of Israel." 25 But she came and knelt before him, saying, "Lord, help me." 26 He answered, "It is not fair to take the children's food and throw it to the dogs." 27 She said, "Yes, Lord, yet even the dogs eat the crumbs that fall from their masters' table."
> *Closing*
> 28 Then Jesus answered her, "Woman, great is your faith! Let it be done for you as you wish." And her daughter was healed instantly.

Looking at the passage as a rhetorical unit (see above),[9] the opening-middle-closing texture provides a look at how the encounter plays out. Just as in Matt 12:15 (when Jesus became aware that the Pharisees were conspiring against him) and 14:13 (when Jesus heard that John was beheaded and his body buried), the opening unit (vv. 21-22) starts with a "withdrawal."[10] But while 12:15 and 14:13 are preceded by the news of a conspiracy and a beheading, the withdrawal to Tyre and Sidon is preceded by a confrontation with the Pharisees on defilement (v. 12). Thus, in v. 21 the storyline pans out from a group of Jewish leaders confronting Jesus to focus on a lone woman, a gentile woman. In a way, it is a deflection of the previous storyline in favor of a new one, one that spotlights a Canaanite woman.

It is important also to note the contrast between Mark 7:24-29 and Matt 15:21-28. Matthew's unique self-designation of a Canaanite woman is singular in the New Testament, suggesting an intent to re-situate the narrative outside of traditional Judaic institutions—rules, rituals, and traditions—thus, creating a sense of something outside of the norm. This is

---

9. For further reading on locating the rhetorical unit and determining the opening-middle-closing texture, see Kennedy, *New Testament Interpretation*, and Robbins, *Exploring the Texture*.

10. The Greek ἀναχωρέω has a range of meanings that include "withdraw," "retire," or "take refuge" (Danker et al., *Greek Lexicon*, 66).

further enhanced by the use of the imperative aorist resulting in a rendering that is peculiar for a male-dominating society. The effect is to re-situate the story on the "margins." This re-situation is followed by a request for mercy (v. 22) setting the parameters for the subsequent dialogical encounter. Matthew is simply engaging in the "deflection" of a dominant narrative.

The middle segment (vv. 23–27) is distinctively dialogical in nature. Yet, the brief silence and the interjection of the disciples in v. 23 impregnates the storyline with a sense of anticipation. From the subsequent cyclical exchange in vv. 24–27 conjures up an image of two *failauga*, orators, engaging in a *talanoa*. In v. 24, Jesus "deflects" any notion that he has the ultimate authority. From this perspective, it is not a rejection but a "lowering" of expectation, humbling of the self in the face of praise rendered in verse 22.

The closing in v. 28 exonerates the Canaanite woman. She is highlighted for her faith. More importantly, for her capacity to "deflect" any presumption of unworthiness and inadequacy.

FAAUSUGAFA[11]—MARRYING THE MATTHEAN NARRATIVE INTO THE SAMOAN *VAOGAGANA FAAFITIFITI*

Matthew 15:21–28 recontextualizes Mark's Syrophoenician woman (Mark 7:24–30). From the perspective of Samoan rhetoric, it is an attempt to deflect a dominant narrative that continues to pervade the *talanoa*. The implied setting is an encounter between two parties each represented by a *failauga*, an orator. Moreover, it is an encounter between those living in the center and those on the margins. Of concern though is to whom "the Messiah" belongs. The evidence is in Matthew's pinpointing of Tyre and Sidon as the place of the interaction. Intertextually, Tyre and Sidon take the readers back to the Old Testament and, in particular, the conquest story in Joshua and the Canaanite genocide. By re-situating Jesus in Tyre and Sidon, Matthew offers an opportunity to reevaluate and deflect a traditional or dominant narrative, one that is creating a roadblock in the way of the Gospel narrative.

The language of the Canaanite woman in v. 22 can be interpreted as a rhetoric of praise. The use of κυριοσ exemplifies praise[12] and coupled with

---

11. *Usugafa* is "to be married into the family" (Pratt, *Pratt's Grammar Dictionary*, 169). By adding the prefix *faa-* the intended meaning in this construction is to "marry" one narrative to another, resulting in a "newborn" meaning or implications for the studied text.

12. κυριος has a range of meanings that also include someone with authority and power (Danker et al., *Greek Lexicon*, 576). By calling κύριε υἱὸς Δαυίδ, Ulrich Luz argues

the imperative aorist[13] has the effect of a "powerful plea" for mercy. The rhetoric of praise frames the plea for help, for the Lord's mercy. From the Samoan rhetoric perspective, the Canaanite woman speaks not only as a gentile woman but also for all living on the margins. She is seeking a deflection of the dominant mindset by circumventing the "norm." In fact, the initial nonresponse and the subsequent interjection by the disciples (v. 23) reflects extant values and attitude towards women in a first century male-dominant society. It is this unveiling moment in Matthew's storyline that accentuates the comprehensive extent of wisdom in the woman's speech. By "deflecting" the social boundaries put upon her breaks open the chance to challenge all other "negative" constructions in society. She speaks not only for herself, but for the "others" in society.

Jesus initiates the *talanoa* by deflecting[14] that he has the authority to heal the daughter. From the perspective of Samoan *vaogagana faafitifiti*, it is in a way deflecting any notion that the authority resides with Jesus alone. Rather Jesus subsumes his authority to God. Jesus in this incidence shows the importance of maintaining respect for the *vā*, the space in between. To some extent it is laying the foundation for breaking social constructs that continue to impede against building and nurturing good relations within society. The woman adds to the anticipation in the *talanoa* by "deflecting" any social barriers placed in between her and Jesus (v. 25). In that way, she is demonstrating that there is much to be gained from the lowering of the self in relation to the other in society.

It is easy to argue that Jesus may have committed a *mis-talanoa* in his response to the woman's deflecting of the "norm" (v. 27). The implied effect is an immediate threat to the *vā* between the two. Yet, it is reasonable to propose though that this context-specific encounter can be redeemed through the use of rhetoric of deflection. From this perspective, Jesus is re-situating any notion of authority by deflecting praises to God. It is God alone that has the authority to bring salvation. The woman's response is in the manner of *tasi ae foi atu*. She deflects any notion that she is insulted or offended. By her response, Matthew is accorded space to re-situate what some may have read

---

that the Canaanite woman already knows that Jesus is the Messiah for the Israelites (Luz, *Matthew 8–20*). By implication I add that it is in a way Matthew's characterization of the woman as the "orator" for all "others," non-Israelites pleading for "deflection" of the dominant narrative that has created boundaries between them and the center.

13. Ἐλέησόν με is in the imperative aorist form.

14. I find the double use of the negative particle and a conditional clause in Οὐκ ἀπεστάλην εἰ μὴ εἰς τὰ πρόβατα τὰ ἀπολωλότα οἴκου Ἰσραήλ very telling. The statement reflects certainty. In a way, it suggests a sense of strong belief about the nature of divine purpose for his people. God sent Jesus to help his people.

and interpreted as an embarrassing moment in the Gospel narrative. In this perspective, without the woman taking the lower position in the *talanoa*, Jesus would not have been able to emerge as the Messiah for everyone. By taking a lower position in the *talanoa* she presents the true nature of God's redemptive love and the value of the *vā* between humanity and God. Because of her unassuming manners, the *talanoa* ends with Jesus praising the Canaanite woman's faith. Her daughter is healed.

CONCLUSION

This essay draws from the wisdom of Samoan rhetoric and language. It seeks an alternative reading of an odd encounter between Jesus and the Canaanite woman. Rather than seeing it as the usual escalation of competing views, the Samoan rhetoric of deflection perhaps offer a different perspective. Jesus is engaging in a re-situating of a dominant narrative regarding honor and status. Rather than taking claim of authority to bring salvation, he subsumes his authority to the overall love of God. This re-situating of authority deflects conventional notions of honor and status where the goal is to seek the highest position. Rather, the encounter provides a clear illustration of how seeking the "lowest ground" diffuses dominant culture and narrative.

This is a timely reminder in today's ultra-competitive environment which often favors the "most profitable" position. The encounter between Jesus and the Canaanite woman deflects that conventional understanding. Rather than striving to maximize interest, it offers a new paradigm where the aim is to strive for the lowest of the low. The low is the new high. To preserve and nurture relations is to subsume individual interests to the common good. To do this warrants a deflecting of the dominant narrative that prioritizes individual honor and glory over the well-being of the community. Jesus in subsuming himself to the authority of God illustrates what is needed to remove social impediments to community growth and solidarity. A healthy community warrants deflecting a dominant narrative that prioritizes individual competition and achievements.

I find also that there is much to gain from cross-contextualizing and intercultural studies. While the risk of personal biases and predispositions is higher, the promise for greater return from using indigenous language in biblical hermeneutics is too good to ignore. The bridge to relevancy is to utilize what is currency in our current context. To many Pacific Island countries and territories—that would be engagements around indigenous language and rhetoric. Language constitutes a significant aspect of the identity and way of life of a people. In that sense, integrating biblical hermeneutics within the context of indigenous language can anticipate alternative and varying interpretations.

In connection to the overall theme of well-being, the encounter between Jesus and the Canaanite woman sheds light on an important element of Pacific epistemology. Well-being is defined within the nebulous network of *fāiā* which the individual and the community are part of. Re-situating the story of the Canaanite woman within this paradigm shifts our interpretive understanding outside the norm. More significantly, it sheds light on navigating the complex system of *fāiā* that effectuate the well-being of the individual and the community. Matthew's re-situating of the Markan tradition parallels this understanding of communal and individual well-being—finding balance and harmony warrants awareness and appreciation of relational spaces.

BIBLIOGRAPHY

Danker, Frederick W., et al. *A Greek Lexicon of the New Testament and Other Early Christian Literature*. 4th ed. Chicago: University of Chicago Press, 2021.

Efi, Tui Atua Tupua Tamasese Ta'isi. *Su'esu'e Manogi: In Search of Fragrance; Tui Atua Tupua Tamasese Ta'isi and the Samoan Indigenous Reference*. Edited by Tamasailau M. Suaalii-Sauni et al. Lepapaigalagala, Samoa: Center for Samoan Studies of National University of Samoa, 2009.

Eteuati, Vaiao, and Mataafa Elia. "*Talanoa* on July 29, 2022 at the Ministry of Education and Culture, Malifa." By Fatilua Fatilua. 2022.

GOODNEWS. "Kolisi i Malua Faauuga 2001." YouTube, Sept. 17, 2001. https://www.youtube.com/watch?v=an5t7ECYcFo.

Havea, Jione. "Islander Criticism: Waters, Ways, Worries." In *Sea of Readings: The Bible in the South Pacific*, edited by Jione Havea, 1–20. Semeia Studies 90. Atlanta: SBL Press, 2018.

Ipiniu, Kara Siaosi. "*Fafaga* Model: A Pastoral Care Approach to Revisit *Fa'aaloaloga* in the Congregational Christian Church Samoa (CCCS) Today." MTh thesis, Pacific Theological College, 2017.

Kennedy, George. *New Testament Interpretation through Rhetorical Criticism*. Chapel Hill: North Carolina University Press, 1984.

LeMarquand, Grant. "The Canaanite Conquest of Jesus (Mt 15:21–28)." *ARC, The Journal of the Faculty of Religious Studies* 33 (2005) 237–47.

Luz, Ulrich. *Matthew 8–20: A Commentary*. Translated by James E. Crouch. Minneapolis: Fortress, 2001.

Pratt, George. *Pratt's Grammar Dictionary and Samoan Language*. Edited by J. E. Newell. Apia, Samoa: Malua, 1911.

Robbins, Vernon K. *Exploring the Texture of the Texts: A Guide to Socio-Rhetorical Interpretations*. Harrisburg, PA: Trinity, 1996.

Tagaloa, Aiono Fanaafi Le. *O Le Fa'asinomaga*. Apia, Samoa: Le Lamepa, 1986.

Tuisuga-le-taua, Fa'alepo Aveau. "*O Le Tofa Liliu a Samoa*: A Hermeneutical Critical Analysis of the Cultural-Theological Praxis of the Samoan Context." PhD diss., Melbourne College of Divinity, 2009.

Wendt, Albert. "Afterword: Tatauing the Post-Colonial Body." In *Inside Out: Literature, Cultural Politics, and Identity in the New Pacific*, edited by Vilsoni Hereniko and Rob Wilson, 399–412. Lanham, MD: Rowman & Littlefield, 1999.

Part Three

WELL-BEING OF IMAGINATIONS AND WORLDVIEWS

11

REIMAGINING IMAGES OF GOD FOR MULTIETHNIC PACIFIC WOMEN

Therese Lautua

NEW GENERATIONS OF YOUNG Pacific people living in Aotearoa New Zealand are more likely to have multiple ethnicities woven together in their genealogy. This presents a complex of new challenges and opportunities for church communities and families to *talanoa* and reimagine what images of God are most meaningful to multiethnic women in particular. The image/s one has of God can harm or aid a positive state of mental well-being.

THE STUDY

This chapter draws on unpublished doctoral research completed in 2020, and focus-group interviews with young multiethnic Catholic women in Auckland. The Catholic Church in Aotearoa and Oceania has the opportunity to contextualize images of God through artwork within local parishes and schools, even more so than it currently does. While this essay is specific to the Catholic community in Aotearoa, it is relevant to any Christian community who are grappling with how to best build the mental resilience of Pacific young peoples from a faith perspective. Social Trinitarianism is used as a model of intersectionality and a means to renew our understanding of what it means to live in the image of God. Radically equal relationships in one's identity with culture, family, spirituality, physical environment, and body generally equate to being mentally well.

The variety of ways which young people in the Pacific name and perceive God is as vast as Te Moana-Nui-a-Kiwa (the Pacific Ocean) that connects us. The enmeshing together of Western Christianity's teaching and artwork of the Persons of the Trinity and the various cultural traditions of the Pacific, including those in the diaspora, presents a complex of new challenges and opportunities. This essay argues that images of God are a starting point for church communities and families to *talanoa* (share stories, have conversation) and reimagine what images of God are most meaningful to assist in building the mental resilience of multiethnic Pacific youth. This argument draws on my unpublished doctoral research completed in 2020, and focus-group interviews with sixty-four multiethnic, Pacific, seventeen- to twenty-four-year-old Catholic women in Auckland, Aotearoa New Zealand.

Reflecting deeply on Jesus's question "who do you say that I am?" (Matt 16:13–18), the research participants shared their experiences of having multiple ethnicities woven together in their genealogy, Catholicism, views on the Trinity, and personal images of God and how these different strands of their identity impacted their mental well-being. Images of God have a direct link to one's relationship to authority figures or attachment figures to whom one has an emotional bond, such as parents and caregivers.[1] Thus, when local churches and families create safe spaces for young Pacific people to describe who they think God is and their relationship with God, *talanoa* can also begin about their relationships with others and past trauma which might currently affect their mental well-being. Renewing an understanding of the Trinity through the lens of Pacific ideas around relationality further renews our understanding of what it means to live in the image of God and have life to the full (John 10:10).

In the Pacific, the number of female Catholic theological views on who God is and how God is perceived are few and far between. My positionality of being a lay female Catholic theologian of mixed Samoan and New Zealand European heritage will always be tightly interwoven with my research process and methodology in approaching any contextual, practical theology projects. It is precisely in this positionality that I also acknowledge the privilege I have in being able to study and write theology at all. Chantelle Kahn, a lay Catholic woman, shared the perspectives of her fellow female parishioners in Fiji when they were preparing a dramatization of the Gospel

---

1. Stroope et al., "Images of Loving God," 28.

for Easter.[2] Many of the women opposed the idea of referring to God in a feminine way, and Kahn argues that in her own experience in Fiji the church does not often refer to God as having both masculine and feminine characteristics. It is a challenge for young, Pacific women to wrestle with understanding contemporary Western definitions of gender, which have strongly influenced how churches insist how both women and men should perceive God and behave in their lived realities.

LIVING *IMAGO DEI*—SOME PACIFIC VIEWS

Across Te Moana-Nui-a-Kiwa there are many different theological expressions of what it means to live one's life, created in the image of God. Methodist theologian Upolu Vaai highlights that it can be difficult for those in the Pacific to navigate what it means to live in the image of a God who is defined by a Western worldview, far disposed from the fluidity of life on the other side of the globe.[3] The natural environment with its seas, stars, the land, and vegetation is a mutual part of existing, thriving, and life for everyone. The same can be said of relationships with family and the fluidity of how gender is understood as women and men move between "domestic versus municipal, private versus collective, masculinity versus femininity."[4] Being created in the image of God and living life to the full is grounded in relationality and earnestly seeking to have meaningful relationships with all aspects of the created cosmos. One's personal identity is woven into each of these strands and has an impact on mental well-being and one's perception of who God is. The Trinitarian Persons of God, in whose image we are created, flow and dance in perichoretic union with their unique roles and actions in the world and within Godself. This multistranded, myriad of ways to respond to God's call to relationship with Godself, within our very identity, speaks to how Pacific peoples can conceptualize holiness. Holiness found in the fluidity of everyday life reflects God's dance of celebration throughout and over the cosmos as each individual searches for deeper connection with creation and the Godhead.

WOMEN'S RESPONSES TO GENESIS 1:26-27

Shared conversations allowed the research participants to communicate who they thought God was, which was grounded in their understanding

---

2. Kahn, "Looking for God."
3. Vaai, "From *Atutasi* to *Atulasi*," 247.
4. Vaai, "From *Atutasi* to *Atulasi*," 247.

of Gen 1:26–27. The sixty-four research participants were each invited to read the passage and share what it meant to them and what it might say about one's self-worth. Stewardship of creation was a strong theme among the responses, as well as having free-will and a sense of God's grace existing within everyone.

> [Interpretations of the passage] like the domination of the world, instead of like being a steward, and just how [to be a steward], well I see it as how humans have tried to assert their superiority in creation by saying they are made in God's image and trying to make themselves God. But it [the passage] still makes me feel special.—Zoe, twenty-four years old, New Zealand–born Tongan

> God loves us so much that he's willing to give us free will to do whatever we want. That's what it means to be created in the likeness. Free will and image, it's to understand more about the world and how God is. His mercy for us is the ability to choose whether to serve him or not.—Susana, eighteen years old, Tokelauan/Wallis and Futuna/Rotuman

A desire to protect the environment for future generations became more apparent through this section of the focus-group interview questions, and the women expressed this in terms of their faith and belief that this was what God intended at creation. Susana described the passage as an insight into what she believed God intends for each individual—that they simultaneously engage in relationships with the whole of creation and God. Susana also discussed serving God, as loving Creator of the universe, as a choice humanity has the freedom to make. The repetition in the first creation account of Genesis and particularly vv. 26–27—"So God created humans in his image, in the image of God he created them; male and female he created them"—suggests that right relationship with creation has its foundation in reflecting the face of God.

Both Zoe's and Susana's quotes demonstrate an awareness of the serious harm humankind can commit against the earth, yet also that God seeks an intimate relationship with everyone. A holistic understanding of self-identity centered on *imago Dei* is crucial to forming a Catholic human anthropology and theology of mental well-being for young Pacific women.

GOD AS *ABBA*, FATHER

Naming God as a Father figure and generally using a male pronoun was the most common way research participants talked about God in positive terms. Zoe was the only woman who described God as a mother; she had studied undergraduate theology and also had been raised by a single mother in a very patriarchal family.

> The God that is important to me now is the image of God who is Creator, source of life like those things. I see that everywhere and when I see each person, I try to see like oh wow God made that, that's amazing. It just makes me really appreciate nature even more, just how beautiful everything is like God made this like this didn't come from nothing. The more I think about it, the more I think of God as a mother, just life-giving, nurturing, loving.—Zoe, twenty-four years old, New Zealand–born Tongan

> Yea especially in this age when there's people having preferred pronouns and we question everything. There's those that don't have mothers and fathers, but they find that in God and strength.—Lilika, twenty-three years old, Tongan/Fijian

Feminist biblical scholars of the New Testament, such as Martina S. Gnadt, argue that the use of Jesus's title for God, *abba*, suggests an intimate parent-child relationship with humanity.[5] The use of Jesus's *abba* also depicts the everyday reality of mothers who are responsible for making food and caring for children. This echoes Vaai's proposal that in a truly Pacific relational way of living, both men and women can take on masculine and feminine roles.[6]

Images of God, such as "Father" and "Mother," have been studied in relation to mental well-being from various angles and particularly in regard to being a buffer against stress.[7] Positive images of God, such as one who is loving and involved in the everyday life of a person as opposed to a judgmental, punishing image of God, are more likely to boost self-esteem and mental well-being.[8] Images of God are also often reflective of one's relationship with authority figures, such as parents or caregivers; if the relationship with authority figures is strained, then the attachment to God either fills this

---

5. Gnadt, "Gospel of Matthew," 610.
6. Vaai, "From *Atutasi* to *Atulasi*," 247.
7. Stroope et al., "Images of Loving God," 27.
8. Stroope et al., "Images of Loving God," 28.

void and compensates or the relationship with God is also strained, as Lilika describes above. Therefore, it is essential that when church communities portray God as a parent figure, they are sensitive to the pastoral, mental well-being needs of congregation members. This requires genuine accompaniment and a disposition of listening to the interwoven strands of their identity as opposed to preaching one Western way of knowing God and self.

JESUS AS SON OF MARY

The Rosary was a popular form of devotional, meditative prayer used by many of the research participants and their families on a regular basis. This reinforcement of the image of Jesus as Son of Mary was evident in many of the women's descriptions of their experiences of Catholicism, the way they understood the Trinity and Jesus's humanity and divinity.

> When I was in Year 7, I got really sick, going in and out of hospital, losing weight and deteriorating. They couldn't find what was wrong with me. The doctors thought I was doing it to myself psychologically. We went to Samoa for a week-long Divine Mercy thing, and I slowly started getting better. There's a witch doctor guy on my Tongan side, and he came to *fofo* [traditional massage] me along with prayers. After a week of his massages, I just threw up all this stuff after that I got better. We believe Divine Mercy cured me and so my family believes in miracles. I believe it did too.—Vaelenoatia, nineteen years old, Samoan/Tongan

The Divine Mercy devotion is a set of extra invocations used when praying the traditional Rosary prayers and meditates on Jesus's death being a merciful act for the world. Vaelenoatia's story demonstrates the mix of indigenous practices of healing and Catholicism that she believed resulted in her physical healing. Sr. Vitolia Mo'a notes that from a Samoan perspective, sickness as a concept or *ma'i* is, in a nutshell, an "integral imbalance in the human system, which affects the wellness of the whole person."[9] Therefore, the care of an individual who is *ma'i* must realign not only the physical, but also the spiritual, emotional, and relational connections with others.

Other women commented on being forced to try and pray the Rosary in Samoan during their family night prayer, without understanding the words. They felt as though they could not freely address this with their parents for fear of being disciplined and therefore also felt distanced from the

9. Mo'a, *Culture as a Foundation*, 4.

church in general. For these women, the image of Jesus as Son of Mary was associated negatively with the lack of communication between the different generations in their household and a reminder of their inability to speak their parents' first language. Nonetheless, many of the research participants described having small shrines dedicated to Mary in their homes or having rosary beads hanging in their car. Jesus as the Son of Mary reaffirmed the importance of family in God's vision for humanity.

GOD AS HOLY SPIRIT

The image of God as Spirit was not frequently mentioned by the research participants as one that stood out to them, thus reflecting how the Holy Spirit is often the forgotten third Person of the Trinity. Nonetheless, Iutita commented on the Holy Spirit as an important part of her understanding of the Trinity:

> I focus on the Father and Holy Spirit part. The Holy Spirit because everyone has that in you and it helps you make decisions. It's your built-in intuition, sometimes it's conscious and sometimes it's not. But then at the same time I feel the Father part but because I've never really had a dad. I've had a grandad, but we've very firmly established that he's my grandad in cultural terms.— Iutita, twenty-two years old, Samoan/New Zealand European

First, Iutita's experience of not having her biological father a stable presence in her life displays how seeing God as a father figure compensates for the lack of connection with her biological father. Second, she describes the Holy Spirit as a guide in her everyday decisions.

There are few Pacific theologians who have pursued a contextual pneumatology. Tongan theologian Sioeli Felekoni Vaipulu offers a reconstructed name for the spirit: *laumālie*.[10] Its literal translation is "good news," though *mā* denotes endurance and humility found in the ordinary, everyday tasks of life. Thus, Vaipulu argues that the Holy Spirit as *laumālie* is concerned for the other, uncontainable but quietly acting in the world with humble endurance. Considering both Iutita's image of God and Vaipulu's proposal, a reflection on Ezekiel's vision of the Valley of Dry Bones (Ezek 37: 1–14) crafts a way to weave together the research participants' narratives and fashion a relational theology of mental well-being.

> Thus says the Lord God to these bones: I will cause breath [*ruach*] to enter you, and you shall live. I will lay sinews on you,

10. Vaipulu, "Naming the Spirit A-*niu*," 99.

and will cause flesh to come upon you, and cover you with skin, and put breath in you, and you shall live; and you shall know that I am the Lord....

I will put my spirit [*ruach*] within you, and you shall live, and I will place you on your own soil; then you shall know that I, the Lord, have spoken and will act, says the Lord. (Ezek 37:5–6, 14 author's translation)

In Ezekiel's context, the scattered bones—shattered and dispersed skeletons—are representative of Israel's disarray post the Babylonian exile.[11] Ezekiel is able to speak words that do what they say only because God's own *ruach* (*ruach 'elohim*—breath, wind, spirit of God) is immersed in the *ruach* of Ezekiel, enabling him to prophesy (Ezek 37:7).[12] The restoration of Israel and placement of the people of their own soil is achieved in the context of each individual knowing their cultural and spiritual identity as part of a collective group. One is created in the very image of God, breathed into life within a community and flourishing under the aegis of the Lord.

RE-STORYING

Fifty-two of the sixty-four research participants stated that their image of God was a significant aspect of their identity and for maintaining a positive state of mental well-being. Whether it was a variation on the Father, Son, or Spirit or commenting on the ubiquitous nature of the Trinity, it was clear that the way each individual spoke about God was impacted by their relationship to their parents or authority figures in their lives as well as the church. I wanted to respect the narratives my participants offered—as young multiethnic women, their words and beliefs are too often critiqued or questioned by those in positions of authority. As a researcher, I wanted to avoid the colonial and patriarchal enterprise of shutting their narratives down or challenging and questioning them. Their multiethnic identities shaped their views—not all participants had entirely Pacific heritage also.

It would also be a generalization to say that there is a "specifically Islander way" of interpreting images of God. This idea is problematic, given the diverse ethnicities of my participants. This is again the reason I chose not to contextualize and decolonize their chosen images of God as I would

---

11. Greenberg, *Ezekiel 21–37*, 742.
12. Grey, "Acts of the Spirit," 79.

have had to discuss, for example, a Samoan God the Father, then a Samoan–New Zealand equivalent, Tongan, Niuean, Tokelauan, and so on.

The opportunity to allow both young Pacific men and women to re-story how mental well-being is envisaged in both churches and families can start with their images of God. Delving into how a young person perceives God reveals the nature of their upbringing, their connection to family members, experience of Catholicism and cultural identity.

Intergenerational communication about the multiple issues young women and their peers face was often seen as problematic for many of the research participants. This ranged from understanding how femininity is conceptualized in their various cultures, strongly desiring to support non-heterosexual loved ones in their family context and the church as well as language fluency and thus at times feeling isolated from their family. While it is not the sole responsibility of the family to build mental resilience in a young person's life, it is important that conversation tools specific to the local context of Te Moana-Nui-a-Kiwa are created for families to use in a Christian environment.

THE POWER OF ARTWORK

It is necessary to have culturally specific and denomination specific responses to mental well-being. From an international perspective, Catholic mental well-being resources and pastoral programs utilize what is already in the tradition—using examples of saints who faced mental health issues, meditative prayer such as *lectio divina* reflecting on Scripture, *visio divina* where artwork aids meditation or Ignatian spiritual exercises, Taizé or workbooks that use particular passages of Scripture to reflect on their situation. Individuals who face mental distress on some level—from being clinically diagnosed with a severe mental illness or experiencing mild anxiety—"desire to have their spiritual experiences accepted as both real and significant" by those who have caring responsibility of them or are considered a part of their support network.[13]

Using creative tools when words cannot express difficult experiences a young person is going through are important. While it is unrealistic to expect families to know where to find these tools, many Catholic parishes across Aotearoa New Zealand have the capacity to display more contextual artwork (see, e.g., fig. 1.1 and 12.1), which can be used as a starting point for discussions around mental well-being. It is essential that as Aotearoa New Zealand becomes increasingly culturally diverse that whitewashed Western

13. Swinton, *Spirituality and Mental Health*, 135.

depictions of biblical stories and Christian tradition are not the only options available. As has been expressed by the various research participants, images of God are often reflections of one's relationship to their parents or authority figures in their lives. If one's image of God is compensating for the lack of relationship with parents or authority figures, it is imperative that portrayals of the Creator of the universe are not limited by one worldview in local churches. In a sense, this fails to recognize holiness found in other migrant cultures who in recent times in the Catholic Church in Aotearoa New Zealand are more likely to be seated in the pews.

REWEAVING TOWARDS MENTAL RESILIENCE

Pacific theologians have deliberated what it means to be created in the image of God, who is inherently relational and engaged in everyday life. Social Trinitarianism is a Western concept where the starting point of theology and model of human unity and ethics is the dynamic unity of the Trinity. On the other hand, Upolu Vaai has an emphasis on cultural epistemologies as the starting point for revealing Trinitarian ontology.[14] It is not difficult for everyday lay Pacific parishioners, who are the focus of this research, to make connections between Vaai's worldviews and Social Trinitarianism. Vaai theologizes from a social location where he is an expert in Samoan culture. His *tino* theology stresses that through Jesus, God moves in deep relationship with the whole *tino*—translated as "body"—but is also fully embodied symbolically in relationships, community and genealogical ties, the experiences of an individual, birth, and truth. This relationship includes the natural environment and ancestors. Vaai is strongly opposed to the notion that God is beyond the *tino* and insists that through Christ and intimate union with the Spirit, God moves through the whole *tino*, communities, ancestors, and the natural environment.[15]

The Trinity is the fundamental example of intersecting identities and is the center of how humanity can understand what it means to be created in the image of God. Each Divine Person—Creator, Son, and Spirit—in radical, harmonious relationship with one another, is aware of the tasks they each perform both within Godself and in the universe. Living in the image of a social Trinitarian God from this contextual theological standpoint sees that Pacific ways of being can be incorporated in the process of affirming the work of the Trinity in the world.

---

14. Vaai, "Tino Theology," 223.
15. Vaai, "Tino Theology," 234.

In the Aotearoa New Zealand Catholic setting, the journey to feeling secure in one's self-identity and understanding what *imago Dei* means today and in the future is more than acknowledging the Trinity by doing the sign of the cross to begin and end prayer, or during the eucharistic prayer at Mass. The search for identity is bound up with the challenge for local parishes and families to better support and teach young multiethnic Pacific women to live out their baptism, which upholds belief in the Trinity as basic to Christian identity. God the Creator journeys with people; Jesus, who is both divine and fully human, understands the depths of our human existence, which includes mental well-being; and the Holy Spirit is the Comforter in all the events of human life: God is a personal God. Social Trinitarianism emphasizes that God is being-in-relationship; this very existence causes love to flow forth, a spiritual *mana* (spiritual power and authority), which sets up everything which is not divine, to be in relationship with God's being.[16]

What do these reflections on *imago Dei* and the different strands of identity mean practically for the church and the lives of young, multiethnic Pacific women of the future? The demographic of participants chosen for the research project has been, and will be, exposed to competing definitions of womanhood via social media, the church and within their families and cultural traditions. Relooking at social Trinitarianism with an intersectional, Pacific lens and offering denomination-specific approaches to discussions about mental well-being and faith offer a way forward into the future. For the multiethnic Pacific woman, there will always be a challenge in holding the tension of the in-betweenness of her ethnic background in balance with the love of a relational God, her whole family, the natural environment, and her ancestors. Despite this, it is possible to find joy in being created in the image of a living God and all the diversity this brings in the church and the world.

BIBLIOGRAPHY

Gnadt, Martina S. "Gospel of Matthew." In *Feminist Biblical Interpretation: A Compendium of Critical Commentary and the Books of the Bible and Related Literature,* edited by Luise Schottroff and Marie-Theres Wacker, 607–25. Grand Rapids: Eerdmans, 2012.

Greenberg, Moshe. *Ezekiel 21–37*. Anchor Bible 22A. New York: Doubleday, 1997.

Grey, Jacqueline. "Acts of the Spirit: Ezekiel 37 in the Light of Contemporary Speech and Act Theory." *Journal of Biblical and Pneumatological Research* 1 (2009) 69–82.

---

16. Tate, "Stepping into Māori Spirituality," 39.

Kahn, Chantelle. "Looking for God with New Eyes." In *Weavings: Women Doing Theology in Oceania*, edited by Lydia Johnson and Joan Alleluia Filemoni-Tofaeono, 186–91. Suva, Fiji: University of the South Pacific Press, 2003.

Mo'a, Vitolia. *Culture as a Foundation for Care: Paper Presented at the Aniva Pacific Health Workforce Fono 25 November 2015*. Wellington: Pacific Perspectives, 2015.

Stroope, Samuel, et al. "Images of a Loving God and Sense of Meaning in Life." *Social Indicators Research* 111 (2013) 25–44.

Swinton, John. *Spirituality and Mental Health Care: Rediscovering a 'Forgotten' Dimension*. London: Kingsley, 2001.

Tate, Henare. "Stepping into Māori Spirituality." In *He Kupu Whakawairua: Spirituality in Aotearoa New Zealand: Catholic Voices*, edited by Helen Bergin and Susan Smith, 37–53. Auckland: Accent, 2002.

Vaai, Upolu Lumā. "From *Atutasi* to *Atulasi*: Relational Theologizing and Why Pacific Islanders Think and Theologize Differently." In *Theologies from the Pacific*, edited by Jione Havea, 235–49. Postcolonialism and Religions. Cham, Switzerland: Palgrave and Macmillan, 2021.

———. "Tino Theology." In *The Relational Self: Decolonising Personhood in the Pacific*, edited by Upolu Luma Vaai and Unaisi Nabobo-Baba, 223–42. Suva, Fiji: University of the South Pacific Press and Pacific Theological College Press, 2017.

Vaipulu, Sioeli Felekoni. "Naming the Spirit A-*niu* (Anew): Re(is)landing Pneumatology." In *Theologies from the Pacific*, edited by Jione Havea, 89–101. Postcolonialism and Religions. Cham, Switzerland: Palgrave Macmillan, 2021.

12

SĀPATE FAʻĒ
Art and the reStorying of Theology

'Elenoa Telefoni

THIS SHORT ESSAY IS a personal reflection on the question—Do we need God(s) in our communities? I answer the above question through my artwork titled *Sāpate Faʻē* (Mother's Day; see fig. 12.1), and two questions that beg attention to the place of art in the weaving of memory and the wellbeing of theological imagination in Pasifika.

1. How does art help us remember?
2. How does art awaken our theological imagination?

Through *Sāpate Faʻē* I affirm my identity as a Tongan woman and locate my faith upon my ancestors. Comprehending God(s)—who are central in my community—involves grasping my inner self in the context of the people within my environment, past and present, and the world. The links between these strands interweave in my spiritual journey, which is always in the context of and in relation to my Tongan identity.

The manifestation of God(s) appropriated through visual expression allows freedom of thoughts and permission to explore my spiritual and religious identity. I compare this to the way I find meaning from the Bible, community rituals, and cultural and religious teachings. Artwork is sacred text also.

ART AND MEMORY

The study of an artwork involves re-membering personal experiences, and this includes joys and frustrations, pains and longings. I view this re-membering event as a language implementation to express ideas or feelings with God and with life.

Sāpate Fa'ē (Mother's Day) involves compositional arrangement of certain elements with the focal portrait of my great-grandmother, who was an important figure in my life. The message behind the title reflects women as the cultural backbone in my context; in other words, the title values women as the strength of life. Both—the significance of my great-grandmother to me, and the valuing of women in my culture—are woven together to present conceptual meaning to the artwork.

Figure 12.1: *Sāpate Fa'ē* (2012)

The artwork is created using a relief and reduction printmaking technique. The visual images are originally carved into custom wood at three millimeters depth. The white areas protrude as the areas that are carved out, then the areas showing the visual images are interpreted as the positive areas that produce the image. The relief process involves two colors—black and white—and the reduction print process is the red color. I created the artwork by printing the black-and-white colors first, then reprinted, adding the red color of the cross. The whole process is created by printing onto fine fabriano paper specifically used for printing.

The work is divided into four quadrants to reflect Tonga's coat of arms. The woven *fala* (mat) in the four quadrants represents the interwoven history of genealogy, tradition, culture, and religion that formulate the weaving of my great-grandmother Limiteti Lakai Fieʻota Kanahe ʻa Tungi Mailefihi ʻOfa-Tuʻitupou—whose image is at the center of this artwork.

The color of the horizontal and vertical dividers that mark the four quadrants is dark red, to symbolize the color of blood, genealogy, ancestors, and the inheritance of the sacrifice that my ancestors endured—at the hands of colonialists—and which have become critical in forming my inner self. The black-and-white colors reflect the linkage to historical events that have molded me and are woven into my genealogy.

Language is conveyed through the colors. The artwork contains colors—red, black, white—and the colors convey language. The interpretations from the viewers will vary with entirely different viewpoints. The language is in the artwork, and the message is in the eyes of the beholder.

In Christian eyes, the dividers that mark the four quadrants—which cross at, and thus centralize, the face of my great-grandmother—re-member the cross of Jesus, a symbol of the constitutional sacrifice of his life. Symbolism is strongly emphasized in portraying meaning, and viewers could state that the artwork has a cross (instead of dividers) in the background, so it also has religious significance. This highlights how art helps to explore human creativity through remembrance and is an outgrowth of God's good creation.

Identifying certain compositional elements and colors portrays the value of memory that links to the human expression of symbolism. My identity through a strong female is reflected through the elements of a red cross, which correlates to my faith juxtaposing with my relationship to God.

ART AND IMAGINATION

The place of God(s) in communities emphasizes the desire to connect with our surroundings—with Moana [sea], Whenua [land], Rangi [sky] and Pulotu [underworld]. The connections can be affirmed through the artwork when we are searching for meaning.[1]

Human nature reveals the curiosity to explore because the supernatural, divine God(s) is a mystery. God(s) is present, but unknown. God(s) is in our communities, and they are not the privilege of churches or religions. The separation of religion from communities has never been achieved at any given time.

There is a false notion that sin lies in not having a God(s) in communities. Sin is not the absence of God(s). Rather, sin is the separating of oneself from a God(s) who is present. God(s) is not present because of churches or religions, but because of communities.

We can argue that communities and religions do not need a God(s) because Western influences brought the need to follow a system of rituals and monotheist thinking. However, God(s) has always been an influential value to Pasifika communities and plays a major role in our lives.

Freedom of expression within artworks requires no God(s) or godliness. But clearly, expression or creativity is a form of cultural art, and it is strongly infused with spiritual connections.

MOTHER'S DAY

In Tongan communities, Mother's Day is one of the most special of the special Sundays. Families go to church and then gather to remember their mothers and grandmothers—to many generations prior. What is remembered the most are the sacrifices that mothers and grandmothers made, for the sake of their families. Their sacrifices echo the sacrifice that Jesus made, but no one takes this kind of reStorying leap. Such a theological leap is one of the imaginative steps that my *Sāpate Faʻē* invites and permits.[2]

Sāpate Faʻē prompts thinking of the death and sacrifice of Jesus. But the story of Jesus did not end with death. Resurrection came next, and that element invites me to appropriate the story of the resurrection of Jesus Christ to my artwork resurrecting the memory of my great-grandmother. The intention to appropriate within the compositional structure of the artwork justifies my weaving of the relationship between my experience and my faith. Pursuing God(s) allows me to affirm my reflections and experiences through an ancestor, my culture and heritage.

---

1. Jione Havea, *talanoa* with author, Apr. 11, 2022.
2. I owe this reStorying leap to Jione Havea, *talanoa* with author, Sept. 11, 2022.

Truth be told, Mother's Day is a painful day for women who tried but could not become mothers. Mother's Day is a day of grieving for them, and this reality is affirmed in the colors of *Sāpate Faʻē*.

CONCLUSION

The value of having God(s) in our communities influences my attempt to create meaning with my artwork, a sense of belonging through an ancestor. Vitally important in this venture is the diverse reStorying opportunities. It is evident in *Sāpate Faʻē* that God(s) plays a significant role in the understanding of my experiences and my faith.

I affirm that nature, spiritual divine powers, and sin form my understanding of life. God(s) in our communities builds bridges of understanding, goodwill, and respect for everyone involved.[3] God(s) holds valuable significance in maintaining our spiritual and religious journey in search of meaning—a journey in which art is a sacred text.

BIBLIOGRAPHY

Browning, Bob. "Why Is Community So Important to God?" Good Faith Media, Feb. 3, 2021. https://goodfaithmedia.org/why-is-community-so-important-to-god-cms-17404/.

---

3. Obviously, God(s) in our communities enables us to reach out to those who are struggling, with words of encouragement and deeds of compassion (Browning, "Why Is Community").

13

THE *TAPU* OF *FANUA* (WOMB)
A Sermon on 1 Thessalonians 4:1–8[1]

Nikotemo Sopepa

As for other matters, brothers and sisters, we instructed you how to live in order to please God, as in fact you are living. Now we ask you and urge you in the Lord Jesus to do this more and more. 2 For you know what instructions we gave you by the authority of the Lord Jesus.

   3 It is God's will that you should be sanctified: that you should avoid sexual immorality; 4 that each of you should learn to control your own body in a way that is holy and honorable, 5 not in passionate lust like the pagans, who do not know God; 6 and that in this matter no one should wrong or take advantage of a brother or sister. The Lord will punish all those who commit such sins, as we told you and warned you before. 7 For God did not call us to be impure, but to live a holy life. 8 Therefore, anyone who rejects this instruction does not reject a human being but God, the very God who gives you his Holy Spirit.
(1 Thess 4:1–8 NIV)

---

   1. This sermon was delivered at the morning devotion of Pacific Theological College, Suva, Fiji, July 17, 2023.

It is becoming common to read in local newspapers of the sexual violating of women and young girls. Our society today is sick. When I say sick, I am referring to such gruesome acts such as the (allegedly) sexual violation of a two-month-old girl by her father,[2] the sexual violation of a fourteen-year-old girl by her grandfather,[3] and the selling of a girl for sex by her mother.[4]

In this sermon, I posit a (k)new *fanua*[5] *tapu* reading of our text. The idea surrounding (k)new is borrowed from Manulani Meyer's new-old wisdom,[6] wisdom that was understood and practiced in the past, downplayed along history lines due to factors that have contributed to our current predicament, but now we need to retrieve, reclaim, and relive it.

In light of what we read in 1 Thess 4:1–8, we find ourselves at the crossroad where texts, epistemologies, and hermeneutics meet. We are presented with a biblical text on sexual taboo that contradicts our Pasifika understanding of sex. Sex is one of those biblical themes that has evaded Christian pulpits across Pasifika, and modern Pasifika civil society has blamed this evasion as one of the leading causes for the rise of sexual violence in our region. Even human rights agents working in Pasifika loathe our silence on the issue of sex.

Some have suggested that families should begin discussing sex during family mealtimes—our problem is we do not talk when we eat, it's rude to do so. Some suggested we should include sex education in our primary and secondary educational curriculums—the last I checked we've not gone beyond the reproductive systems of biology class. Some have asked the church to start preaching about sex from the pulpits, but Pasifika pulpits continue to evade the subject. And all these boil down to one fact—sex is *tapu* in Pasifika.

TAPU

But we have lost the meaning of *tapu* through misrepresentation and misinterpretation of it to mean taboo in the work of anthropological researchers; therefore, there is a great need for us to retrieve and resurrect *tapu* in Pasifika. In other words, to (k)new *tapu* once again.

In Tuvalu we do not have a word for "sex" in the way that it is understood in Western cultures. We do have words for sexual intercourse, and

---

2. *Fiji Times*, "Father Allegedly Rapes Baby."
3. Savike, "Grandfather Pleads Not Guilty."
4. Reece, "Mother of Teenage Daughter."
5. The Tuvaluan term for "land" and "womb." In Fiji, *vanua*; Samoa, *fenua*; Māori, *whenua*.
6. Meyer, "Holographic Epistemology."

they have to do with the idea of communality and gathering. The silence in Tuvalu and many Pasifika islands on the subject of sex[7] does not derive from the fact that we do not have a word for it, but the fact that the word or idea of sex portrayed in Western cultures does not exist in our daily vocabulary contributes to our silence. In Tuvalu, we do not conceptualize sex. We live it. We embody it. And because we live it in our bodies and not in our minds, it is *tapu*. This is basically why we do not speak of it in our family circles, for within the family circles there exist relationships that teach us how to carry ourselves around the community as sexual beings.

In my Tuvaluan culture, I am not to even speak to my female third cousins. I refer to them as my *tuagane tapu*, or *tapu* sisters. This is because a third cousin is still treated like an immediate sister (sibling), and she is within the circle of sexual *tapu*. In that case, fourth, fifth, sixth, and even seventh cousins (in Tuvalu) are treated as first, second, and third cousins (in Western cultures), and are still within the peripheries of sexual *tapu*. And not just them, their children and grandchildren are also included in this *tapu* sexual circle. That is why when we say that we are related to three-quarters of the villagers, it really means that we are related to three-quarters of the villagers. The transgressing of this sexual *tapu* is called *mataifale*, loosely translated "a stranger/visitor in the *fale* (home)." And if you commit *mataifale*, you have transgressed the circle of sexual *tapu*. When this happens, the common Tuvaluan judgment given is *koulua ko se kai I te kaitasi/mataniu* (you will not eat of your portion from the *fenua*).

Celebrate Sex

The text for this reflection provides another view of sex. Influenced with the culture of the day, coupled with religious convictions and theological reflections, we find a text that is an amalgamation of cultures and belief systems. From this fusion, we find the forging of a legalistic view of sex where the human body is subjected to the law, and anything that falls outside of those laws is immoral, unholy, and unclean. The sexual *tapu* space found in the text is limited to morality based on an individual choice. The violation of such sexual spaces, as provided by our text, often results in retributive justice. In this view justice is served only if the retribution satisfies the law, and not the healing of both victim and perpetrator.

Our Christian understanding of sex in Pasifika is driven by the conventional narrative where the human body is shamed and not celebrated.

---

7. One of the few theological engagements with the subject of sex in Pasifika is Havea and Havea, "Sex."

Today in Pasifika, we disdain the celebrating of our bodies; celebrating our bodies as sexual beings is lost to the Christian sexual concept of lust—thus the exhortation found in our reading this morning.

If you want to see what celebration is within the *tapu* space of sex in Pasifika, just listen to the love songs from Pasifika. They are decorated with stars and flowers, fishes and mountains, rivers and waves—the density of metaphors and the aesthetic of sex as *tapu* is celebrated in our love songs.

Fanua

But the issue remains, sexual violence in Pasifika is rising. And while we know that our sisters, mothers, and daughters are the victims, we must not forget that our brothers, fathers, and sons have also forgotten the *tapu* that flows in the relationships we have in our *fanua* (*fenua, vanua*).

The *tapu* of the *fanua*, which means both "land" and "womb," is sexual. The *tapu* of sex is the *tapu* of the *fanua*—and that is why we do not discuss them openly. Those who do not understand our ways and have a more open, straightforward approach to issues like sex find this problematic. But like our aspiration to find alternative developmental strategies and alternative climate change narratives with Pasifika ecological understandings, we should also aspire to the calling of our people to return to the *fanua*.

We need to recall our children to—so that they may again (k)new—the *fanua*. We have written extensively about the *fanua* being our mother,[8] the source of life for us Pasifika people, yet our people are so detached from it. The silence of sex as a topic in Pasifika spaces has now become one of shame and fear, rather than one of *tapu*.

The *tapu* of the *fanua* is the *tapu* of the womb, a *tapu* that is specifically given to mothers and is carried in the bodies of our sisters and daughters. That is why the sexual violation of a woman goes beyond the violated individual; it is the violation of the family, the community, and the *fanua*. Our violent and predatorial men have forgotten this *tapu*. They are living superficial lives based on what is available to satisfy their craving. There is no connection to the *fanua*, the womb from which we derive. Due to this disconnection, Pasifika patterns of life that connect no longer have any bearing or meaning to us.

The respect and honor we give to our mothers through cultural practices during pregnancy are done out of respect for life and *fanua*.[9] That is why the spaces of birth are forbidden to men. Men show up to these

---

8. Hoiore, "Maohi Perspective."
9. In the past, Pasifika islanders went to war due to the violation of sexual *tapu* spaces.

forbidden spaces only to provide sustenance for the midwives, the mother, and the new life embodied in the child. We have forgotten this cycle of life, where the spirituality that is embodied in the bodies of our mothers, sisters, and daughters no longer makes sense to us.

It is this respect for life, the energy and enthusiasm we give to life, that should prompt in us the need to retrieve *tapu* in sex spaces, and to return to the *fanua*. And this should be the same respect, the same energy we give to the protection of our mothers, sisters, and daughters from the fathers, brothers, and sons who have lost respect of the *fanua*, thus their violating of sacred bodies where life is nurtured, nursed, and safeguarded. What we need is not a retributive justice governed by the moralistic legalization of human bodies, mainly of women bodies, but a restorative justice that emanates from the respect we have for life—which in our (k)new Pasifika epistemologies is embodied in our mothers, sisters, and daughters.

LET'S TALK ABOUT SEX

Should we talk about sex in the church? Yes, we should! But we should speak about it in a *tapu* of *fanua* way; we should not speak of it as a moralistic legal issue like the one presented in our text, or in traditional interpretations of this text, because those, too, have oppressed our women, by creating Pasifika cultures that for instance make us require women to be fully covered from head to toe because that is the modest thing to do.

At the same time, we should call the church to the *fanua*, to the womb. The church cannot continue to operate in a form of Christianity that is separated from the *fanua*. An ecclesiastical operation based merely on theological arguments kept in church dogmas and creeds, and current cultural rationality, has no bearing on and for our people—and most especially if our energy lies in defending doctrines as truths, rather than in making them life affirming.

We should also call biblical texts to the *fanua* Pasifika if those texts are to be relevant to our current predicament. I strongly believe that we are not answerable to the Bible. But we, together with the Bible, are answerable to the *fanua*, where God lives and interacts with life. God instilled life in the *fanua*, and the *fanua* gave birth to us and our texts. The embodiment of that life is in our mothers, our sisters, and our daughters. We should therefore protect them with all our love, and life. "Protect" here is not about power, whether one is superior or inferior, but about a responsibility to life.

Last night my wife asked me, "Don't you think that you sound a bit off?" I said "Why?" She said, "I mean preaching about sex?" This is the problem we face when we privatize and individualize sex, buttressed by the doctrine of individual salvation in Christ. This is also the problem we find in the interpretation of 1 Thess 4:1–8 based on moralistic legality. Sex was a communal matter in Pasifika; it was not hidden; it is *tapu*. That is why we don't take our girlfriends to a fancy restaurant and go down on one knee and ask, "Will you marry me?" We go to the *fanua*, to communities with *kava* and *tabua*, shells, yams, and best produce of the land, we take the finest mats, the finest of *tapa*, both decorated with designs of life whose meanings are buried in our bodies and *fanua*, to seek approval for marriage. This is the respect we give the *fanua*, life, and women. These are not prices, nor are they dowries. This is life lived in respect within the *tapu* of sex in our *fanua* epistemologies. And we must retrieve that (k)new wisdom and look intently and intentionally into it to restore and heal our *fanua* Pasifika.

Well-Being

The well-being of Pasifika, the healing of *fanua* Pasifika also depends on our celebration of sex within the *tapu* of the *fanua*, the *tapu* of our mothers, our sisters, and our daughters. We cannot separate human well-being from the well-being of *fanua*, and the honoring of *fanua*. Honoring the *tapu* space of sex within the *fanua* heals not just a community of people, but the *fanua*—which is the embodiment of the whole of life.

BIBLIOGRAPHY

Fiji Times. "Father Allegedly Rapes Baby Girl." *Fiji Times*, Feb. 16, 2016. https://www.fijitimes.com/father-allegedly-rapes-baby-girl/.
Havea, Jione, and Diya Lakai Havea. "Sex: Suicide, Shame, Signals." In *Theologies from the Pacific*, edited by Jione Havea, 323–36. Postcolonialism and Religions. New York: Palgrave, 2021.
Hoiore, Céline. "A Maohi Perspective on Birth and Belonging." In *Weaving: Women Doing Theology in the Pacific*, edited by Lydia Johnson and Joan Alleluia Filemoni-Tofaeono, 43–48. Suva, Fiji: University of the South Pacific Press, 2003.
Meyer, Manulani A. "Indigenous Epistemology: Spirit Revealed." In *Enhancing Mātauranga Māori and Global Indigenous Knowledge*, 151–64. Wellington: NZQA, 2014.
Reece, Lena. "Mother of Teenage Daughter from Fiji Jailed 6 Years and 11 Months for Keeping Daughter as Sex Slave." *fijivillage*, Apr. 18, 2018. https://fijivillage.com/t/Mother-of-teenage-daughter-from-Fiji-jailed-6-years-and-11-months-for-keeping-daughter-as-sex-slave-2s9rk5.
Savike, Jessica. "Grandfather Pleads Not Guilty to Alleged Rape of Granddaughter." *Fiji Times*, Dec. 5, 2018. https://www.fijitimes.com/grandfather-pleads-not-guilty-for-alleged-rape-of-granddaughter/.

14

"I AM FEARFULLY AND WONDERFULLY MADE"[1]

Takatāpui (LGBTQ+), God's Call, and the Church's Dis-Ease with the Bedroom

Paul Reynolds

AT THE BEGINNING OF 2022 a friend shared with me a story of someone who I know who is *takatāpui*[2] and felt the call to be ordained in the Anglican Church of Aotearoa New Zealand and Polynesia—Te Haahi Mihinare. What troubled me about this story was that the potential ordinand was refused the possibility of ordination, not because of his sexuality but because he is in a loving same-sex relationship that was declared to the world in a civil marriage ceremony. The Anglican Church currently does not fully accept this as a covenantal, godly marriage, or in Anglican-speak, as a "right relationship."[3] This stance, I believe, not only is detrimental to the health and

---

1. Psalm 139:14.

2. *Takatāpui* is a Māori word, historically meaning "intimate companion of the same sex." The use of this term is recorded in the *Dictionary of Māori Language* compiled by missionary Herbert Williams in 1832 (https://takatapui.nz/definition-of-takatapui#takatapui-meaning). See the glossary at the end of the essay for the meaning of other Māori terms used in this essay.

3. A "right relationship" or a "rightly ordered relationship" is defined in the canons as someone who is chaste. However, the Anglican Church does not fully define what chaste means. Currently, a bishop may determine whether a civil marriage, which has

well-being of *takatāpui* who have felt the call to ordination, but also clearly illustrates an institution that does not fully understand how to be welcoming, inclusive, and Christian, nor are its actions *tika, pono,* and *aroha*.

For some time now, I have been thinking of writing an article about being *takatāpui* (LGBTQI+) and ordained in Te Haahi Mihinare. There is an obvious tension here because the church does not recognize same-sex marriage, restricts same-sex blessings in church, and places limits on the ordination of *takatāpui*. Despite this overt discrimination, some *takatāpui* remain in the church—an institution that does not fully accept them as loyal and faithful servants—with some feeling the compelling call from God and their community to be ordained.

I felt God's call and was obedient—both to God and to the people who discerned my faith and call to ordination. The Māori bishops who ordained me deacon and then priest were fully aware of my *takatāpui* sexuality, and yet still ordained me. However, where the church departs from the welcome of *takatāpui* ordinands is over the issue of "right relationship." It is apparent that the church allows individual bishops to determine what they consider is a "right relationship," with some bishops defining a "right relationship" as a married heterosexual couple only. Many, myself included, would challenge this interpretation of the church's canons and teaching and argue that civil marriage equally constitutes a declaration and state of "right relationship." Civil marriage is, I believe, a sacred covenantal relationship between two people who love one another and, if the couple are Christian, who also love God. In this regard, I believe that Te Haahi Mihinare deserves to be challenged by those whose lives have been impacted by the church's stance on sexuality. This response from the church to *takatāpui* illustrates dis-ease with what it constitutes as a sacred covenantal relationship.

The *kaupapa* for this chapter is the well-being of *takatāpui* who haven't already left our churches, and in particular their sense of welcome or not within our churches. A key question I ask is "What messages are we sending to the *takatāpui*/LGBTQI+ members of our church?" This chapter will focus on three key areas:

1. An indigenous call to servanthood.
2. What messages are we sending to *takatāpui*/LGBTQI+ seminary students being discerned for ordination?

---

been blessed by the church, may, or may not, be considered "rightly ordered" (Anglican Church, "Canons and Statutes," canon 1, title D, clause 25, "Chastity").

3. Pope Francis's statement: "If someone is gay and he searches for the Lord and has good will, who am I to judge?"[4]

AN INDIGENOUS CALL TO SERVANTHOOD

God chooses people to do his work.
(Dr. Rose Elu, Torres Strait Islander elder)[5]

Many people are called to serve. There are servants who would not consider themselves Christian, for whatever reason, yet they serve God by their very actions of serving others, by serving their neighbor. Often, these servants are serving the "down and out," the marginalized, the ostracized, the forgotten or silenced; those who may be invisible to some members of the church, yet are our neighbors.

For Māori and Indigenous peoples, faith and servanthood are part of the very fabric that is richly textured and woven together in a *kaitiaki* relationship with all our neighbors, including *whānau*, *hapū*, and *iwi*, as well as the integral relationship with *whenua*, *maunga*, *moana*, and *awa*; all of God's creation are our neighbors. Colgan et al. believe,

> There are deep resonances between biblical thought and practice and indigenous thought and practice. These resonances are particularly felt in a common perception of the sacred and inseparable connection between God, people, and Earth, which has been all but lost within many Western societies. . . . Without a connection to our traditional lands, the lands of our ancestors, our connection to God and to indigenous ways of being will simply cease to exist.[6]

Wirihana and Smith define this connection between God, people, and earth as strongly associated with well-being: "Māori well-being incorporated a complex holistic process which relied on whakapapa relationships and knowledge, connections to the environment (physical and natural), and an intrinsic spirituality."[7]

Underlying this relationship with God and all of creation then, are a number of key principles. There are four critical understandings of

---

4. McGregor, "Pope Francis," para. 3.

5. Rose Elu, interview with author, July 30, 2022. Dr. Elu is a member of the Anglican Indigenous Network Executive.

6. Colgan et al., "How Long," 18.

7. Wirihana and Smith, "Historical Trauma," 205.

servanthood and faith from a Māori, Oceanic, and Indigenous perspective that I would like to focus on in this section:

1. Faith is a lived experience.
2. People of faith must show respect for difference and hospitality toward the stranger.
3. Social justice is embedded in the practice of faith.
4. "God chooses people to do his work,"[8] and this is confirmed by community endorsement.

Inuit elder Colleen Swan believes that the values within the Bible, and therefore in Christianity, are those lived and practiced by Indigenous people: "If you study the Bible, what you find there is what we already practice."[9] Rev. Māori Marsden (Ngā Puhi), priest, healer, *tohunga*, philosopher, and theologian, explains the process of learning tribal life as an apprenticeship that occurs by existence in the cultural milieu.

> The integration of an individual into full membership of society takes place over a long period of time. Not in formal schooling, but in his living situation . . . the instilling of values, norms and attitudes is effected by the apprenticeship to tribal life, that is, by existence in the cultural milieu. Remembering that the cultural milieu is rooted both in the temporal world and the transcendent world, this brings a person into intimate relationship with the gods and his universe.[10]

Put simply, faith for Indigenous peoples is a lived experience. What then underpins this lived experience?

Indigenous values include generosity, hospitality, extending relationships, and respect for difference—all values that are embodied in being Christian, and which also encompass all it means to love our neighbor and God. Rev. Randy Woodley explains key values for Indigenous peoples that align perfectly with the values of Christianity:

> The qualities in Indigenous cultures are generosity, hospitality, extending relationships, respect for difference . . . not simply teachings: they are life values. Almost all Indigenous values

---

8. Rose Elu, interview with author, July 30, 2022.
9. Cited by Rose Elu.
10. Marsden, *Woven Universe*, 23.

align with the teaching of Jesus. Wouldn't it be wonderful if Christianity aligned itself with the teachings of Jesus?[11]

In terms of respect for difference, Bishop Steven Charleston outlines what hospitality means for Indigenous peoples, which aligns with the notion of always expecting the stranger and, whenever you encounter a stranger, ensuring that you offer an open welcome, that you *manaaki* the visitor/stranger.

> Hospitality assumes diversity. It expects the stranger. When the Hopi People, for example, first encountered the Spanish conquistadores, they were not shocked. Their reaction was not fearful because their prophecies, their spiritual way of life, taught them to expect strangers and most importantly, to welcome them.
>
> Europeans, on the other hand, were busily conquering peoples they had never imagined and could not understand. The history between the two spiritualities is tragic, but the lessons are there for all to see: the Native cultures were able to adapt to diversity. They did not have to kill what they could not comprehend. Instead, they could exercise patience, a forbearance that is remarkably advanced in its sophistication.[12]

Rev. Randy Woodley would recognize this hospitality and welcome it as a Christian response to the stranger in Matt 25:35, remembering also that Christ too was a stranger. As stranger, Christ was sometimes welcomed but not always (for example, John 1:11). There are many stories of Christ being treated with hostility, and ultimately ending with death on the cross. Indigenous people have also been the recipients of welcome by some, but with colonization, genocide ensued. This offering of hospitality is integral to the values that Indigenous people hold worldwide and is also interwoven into the lived experience—the praxis—of doing and living faith.

The praxis of faith for Indigenous people is also intimately woven with a rich and deep resonance of being just, of being *tika*, *pono*, and *aroha*. For Rountree and Reynolds, this is a calling, and in particular a remembering and memory of historic and intergenerational trauma through colonization, which is ongoing, requiring constant vigilance and challenge.

> Whenever we are challenged or attacked as a people, we come together to protect one another, we speak out about any injustice, and we take action to ensure the wellbeing of all whānau, hapū and iwi. This is what we are called to do. We must turn hate

---

11. MacMath, "Interview," para. 11.
12. Charleston, "Global Tribe," 25–26.

into wellbeing for all, and Māori and Indigenous people worldwide have practiced this walk of what it is to be Christian and a good neighbor since the inception of colonization. We are called to live out our lives as guided from scripture and our tūpuna to prioritize the focus on wellness for all. Our actions need to be tika, pono and aroha—this is what we are called to be and do.[13]

When God calls us to serve in the church, sometimes we may hear and know the call as something that strongly wells up within us and we have no control over it. Sometimes it is more like a gap which we know has not yet been fulfilled, but we are unsure how to articulate this knowing, or even what this means for us. Sometimes this God heart resides within us, and we do not yet recognize it ourselves, but others see that light of God's calling in us. However, this calling manifests within each of us, this calling is divine. Aunty Rose Elu says, "God chooses people to do his work."[14] This calling is also confirmed by many people who witness it and who support the call to ordination for one of their own. We are called by God, but we are also endorsed by our communities when they too discern this vocation.

For some, this call to serve in the church is sometimes felt to be too much of a responsibility. They may experience a personal sense of unworthiness or feel unprepared for such service. I will always remember the wisdom of a friend and mentor, a *kuia* within Te Haahi Mihinare who replied, when I was questioning God's call and harbored all of the above concerns, "If God calls you, you need to obey."[15] It is that simple. God and community choose ordinands. For Māori and Indigenous peoples worldwide, this divine calling is life-long in serving their community, however for others it is a specific calling to serve within the ministry and life of the church.

WHAT MESSAGES ARE WE SENDING TO LGBTQI+ SEMINARY STUDENTS BEING DISCERNED FOR ORDINATION?

The church has created its own "untruthfulness" in that takatāpui who inherently discern God's call to ordination find the need to conceal their "bedroom" activity to answer that call![16]

---

13. Rountree and Reynolds, *"Tuia I te here tangata!,"* 35.
14. Rose Elu, interview with author, July 30, 2022.
15. Whaea Wyn Ehau, conversation with author, 2016.
16. Anonymous *tikanga* Māori (someone who follows the Māori culture) priest and friend, email to author, Sept. 20, 2019.

The theme for the 1994 St. John's Theological College Selwyn Lecture was "Human Sexuality: Christian Perspectives." One of the four speakers for the Selwyn Lectures was Bishop Muru Walters, whose presentation was entitled "Kahui Tane: An Experience of Tane Sexuality." In the introduction to his published talk, Bishop Muru recalled an incident at the college in his first year as lecturer.

> I was surprised to hear spiritually filled, enlightened and academically able students denigrating, exposing, and humiliating three students who dared, either foolishly or bravely, to announce their different sexual orientations. Letters were dispatched to bishops to remove these sinful students from St. John's. At that time my wife and I offered these students support, hospitality, aroha, and the use of our home, provided they cared for our home, our two cats and our dog whenever we were away. To this day, these persons continue to be our trusted and loyal friends. Later, I heard that I was reported to the Warden for maintaining dishonorable relationships with homosexuals.[17]

In 2024, you may ask whether the situation for *takatāpui*/LGBTQI+ seminary students has improved. The simple answer is—not much. Although the Anglican Church in Aotearoa New Zealand and Polynesia finally approved same-sex blessings at the General Synod in 2018, after decades of painstaking deliberation and debate, there was still dissension within the church, with some choosing to fracture and form what I would call a "claytons"[18] version of what it is to be Anglican, largely influenced by an aggressively anti-LGBTQI+ group of Anglicans called GAFCON.[19] This "claytons" version of being an Anglican is enacted when anti-gay Christians race to seek an opt-out by setting up what is called "alternative episcopal

---

17. Walters, "Kahui Tane," 43.

18. *Claytons* is a slang term used in New Zealand and Australia that has a variety of meanings, including a compromise that satisfies no one, inferior substitute or low-quality imitation, or something essentially the same but referred to by a different name. The term derived from the name of a nonalcoholic beverage promoted in 1979 as "the drink you have when you're not having a drink."

19. "The Gafcon movement is a global family of authentic Anglicans standing together to retain and restore the Bible to the heart of the Anglican Communion. Our mission is to guard the unchanging, transforming Gospel of Jesus Christ and to proclaim Him to the world. We are founded on the Bible, bound together by the Jerusalem Statement and Declaration of 2008, and led by a Primates Council, which represents the majority of the world's Anglicans. Gafcon works to guard and proclaim the unchanging, transforming Gospel through biblically faithful preaching and teaching which frees our churches to make disciples by clear and certain witness to Jesus Christ in all the world" (https://www.gafcon.org/about).

oversight" if their bishop decides to support gay marriage. This fracturing of the church has occurred in Aotearoa New Zealand, with a splinter group of Anglicans in Christchurch, for example, establishing their own bishop and diocese, forming the Church of Confessing Anglicans Aotearoa New Zealand.[20] I wonder if this group has thought about the real impacts of their actions on LGBTQI+ members of the Anglican Church—the hurt they have caused and the violence they have inflicted on others. I wonder if they have even considered the impacts on their own *whānau* if one of their *whānau* members happens to be LGBTQI+. This determination to fracture the church shows that the dogma of a few has the very real potential to derail and destabilize the Anglican Church worldwide.

Anglican Church Exclusion through the Canons

Unbeknownst to some within Te Haahi Mihinare (it seems), *takatāpui/* LGBTQI+ students do attend our seminaries and are called to ordination, yet they are rendered invisible within our wider church. Key decisions in New Zealand that affect what I would call the "welcome" that is extended to *takatāpui/*LGBTQI+ members in the Anglican Church, and our *takatāpui/* LGBTQI+ seminary students, include:

1. In 2013, same-sex marriage through a civil ceremony was legalized in New Zealand. This was after the decriminalization of homosexuality in New Zealand with the passing of the Homosexual Law Reform Act in 1986.

2. Prior to 2018, the Anglican Church in Aotearoa New Zealand and Polynesia did not recognize same-sex civil marriage. In 2018 the church compromised with the anti-LGBTQI+ Anglican sect to approve same-sex blessings in an Anglican Church, so long as the couple had been married in a civil ceremony first. According to the canons, the church sanctioned a blessing not a marriage.

3. In terms of ordination to the holy orders of diaconate or priest, any person being considered and discerned for ordination must be living in a "right relationship." The Anglican Church has outlined what it considers a "right relationship": "Chastity is the right ordering of sexual relationships. Ministers are to be chaste. Promiscuity and adultery are incompatible with chastity."[21]

---

20. See https://confessinganglicans.nz/documents/.
21. Anglican Church, "Canons and Statutes," canon 1, title D, clause 25, "Chastity."

4. According to Rev. Richard Bonifant, because the "right ordering of sexual relationships" is not defined by the Anglican Church anywhere currently, bishops within the province may determine that a same-sex blessing is a "rightly ordered relationship." A same-sex blessing of someone who has had a civil marriage is therefore the mechanism that can be used within the church in order to meet the threshold of a "right ordered sexual relationship."[22]

5. Furthermore, "any authorising Bishop, or any person using such a service once it has been authorised, will not be subject to any process of investigation or discipline under Title D Canon I or Title D Canon II."[23]

6. Similarly, "any Bishop who does not authorise a service pursuant to clause 8, or any Ordained Minister who refuses to use such a service once it has been authorised, will not be subject to any process of investigation or discipline under Title D Canon I or Title D Canon II."[24]

Let us break this down as to what this indicates to *takatāpui*/LGBTQI+ members within the Anglican Church:

1. A same-sex blessing may be approved by the Anglican Church only if two key requirements are fulfilled. Namely, that the couple must have been civilly married first, then that a bishop is willing for a blessing to happen within their *amorangi* or diocese.

2. *Takatāpui*/LGBTQI+ same-sex (civil) marriage is not specifically sanctioned as marriage by the Anglican Church.

3. A *takatāpui*/LGBTQI+ member of any Anglican parish, *amorangi* or diocese, may be considered and discerned for ordination. However, as the canons currently stand, in order to meet the conditions for ordination, they must be in a "right relationship," or be celibate. This same standard applies to heterosexuals as well.

4. As the canons currently stand, a bishop *may* choose to allow a same-sex blessing of a *takatāpui* couple who have had a civil marriage. Equally, they *may* choose not to allow a same-sex blessing to take place within their *amorangi* or diocese.

5. Further, a bishop *may* choose to approve the ordination of a *takatāpui* ordinand who is in a civil relationship, and who has had a same-sex

---

22. Richard Bonifant, conversation with author, Dec. 8, 2022. Rev. Bonifant was a Tikanga Pākehā representative at General Synod in 2018 where the same-sex blessings wording in the canons was debated and then approved.

23. Anglican Church, "Canons and Statutes," canon 14, title G, clause 13.

24. Anglican Church, "Canons and Statutes," canon 14, title G, clause 14.

blessing in the church, considering the same-sex blessing as a "rightly ordered relationship."

6. However, a bishop *may* equally choose not to approve the ordination of a *takatāpui* ordinand who is in a civil relationship, even if a same-sex blessing has occurred, because they personally do not consider a same-sex blessing as a "rightly ordered relationship."

7. The canons therefore are highly ambiguous and are interpreted at the whim of the bishop.

Takatāpui who are in a loving, same-sex relationship and have had a civil marriage, are not considered to be in a "right ordering of sexual relationships" by some bishops in the Anglican Church in Aotearoa New Zealand and Polynesia. For some *takatāpui*, this meant that they have no choice but to hide their relationship if they feel that they have been called to be ordained, or they have chosen to remain celibate in their relationship in order to comply with the church canons as interpreted by their bishop. For some, they have decided, in order to follow their calling, to change their *tikanga*, or change their *amorangi* or diocese, to be able to move within the jurisdiction of a bishop who interprets the canons with an inclusive and loving lens.

As a current faculty member of St. John's Theological College, I have had students come to me worried about their call to ordination because they have seen the negative reaction to the *takatāpui*/LGBTQI+ community from within the Anglican Church nationally and internationally, with some bishops, clergy, and lay people constantly challenging and attacking the church when it attempts to be inclusive of everyone, including *takatāpui*/LGBTQI+ members and clergy. Significantly, in 2022 the archbishop of Canterbury welcomed *takatāpui*/LGBTQI+ bishops to the Lambeth Conference in the United Kingdom, but he did not extend the welcome to their partners. All other (heterosexual) bishops' partners were able to attend. Some of the bishops who are members of GAFCON decided to boycott the Lambeth Conference because of what they seem to consider as the church's perverse welcome of *takatāpui*/LGBTQI+ bishops. That is, they could not sit at the same table, including the communion table, with their brother and sister bishops because of their differing sexualities. GAFCON presents itself as an alternative and more "authentic" Anglican voice and community than the rest of the Anglican Communion.

These so-called Christians repeatedly ignore the inclusive message of the Gospels to willfully misinterpret a select few passages of Scripture in their attempts to justify their violent stance toward the *takatāpui*/LGBTQI+ community. I do not intend to refute their interpretation of these texts here as many biblical scholars and theologians have done so more than adequately.[25]

What I want to highlight is that this vehemence and violence has consequences; for our church, for our communities, for how the church and Christians are perceived, for how we, as Christians, show welcome—or not, and not least for the direct impact on the health and well-being of *takatāpui/* LGBTQI+ Christians, including those in our seminaries. This vehemence and violence will further fracture the already diminishing relevance of the Anglican Church to wider society internationally, and to those who are steadfastly hanging on to the belief of Christian love within our churches.

Takatāpui/LGBTQI+ Community Health and Well-Being

Analysis of the results of national and international (secular and Christian) surveys of LGBTQI+ communities highlight some disturbing trends, which churches need to be cognizant of when considering how welcoming and inclusive they are.

In 2018 a survey entitled "Faith and Belief in New Zealand" was funded by the Wilberforce Foundation to identify views on Christianity in New Zealand.[26] The survey highlighted some significant problems that Christian churches need to address. A significant finding was that many New Zealanders view Christians as hypocrites—Christians preach about loving one's neighbor, yet many behave in a completely opposite way. This perception was partly influenced by the incidence of church-based abuse reported in the media. Another key factor influencing the negative perception of the church is the church's teaching on homosexuality. From these two indicators alone, it is clear that the general perception of Christianity within New Zealand is poor. Churches need to address this negative perception urgently, not by employing PR consultants—but by actually being Christian.

In 2019, the first health survey of transgender and nonbinary people in New Zealand, "Counting Ourselves," was conducted. Key findings identified in this survey were:

- Transgender and nonbinary people have higher risk of experiencing sexual violence—one-third had experienced nonconsensual sex since the age of thirteen.

- Seventy-one percent of transgender and nonbinary people aged fifteen and over had high or very high psychological distress.

25. See, for example, Brueggemann, "How to Read Bible."
26. McCrindle, *Faith and Belief.*

- Fifty-six percent of transgender and nonbinary people had seriously considered suicide in the last twelve months, and 12 percent had attempted suicide in the last twelve months.

- Sixty-seven percent of transgender and nonbinary people had experienced discrimination at some point, and 44 percent had experienced discrimination in the last twelve months.[27]

These findings are of concern to all New Zealanders. The authors state, "Our findings illustrate the stark contrast and health inequities between trans and non-binary people and the general population, especially in the areas of mental health and wellbeing, including the very high rates of psychological distress and suicide attempts within our communities."[28]

As Te Haahi Mihinare, we need to consider how our churches make transgender and nonbinary people feel welcome.

The "2021 Safeguarding LGBT+ Christians Survey," which surveyed the safety of LGBTQ+ Christians attending church in the United Kingdom, has significant implications for the church going forward. The findings from this report are disturbing and should make churches examine how they show hospitality to regular congregants, let alone how they welcome strangers. Approximately 60 percent of the 754 respondents who regularly attend church are affiliated with the Church of England. Two of the key findings from the report are that:

- Only one third of respondents felt safe to be out and to be themselves as LGBTQ+ in their local church, while lesbians, bisexuals, trans- and nonbinary Christians felt less safe in church.

- The attitudes of church leaders have a significant impact on whether LGBTQ+ people feel safe in their church. Examples include a church leader's stance on conversion therapy,[29] whether they use inclusive language, and sermons that indicate inclusiveness and welcome.[30]

Dr. Sarah Carr, independent research monitor for the UK survey, states:

> Whilst faith and belief can have known positive benefits for many people's mental health, it can sadly have the opposite

---

27. See Veale et al., *Counting Ourselves*.

28. Veale et al., *Counting Ourselves*, 113.

29. Conversion therapy is predicated on the belief that a person's sexual orientation and gender identity can and should be changed and the unscientific view that LGBTQ+ people, and other diverse people, are sick and should be "cured." See Ozanne Foundation, "Gender Identity 'Conversion Therapy.'"

30. Ozanne Foundation, "Safeguarding LGBT+ Christians Survey."

effect on LGBT+ people given that so many have experienced exclusion or judgement by various faith communities. This survey evidences this, with over two thirds of LGBT+ Christian respondents clearly indicating that they don't always feel safe to be themselves in their place of worship.[31]

A key finding from a 2022 Aotearoa New Zealand survey of LGBTQ-IA+ young people similarly highlighted the importance of safe communities in overall well-being, with participants feeling unsafe in schools and universities, and for some in their living situations or communities, as well as two-thirds of participants having thought about committing suicide in the last twelve months.[32]

I believe it is imperative, indeed critical, to gather quantitative data through a national survey of LGBTQI+ Christians in the Anglican Church in Aotearoa New Zealand and Polynesia, to gauge how welcome and safe people feel in our churches and in our Aotearoa/Polynesian Christian context. There are enough "red flag" indicators, as evidenced in the above surveys of well-being, as well as in the current deliberation of the Royal Commission of Inquiry into abuse in state care and the care of faith-based organizations in Aotearoa New Zealand,[33] that highlight the need for investigating how welcoming, how loving, and how Christian we purport to be. Sadly, it takes quantitative evidence to make a case for any kind of response from the church, or a legal case that calls the church to account for not providing a safe environment.

Using Scripture as a Weapon

Many *takatāpui*/LGBTQI+ Christians have already left the church. However, those who remain are watching to see how the church's leaders and members respond to questions about whether they accept *takatāpui*/LGBTQI+ people in Te Haahi Mihinare, and whether they accept *takatāpui*/LGBTQI+ people, particularly those with partners, for ordination.

In the past few years there have been repeated attacks on the *takatāpui*/LGBTQI+ community in Aotearoa and Australia by high profile "Christians" who use scripture to justify homophobia and exclusion. Rugby league player Israel Folau sent out a message on social media in 2018 saying that all homosexuals will go to hell as they are sinners, and Destiny Church leader

---

31. Ozanne Foundation, "Safeguarding LGBT+ Christians Survey," iii.
32. *1 News*, "64%."
33. See https://www.abuseincare.org.nz.

Brian Tamaki blamed the 2011 Christchurch earthquakes on gays, sinners, and murderers in a sermon. Both based their personal opinions on the same old biblical texts that are repeatedly dragged out to batter the *takatāpui/* LGBTQI+ community. As well as the fallout nationally and internationally about these illogical, hysterical, and un-Christian condemnations of the *takatāpui*/LGBTQI+ community, this sends a strong message to anyone who is *takatāpui*/LGBTQI+ and is a Christian, that they are worthless. If the leadership within the different Christian denominations do not stand up and challenge this un-Christian message, this sends an even more powerful message to those who are already feeling marginalized and ostracized. Harriet Winn sums this up well, declaring:

> Silence from churches whenever a public figure uses their faith to justify homophobia has a tangible impact. It breeds institutional complacency which causes queer people to leave the pews, and vulnerable young people to doubt their self worth.[34]

GAFCON and anti-LGBTQI+ Christians, while keen to proclaim the injunction to love one's neighbor, in fact utilize scripture as a violent tool of oppression. Biblical scholar Walter Brueggemann critiques this selective cherry-picking of scripture to support prejudice. Brueggemann advocates instead the "emancipatory work'" of biblical interpretation.

> The reason the Bible seems to speak "in one voice" concerning matters that pertain to LGBTQ persons is that the loud voices most often cite only one set of texts, to the determined disregard of the texts that offer a counter-position. But our serious reading does not allow such a disregard, so that we must have all of the texts in our purview.[35]

For Rae and Redding, who are the editors of a collection of articles written on the theological considerations concerning the ordination of practicing homosexuals, these types of attacks utilize unsound theological thinking.

> In some quarters of the Church the debate about the ordination of homosexuals has been reduced to sloganeering: "Scripture is clear. . ."; "The Gospel is inclusive. . ."; "This is the way God made me. . ." These frequently heard refrains do little to advance the debate and often indicate a paucity of sound theological thinking.[36]

34. Winn, "Church Must Renounce," para. 14.
35. Brueggemann, "How to Read Bible," para. 31.
36. Rae and Redding, *More Than Single Issue*, v.

Rev. Randy Woodley similarly explains his concerns with this "post-Enlightenment" interpretation of the Bible.

> Jesus, and the writers of scripture most likely, were not Enlightenment-bound people. They never meant for their words to be interpreted in the way Christianity has served them up. These people in scripture were storytellers, much like our Indigenous peoples.[37]

Yet the majority of *takatāpui*/LGBTQI+ members are often invisible and silent in the congregation, and some feel as if they are given little choice but to leave the church because they have observed that they are not welcome. Those who have not yet left include LGBTQI+ seminary students who also observe this vociferous and ongoing attack of who they are, which obviously impacts on their very being, as *takatāpui*/LGBTQI+ Christians. Anglican Priest, Rev. Canon Paul Oestreicher poignantly sums this up, saying, "There are many gay and lesbian followers of Jesus—ordained and lay—who, despite the church, remarkably and humbly remain its faithful members. Would the Christian churches in their many guises more openly accept, embrace and love them, there would be many more disciples."[38]

WHO AM I TO JUDGE?

If someone is gay and he searches for the Lord and has good will, who am I to judge?—Pope Francis[39]

We have to call the church out on their stink "colonial" boxing of God's love and mission in/to the world.[40]

Pope Francis as the head of the worldwide Roman Catholic Church in this well-known statement, "Who am I to judge?," sends a strong message to the world. The pope's personal advocacy for the *takatāpui*/LGBTQI+ community is an advocacy for the love of all. This is also apparent in a response to Jesuit Father James Martin's letter to Pope Francis asking,

> "What do you say to an LGBT Catholic who has experienced rejection from the church?" The Pope replied, "I would have

---

37. MacMath, "Interview," para. 9.
38. Oestreicher, "Was Jesus Gay," para. 9.
39. McGregor, "Pope Francis," para. 3.
40. Anonymous *tikanga* Māori priest and friend, email to author, Sept. 20, 2019.

them recognize it not as 'the rejection of the church,' but instead of 'people in the church.'"[41]

The bishop of Oxford, the Rt. Revd. Dr. Steven Croft, is currently the highest-ranking Church of England leader who has spoken out supporting same-sex marriage, saying that the Anglican Church's LGBTQI+ position "is leading to a radical dislocation between the Church of England and the culture and society we are attempting to serve."[42]

The response to the *takatāpui*/LGBTQI+ community is unfortunately the next litmus test of the welcome and acceptance of diversity within Christian churches worldwide. There have been many more before, including the place of Indigenous expressions of faith and Indigenous clergy, the place of divorcees, women priests, women bishops, and LGBTQI+ priests and bishops. I acknowledge that not all of these differences are met with universal acceptance in Christian churches, yet they have been moments where the institution of the church has had to deeply think, debate, discern, and interpret God's word.

This is a time for the church to think, debate, discern and interpret God's word again. This discernment has implications for the *takatāpui*/LGBTQI+ community who remain faithful to God's call. Many have already left the church, and have been severely traumatized spiritually, mentally, and physically by the church's stance on LGBTQI+ people. Some who remain in the church have stayed because of the support of their bishop and *amorangi*/ diocese; others have stayed but remain invisible. Some have stayed and decided to abstain from sex if in a civil partnership, and some have stayed and kept their sexuality and relationship transparent and authentic. Others have kept it secret in order to continue to serve. For LGBTQI+ Christians who are still loyal to the church, there are multiple micro and macro-aggressions, which are daily stressors, and this stress is deeply wounding. Coming from a Catholic perspective, Father James Martin, in his book *Building a Bridge: How the Catholic Church and the LGBT Community Can Enter into a Relationship of Respect, Compassion, and Sensitivity* is clear about what needs to happen, stating:

> The institutional church bears the main responsibility for the ministry of dialogue and reconciliation, because it is the institutional church that has made LGBT Catholics feel marginalized, not the other way around . . . it is the clergy and other church officials who bear responsibility.[43]

41. White, "Pope Francis.," para. 6.
42. Handley, "Bishop of Oxford," para. 2.
43. Martin, *Building a Bridge*, 3.

This is the case for Anglicans also. So, what do Christian church leaders need to do?

- Ask "What would it mean to be a hospitable church?" Because it isn't now. A hospitable church is a Christian church.
- Church leaders need to stand up to hate! Hate comes from both outside of the church and within the church.
- When LGBTQI+ people are attacked publicly using Scripture as a violent tool, our church leadership needs to stand up. If they do not, people either leave the church or stay and hide and feel worthless and disempowered.
- Church leaders are complicit in this violence if they do not say something about this hate speech and behavior when it occurs, especially within the church.
- Church leaders need to consciously work on being inclusive in all that they do and say, and to utilize inclusive language that advocates welcome to all.
- Church leaders need to initiate a survey in Aotearoa New Zealand to gauge the welcome and safety for LGBTQI+ people within our churches, then act decisively on implementing the recommendations for change.
- A same-sex, blessed civil marriage needs to be clearly and explicitly recognized as a "rightly ordered relationship" by the Anglican Church in Aotearoa New Zealand and Polynesia. Legally, civil marriage is recognized by New Zealand law and the government as a solemn covenantal relationship between two people.

POU

I conclude with five Christian *pou*, each able to stand alone in how they can be interpreted, and also able to stand together as a proclamation and a challenge to Te Haahi Mihinare, as well as to sister/fellow churches and faith communities:

1. We are all "fearfully and wonderfully made," as God made us (Ps 139)!
2. For Māori, Oceanic, and Indigenous people, there is a divine calling from birth to serve all in our communities. For some, there is an even more specific calling to serve within the ministry and life of the church.

3. When we are called to be ordained, we are discerned by God, and by many.
4. *Takatāpui*/LGBTQI+ people who remain in the church are obedient to God's call.
5. Christianity, including Te Haahi Mihinare, is called to align itself with the teachings of Jesus.[44]

I started this chapter with a story of someone whom I know who is *takatāpui* and who was called to be ordained in Te Haahi Mihinare. This deeply God-filled person has decided to transition to another *tikanga* in order to be able to fulfil his divine calling to be a servant in God's house, with a bishop who deems a same-sex blessing as a "rightly ordered relationship." Thus far the churches' response to *takatāpui* who believe they have been called to ordination has been unsatisfactorily ambiguous, and the vitriolic attacks on the *takatāpui*/LGBTQI+ community that have been allowed within the Anglican Church worldwide have been unwelcoming, unloving, and violent. I cannot see how this behavior is Christian. Our role as servants of God is simple: "We are called to live out our lives as guided from scripture and our tūpuna to prioritize the focus on wellness for all. Our actions need to be tika, pono and aroha—this is what we are called to be and do."[45]

> As human beings we all long for relationship and intimacy—communion with each other. As Christians we also seek relationship with God in Christ. May we enter that journey together, fully aware that when we talk about our sexuality, we speak of God's gift.[46]

---

44. MacMath, "Interview."
45. Rountree and Reynolds, "*Tuia I te here tangata!*," 35.
46. Coles, "Sexuality and Christianity," 24.

GLOSSARY

Amorangi	diocese
Aotearoa	New Zealand, translated as "land of the long white cloud"
Aroha	love
Awa	river
Hapū	subtribe
Iwi	tribe/clan
Kāhui	group
Kaitiaki	carer, guardian, protector
Kaupapa	topic, issue, purpose
Kuia	elder female
Manaaki	make welcome, hospitality, care, support
Maunga	mountain
Moana	sea
Ngā Puhi	tribal area in the far north of the North Island of New Zealand
Pono	true, truth
Pononga	servant/servanthood
Takatāpui	LGBTQI+, historically meaning "intimate companion of the same sex"
Tane	male
Te Haahi Mihinare	Anglican Church
Tika	correct, right
Tohunga	expert practitioner—healer, priest, carver, navigator
Whakapapa	genealogy/family tree
Whānau	family, including extended
whenua	land

BIBLIOGRAPHY

1 News. "64% of NZ's Rainbow Community Have Thought about Suicide—Survey." 1 News, Dec. 8, 2022. https://www.1news.co.nz/2022/12/08/64-of-nzs-rainbow-community-have-thought-about-suicide-survey/.

Anglican Church in Aotearoa, New Zealand and Polynesia. "Canons and Statutes." Anglican Church in Aotearoa, New Zealand and Polynesia, 2008; last updated 2022. https://www.anglican.org.nz/Resources/Canons.

Brueggemann, Walter. "Walter Brueggemann: How to Read the Bible on Homosexuality." Outreach, Sept. 4, 2022. https://outreach.faith/2022/09/walter-brueggemann-how-to-read-the-bible-on-homosexuality/.

Charleston, Steven. "The Global Tribe: Community in the 21st Century." *First Peoples Theology Journal* 4 (2006) 23–29.

Coles, David. "Sexuality and Christianity in a Changing World." In *Human Sexuality: Christian Perspectives*, edited by Janet Crawford, 5–26. 1994 Selwyn Lectures. Auckland: College of St. John the Evangelist Press, 1996.

Colgan, Emily, et al. "How Long Will the Earth Mourn? Environmental Racism and Its Impact on Indigenous Communities." Presentation at Lambeth Conference, July 26–Aug. 23, 2022, Canterbury Cathedral, Kent.

Handley, Paul. "Bishop of Oxford Calls for an End to Ban on Same-Sex Marriage in Church of England." *Church Times*, Nov. 3, 2022. https://www.churchtimes.co.uk/articles/2022/4-november/news/uk/bishop-of-oxford-calls-for-an-end-to-ban-on-same-sex-marriage-in-church-of-england.

Lima, Luís Corrêa, SJ. "Five centuries after St. Ignatius Loyola's Conversion, Catholics Are Called to Embrace LGBTQ People." Outreach, Nov. 4, 2022. https://outreach.faith/2022/11/five-centuries-after-st-ignatius-loyolas-conversion-catholics-are-called-to-embrace-lgbtq-people/.

MacMath, Terence Handley. "Interview: Randy Woodley, Indigenous Theologian and Farmer." *Church Times*, Aug. 22, 2022. https://www.churchtimes.co.uk/articles/2022/26-august/features/interviews/interview-randy-woodley-indigenous-theologian-and-farmer.

Marsden, Maori. *The Woven Universe: Selected Writings of Rev Maori Marsden*. Edited by Charles Royal. Otaki, NZ: Estate of Rev Maori Marsden, 2003.

Martin, James. *Building a Bridge: How the Catholic Church and the LGBT Community Can Enter into a Relationship of Respect, Compassion, and Sensitivity*. New York: HarperOne, 2018.

McCrindle, Mark. *Faith and Belief in New Zealand*. NZ Faith and Belief Study, May 2018. https://nzfaithandbeliefstudy.files.wordpress.com/2018/05/faith-and-belief-full-report-may-2018.pdf.

McGregor, Gena. "Pope Francis and the Power of Five Words." *Washington Post*, July 29, 2013. https://www.washingtonpost.com/news/on-leadership/wp/2013/07/29/pope-francis-and-the-power-of-five-words/.

Oestreicher, Paul. "Was Jesus Gay? Probably." *Guardian*, Apr. 20, 2012. https://www.theguardian.com/commentisfree/belief/2012/apr/20/was-jesus-gay-probably.

Ozanne Foundation. "Gender Identity 'Conversion Therapy.'" Ozanne Foundation, n.d. https://ozanne.foundation/project/gender-identity-conversion-therapy/.

———. "Safeguarding LGBT+ Christians Survey." Ozanne Foundation, Oct. 10, 2021). https://ozanne.foundation/safeguarding-uk-lgbt-christians-survey/.

Rae, Murray A., and Graham Redding, eds. *More Than a Single Issue: Theological Considerations Concerning the Ordination of Practising Homosexuals*. ATF Series 3. Adelaide: Open, 2000.

Rountree, Te Aroha, and Paul Reynolds. "*Tuia I te here tangata! Tuia I te muka tangata!* Indigenous Maori Wisdoms for the 21st Century." *Anglican Journal of Theology in Aotearoa and Oceania* 1 (2022) 26–41.

Veale, Jaimie, et al. *Counting Ourselves: The Health and Wellbeing of Trans and Non-Binary People in Aotearoa New Zealand*. Hamilton, NZ: Transgender Health Research Lab, 2019. https://researchcommons.waikato.ac.nz/handle/10289/12942.

Walters, Muru. "Kahui Tane: An Experience of Tane Sexuality." In *Human Sexuality: Christian Perspectives*, edited by Janet Crawford, 43–59. 1994 Selwyn Lectures. Auckland: College of St. John the Evangelist Press, 1996.

White, Christopher. "Pope Francis on Gay Catholics: God 'Does Not Disown Any of His Children.'" *National Catholic Reporter*, May 9, 2022. https://www.ncronline.org/news/vatican/pope-francis-gay-catholics-god-does-not-disown-any-his-children.

Winn, Harriet. "Church Must Renounce Biblical-Based Homophobia." University of Auckland, May 31, 2019. https://www.auckland.ac.nz/en/news/2019/05/31/church-must-renounce-biblical-based-homophobia.html.

Wirihana, Rebecca, and Cherryl Smith. "Historical Trauma, Healing and Well-being in Maori Communities." *MAI Journal* 3 (2014) 197–210.

INDEX

abundance, 1, 138
abuse, 13, 44, 89, 102, 103, 180, 182
adoption, 10, 121, 129, 130
ancestor(s), 33, 38, 39, 117, 122, 156, 157, 159, 161, 162, 163
Anthropocene, 27, 29, 54
artwork, 3, 12, 147, 148, 155, 159–63

belonging, 7, 9, 11, 33, 37, 38, 73, 23, 128, 163
betrayal, 10, 113, 114, 116
biodiversity, 7, 28, 36, 53, 54
blackness, 38
body, x, 1, 2, 6, 12, 17, 19, 21, 25, 29, 31, 50, 115, 131, 139, 148, 156, 164, 166

Canaanite woman, 133–43
canoe, 37, 109, 111
capital(ism, ist), 49, 54, 56, 57, 100
clericalism, 98
climate change, 7, 8, 27, 28, 35, 36, 41, 42, 44, 46–51, 53–67, 100, 167
colonialism, 111, 118
colonization, 33, 97, 98, 99, 100, 102–6, 118, 122, 174, 175
conspiracy theories, 74, 77, 84
consumerism, 49
coronavirus, 23
covenant(al), x, 126, 127, 170, 171
COVID, 4, 7, 9, 22, 23, 74, 75, 78, 79, 117, 118
creation, 9, 28, 35, 38, 45, 47–50, 74, 96, 97, 98, 99, 100, 106, 125, 149, 150, 161, 172
cultural diversity, 105

dance, 23, 59, 149
daughter(s), ix, x, xi, 3, 27, 110, 111, 139, 141, 142, 167, 168, 169
deflection, 133–43
delusional religiosity, 7, 9, 73–93
dialogue, 29, 61–62, 66, 81, 87, 90, 135, 185
discrimination, 44, 50, 89, 92, 93, 102, 103, 106, 131, 181
disease(s), 2, 21, 28, 42, 53, 97, 111
disharmony, 11
distress, 78, 81, 82, 83, 85, 86, 155, 180, 181
diversity, 36, 80, 82, 105, 157, 174, 185
domination, 12, 75, 98, 104, 105, 150

ecotheology, 7, 27, 34
election theology, 120, 121, 126
embarrassing, 9, 11, 133, 136, 138, 142
embody, 166
emissions, 46, 49, 54
eroticism, 108, 113
eternity, 31, 32
exile, ix, 125, 154

faith seeking understanding, 28
fanua, 12, 122, 134, 164, 167–69. See also fenua, vanua.
fear(ful), 18, 46, 60, 74, 78, 82, 85, 88, 89, 110, 111, 152, 167, 174
fenua, 166, 167. See also *fanua*, vanua
firstborn, 10, 119, 120, 128, 129
fluid(ity), 2, 28, 33, 38, 149
food, 36, 42, 44, 55, 139, 151
freedom(s), 88, 92, 150, 159, 162
fundamentalism, 84, 90, 91

garden, 9, 10, 112, 113, 114, 115, 116
genealogy, ix, 11, 123, 126, 147, 148, 161, 188
generosity, 33, 38, 173
genocide, 33, 140, 174
granddaughter, 109, 110
greed, 47, 97, 100, 101, 103, 104, 105, 118
greeting, 109, 111, 116
groundedness, 7, 30, 31
guilt, 50, 83, 88, 89
gun, 28

harmony, 42, 87, 104, 136, 137, 143
have nots, 104
healing, 31, 74, 78, 100, 152, 166, 169
heritage, ix, 38, 43, 57, 101, 148, 154, 162
holiness, 149, 156
homophobia, 182, 183
hospitality, 45, 173, 174, 176, 181, 188
household, 42, 50, 130, 153

imago Dei, 101, 149, 150, 157
immorality, 164
impure, 164
injustice, 37, 44, 47, 48, 49, 103, 104, 105, 174
innocent, 48, 125
intellectual archaeology, 29
intersectional(ity), 2, 12, 147, 157
intimacy, 108, 114, 187
isolation, 77, 84, 85, 88

justice, 39, 47, 48, 49, 50, 58, 102, 106, 121, 137, 166, 168, 173

kiss(ing), 9, 10, 108, 112, 114–16
language loss, 104, 105

lagi, 110, 117. See also *rangi*, sky
Last Kai, 3, 4
Last Supper, 3, 4, 113
LGBTQ+. See *takatāpui*
lifestyle(s), 1, 42, 44, 82, 89, 120
lockdown, 74, 79
lost coin, 32
lotu, 9, 74, 75, 76, 77

love, 23, 26, 34, 104, 108, 109, 112, 113, 114, 115, 117, 142, 157, 167, 168, 171, 173, 180, 183, 184, 188
lust, 164, 167

maidservant, 120, 129
mana, 5, 9, 13, 125, 157
maneaba, 7, 8, 44, 45
margin(s), 56, 140, 141
marginalization, 84
marginalized, 103, 104, 105, 172, 183, 185
marriage, 169, 170, 171, 177, 178, 179, 185, 186
masks, 4
massacre(s), 28, 75
media, 74, 84, 93, 147, 180, 182
memory, 12, 109, 159, 160, 161, 162, 174
mercy, 139, 140, 141, 150, 152
migration, 43, 44
miracles, 78, 152
mission, 31, 38, 50, 78, 79, 82, 83, 92, 102, 184
Moana, ix, x, 10, 12, 30, 34, 38, 75, 114, 117, 119, 120, 121, 122, 130, 148, 149, 155, 161, 172, 188. See also sea.
money, 42, 44, 89, 96, 97, 129
multiethnic women, 11, 147, 157
multiple ethnicities, 11, 147, 148

native, 1, 2, 5, 6, 7, 10, 117, 118, 122, 127, 128, 174
neighbor(s), 7, 8, 9, 37, 98, 99, 104, 172, 173, 175, 180, 183
neocolonialism, 122
nonbinary, 180, 181
nuclear testing, 99

oikos, 32, 33, 36
oppression, 102, 106, 183
ordain(ed), 12, 102, 103, 170, 171, 178, 179, 184, 187
ordination, 170, 171, 175, 177, 178, 179, 183, 187

pagans, 164
pandemic, 4, 9, 23, 74, 75, 111

Passover, 112, 113
peace, 21, 48, 58, 81, 136
pedagogy, 56, 57, 59, 60, 62, 66
plastic rubbish, 99
poison(ed), 28, 75
poor, 50, 97, 98, 100, 103, 137, 180
postcolonial(ism), 34, 104, 105, 121
powerless, 48, 97
practical theology, 19, 20, 148
praise, 50, 135, 136, 140, 141
praxis, 36, 174
prejudice, 87, 183
presence of God, 7, 18
pride, 97, 103, 104, 105
promise, 120, 127, 142
prosperity, 1, 49, 117
pulotu, 161. See also underworld.

racism, 36, 44, 98, 106, 131
rangi, 161. See also lagi, sky.
reciprocity, 32, 37, 57, 65, 137
reconciliation, 32, 136, 185
redemption, 32, 136
rejection, x, 9, 74, 88, 89, 90, 91, 134, 140, 184, 185
remember, x, 12, 39, 89, 110, 111, 159, 162, 175
resettlement, 44
resilience, 6, 12, 21, 26, 47, 48, 51, 111, 117, 147, 148, 155, 156
resistance, 91, 104, 106, 137
resurrection, 117, 162
rituals, 59, 74, 78, 91, 123, 139, 159, 162

sacrament, 26
sacred space, 135, 137
sacred text(s), 20, 29, 159, 163
salvation, 141, 62, 169
sea, 1, 2, 7, 27, 34, 43, 57, 58, 109, 161, 188. See also Moana.
sea level (rise), 36, 37, 41, 42, 46, 48, 49, 53, 55
sea of islands, 1
security, 44, 45, 47, 48, 55

servants(hood), 7, 13, 18, 19, 25, 171–73, 187, 188
sexism, 98
sexual violence, 12, 165, 167, 180
sexuality, 12, 13, 108, 113, 170, 171, 176, 177, 185, 187
shame(d), 166, 167
silence(d), ix, 50, 99, 100, 128, 140, 165, 166, 167, 172, 183
sky, ix, 7, 43. See also *lagi, rangi*
slave, 119, 120, 128, 130
solidarity, 48, 142
stigma(tization), 84, 87, 92
strange(r), ix, 7, 8, 27, 30, 32, 35, 36, 44, 166, 173, 174
suicide, 75, 80, 181, 182
supremacy, 9, 73, 75, 90
Syrophoenician woman, 9, 11, 140

taboo, 165
takatāpui (LGBTQ+), 11, 12, 13, 170–87
tapu, 5, 9, 11, 12, 13, 164–69
the Other, 29
trauma, 84, 107, 148, 174

underworld, 162. See also *pulotu*.

vā, 7, 8, 9, 11, 58, 66, 103, 104, 105, 133, 134, 135, 137, 138, 141, 142
vaccination, 17, 18, 78
vanua, ix, x, 7, 34, 43, 167. See also *fanua, fenua*
violence, 12, 43, 75, 86, 88, 89, 90, 92, 93, 100, 101, 105, 106, 137, 165, 167, 177, 180, 186
virus, 24, 74
vulnerable, 17, 36, 41, 49, 50, 55, 84, 87, 97, 100, 103, 183

water, 27, 36, 38, 42, 44, 46, 50, 55, 115
womb, 12, 122, 164, 167, 168
wound(ed, ing), x, 31, 185

youth, 3, 19, 148

www.ingramcontent.com/pod-product-compliance
Lightning Source LLC
Chambersburg PA
CBHW070328230426
43663CB00011B/2253